Wintering

Wintering

Diana Kappel-Smith

Illustrations by the author

LITTLE, BROWN AND COMPANY · BOSTON · TORONTO

FIRST EDITION

Portions of this book originally appeared in Blair & Ketchum's
Country Journal and *Vermont Life.*

LIBRARY OF CONGRESS CATALOGING IN PUBLICATION DATA

Kappel-Smith, Diana.
    Wintering.

    "Portions of this book originally appeared in Country
journal and Vermont life"—
    1. Winter—New England.   I. Title.
QH104.5.N4K37   1984   574.5′42′09744   84-19387
ISBN 0-316-48299-4

VB

Designed by Dede Cummings

Published simultaneously in Canada
by Little, Brown & Company (Canada) Limited

PRINTED IN THE UNITED STATES OF AMERICA

for my father
Albert David Kappel

Contents

Foreword

When I spent my first winter in Vermont, twelve years ago, I bought a pair of snowshoes. They were the only way to get back into the woods. I thought it would be a good idea to learn to tell the trees apart in the wintertime, by their twigs and whatnot, but I made slow progress. After a while I left my field guide and hand lens at home, and went farther into the hills. With three feet of snow on the ground the world was clean, stripped. The snow settled in branches, sifted through the air, or blew into drifts, in ways that I thought were very beautiful. Walking through the countryside in January was like exploring a foreign planet. Aside from a light network of gravel roads, with a few farms and summer cabins here and there, there were not many signs of people. It was easy to pretend that I had the planet to myself.

My sister and I had bought an old falling-apart farmhouse on the ridge of the hill the summer before. We bought it with some money that we had inherited from an uncle. There was enough for a house and six acres, with something left over to live on for a while. We had romantic visions of a simple life. I wanted to keep animals, a garden, cut my own wood, and learn to be a better naturalist. None of these things are simple;

I'm not sure why we thought that they would be. The woods in winter, on the other hand, were peaceful and undemanding. Pushing along through the undergrowth, tracing a river to its source, was easier in many ways than staying home, burning green wood, and expecting to be warm.

One day I floundered down a ravine into a deer yard. The dense little evergreens had been pruned by nibbling deer into tunnels, hedges, and walls. There were deep pathways tramped in the snow, and oval hollows where the animals had slept, and droppings everywhere. I was beginning to notice that the winter planet wasn't empty at all, or uneventful.

After four years on the hill I married a neighbor and we began to farm full-time. Neither farm nor marriage was built to last, but I still live here — writing some, farming some — with my son, Coulter. The woods in winter continue to be a source of wonders.

In the winter everything out-of-doors seems to be gone. But ever since Louis Pasteur exploded the myth of spontaneous generation — which held that frogs could be born out of a spring rain and mice from ears of ungleaned corn — we know that nothing is gone, and that all the rich life of a June morning must be out there on a January morning. These stories are the results of many and varied attempts to find out where it is, and what it is up to.

I have been struggling to define my terms, even to myself; and winter is not an easy thing to define. Most plants are not growing then, it is cold, there is less sunlight, so the season itself translates as a time of energy deficit. The deficiencies are of immediate and tangible things: calories of food, BTU's of heat, quanta of light. The gnawing lack of these basic necessities of life makes itself felt gradually through the autumn months, and spring comes slowly also, so that winter is a turning rather than a coherent event. *Wintering* tries to compass this turning, and so it has come to include a good deal of the year.

This is also a personal journey filled with strayings from the narrow path and burrowings after obscure subjects and wonders; I hope that others will enjoy this convoluted path as much as I have.

I have inevitably made use of the work of a lot of other people, for which it has not always been possible to give due credit. I trust that I will be forgiven for these oversights, and that the people whose work I have used will be pleased with my use of it.

Finally, every observation and event and understanding in here have been powerfully affected by the seasons of my own heart; I believe that this is unavoidable, even good.

When we observe something, what we take in is less that thing itself than its effect on us — the clangor of nerve ends processing chemistry, temperature, reflected radiation, old terror, and private hope. I have come to the conclusion along the way that there is such a thing as the wintering of the human spirit; by spirit I mean the force which we hold, hidden, chrysalised, as it were, under a layered shell of physical necessity and present time. The spirit seems to inhabit no time and no space at all, but it thrashes and resounds when it meets the world, like a tuning fork which has been struck against the edge of a table. By its sudden music we know it is there.

Tuning forks have a strange and almost magical quality; if you hold ten of them up in a room, and strike only one so that it sounds its particular tone, a few other forks will begin to sing quietly as well, in harmony, each absorbing sympathetic vibrations through the fabric of the air. When I have been struck, then, I have tried hard to listen, and to communicate the clear sound.

I have used science as my chief tool here, because I have some experience and training in it, and I like it, and it's handy. The art of science seems to be to look, ask, observe, and ask again. This process gains momentum, though, until it has the intensity of battle. It is the nature of this odd quest that facts dispatch questions as if they were a head of the Hydra; each time an answer is found a dozen fresh questions squirm into grinning life. I dimly remember that I began this journey into wintry things feeling brave and shining, inviting anyone that would to come along, on what seemed to me would be a kind of rout, a morning's joyride into spring. I laugh now because I hardly recognize myself: my armor has a patina of pitch and rust, sticks and burs are tangled in my sleeves; but I can lift my face in the April sunlight and suck air. We have won this. It is no mean prize. That anything lives at all now seems a victory beyond measure.

✦ ✦ ✦

Twelve years ago I used to follow Dr. Steven Young into the woods whenever I could. He was encyclopedic; he knew the names and habits of everything that lived in the hills, and would crash off cross-country, unhill and down, in wholly inappropriate shoes, and arrive twenty minutes later at the bush or the rare four-inch-high fern that he wanted to check up on. Besides, he was and is a great botanist. Once I asked him how he knew the names of the trees so well. He said that it was like recognizing a friend on the street; you just knew. At the time this seemed a miraculous knowledge. I am indebted to Steve for many things, but most of all for the habits of not carrying field guides or sticking to paths but of keeping one's eyes open; and of knowing that you can never keep them open enough.

To Dr. Peter Marchand I owe a different debt of gratitude: that of introducing me to winter ecology as a hard science. To the other professors who taugh with him, both in 1973 and in 1983, I owe a similar debt. My fellow students, especially in the early years, practiced their science in a serendipitous fashion, building snow houses and sleeping in them, soberly taking the temperature of their own toes, and discovering first-hand what it might mean to be a bear. These were exercises in joy. I try not to forget them.

The libraries of Yale University and of the University of Vermont have been constant sources of nourishment. The excitement and frustration of tracking down a paper on "Compensation for Temperature in the Metabolism of Poikilotherms" are not unlike the sensations produced by following an otter trail over the ridge. The Center for Northern Studies has allowed me to use their library as well, and their lab, and the staff there has always been helpful. I hope that they don't take it amiss that I still have one of their microscopes. It was lent me long ago by a staff member whom I dare not name. It has been very useful.

My cousin G. Stuart Keith was responsible for bringing birds into my life very early on. I was not very receptive. I used to trudge along in his wake, binoculars a-dangle, only because I liked being with him. After a while, something rubbed off. His help, both tangible and intangible, has been a simple gift of himself.

I am very grateful to all the people at Cape May who let me follow them and watch them work during the great hawk migration. Some of these are people whom you will read about presently: Pete Dunne, Bill Clark, Dr. Sidney Gauthreaux, Katy Duffy, and many other banders and watchers. Their enthusiasm was inexhaustible. I know I got in their way more than once. And if it hadn't been for Larry Metcalf, my old partner in naturalists' mischief of many kinds, I would never have gotten there in the first place.

In 1979 and 1980, Blair and Ketchum's *Country Journal* published a series of three articles I had written about wintering, which later became the inspiration for this book. I am very much indebted to them, especially to Tom Rawls, for his faith and his criticism. In the winter of 1983 *Vermont Life* published a portion of *Wintering*, which was very exciting, especially because it gave some of my friends and neighbors a chance to see what I had been up to all this time. As a result, my friends and neighbors gave me a boost when I needed it most.

Making a pile of stories and notes and articles into a book has involved a lot of what I believe is called technical support. Technical support is like that crisscross of girders under the railroad trestles in those old Westerns; without them, tracks and train collapse into the Rio Grande. Julia Fallowfield and Ray Roberts have been like literary parents; my sharpest critics and most reliable enthusiasts. Shapleigh Smith, Jennifer Martin, Annette and Christine Whipple and their family, Christine and Rick Bolin and theirs, and my mother and father, Victoria and Albert Kappel, have all taken care of me and of Coulter while I was working. Tom Burke rescued a chapter from electronic oblivion. Fritze Till gave me two birds to draw. Jane and Homer Porter gave me a snowshoe hare to draw, and eat. Lois Budbill taught me about drawing pencils. Carol Clarkson got me into the Bronx Zoo after hours. Suse Lyon did a typing blitz that set a record for such things, I think. Phillip Isom gave me sleigh-rides and snowball fights. These were all, at the time, necessary things. All real gifts are. I hope that I can give them back.

D. Kappel-Smith
Vermont, February 1984

Wintering

COOPER'S HAWK

I   *A Way Away*

> *... their chearfulness seems to intimate that they have some Noble Design in Hand, and some great Attempt to set presently upon, namely, to get above the Atmosphere, high, and flie away to the other World.*
>
> — CHARLES MORTON,
> *London, England, 1703*

> *Just give me the miracles!*
>
> PETER DUNNE,
> — *Cape May, New Jersey, 1982*

News

In August I went to Dead Creek to see what birds were there. While I was easing down close to the water, trying to get a better look at a stump that seemed to be a rare species of heron, I dropped suddenly to my ankles in slick, stinking mud. I slid steadily down and as the mud gathered me in its cool grip I collapsed backward, scrabbling, in the cattails. It took all my strength to haul myself out, and the mud chuckled at me, closing over one lost-forever sneaker like gray, greasy pudding. I was annoyed at losing my sneaker and at having to spend the rest of the day in boots; this isn't my kind of place anyhow, I thought to myself while I scraped the worst of the ooze off my pant legs with a stick; in more ways than one I am out of my depth here — a foreigner, sightseer, tourist. It is small comfort that the birds I have come here to see are foreigners and tourists, too; or that the mud is part of what they come for. The mudflats of Dead Creek are an oasis for shorebirds in the long flight from breeding grounds to wintering grounds; a lucky swatch of fertile muck in a howling wilderness of granite hills.

Actually the wilderness is not as howling as all that. Dick Smythe, my good friend and neighbor, says that sometimes, spring and fall, a pair of spotted sandpipers will visit his home-made pond up on our hill. They stop by there for a rest and a dab of food on their way from Mexico to Labrador, or Labrador to Mexico. Dick's pond has been in existence for only four years, so some birds anyway must fly all that way with their eyes peeled.

With the gray mud drying on my jeans and ankles I went on from one bridge to another, scouting the marsh with my binoculars; the reedy greenery hid much, nearly everything, in fact. I caught the loom of muskrat houses here and there and I saw a muskrat nosing along in the green water. The muskrats make trails up onto the land just like beavers do, hollow muskrat-sized pipes in the reeds and mud and cattails, and autumn wildflowers and grass.

Great blue herons were around every bend of marsh, yard-high graceful birds like something come alive from an Oriental screen. From the side they were dusty blue with white cheeks and black cockades, but their breasts and throats were streaked, so that when they turned toward me they disappeared against the cattails. This was an optical illusion of the first water; I couldn't see them at all and they could see me just fine.

The great blues had bred there along the creek and along the lakeshore, and they wouldn't go far to winter — to Dela-ware, the Carolinas, maybe on to Florida. I wasn't looking for great blues particularly, but all day long I couldn't take my eyes off them; patient, gangling, serene, with their dark-browed warrior's eyes and beaks like swords.

Between stops I drove off on straight roads through fields of alfalfa and corn. This was farm country, old Pleistocene lake-bed, the rectangular level fields bearing crop after crop be-tween straight hedgerows of elms and oaks. This was all only an hour and a half by car from my hardscrabble farm in the hills. There are few elms on my land and no oaks, and we have no rich muddy marshes anywhere nearby. All of our hill water drains downhill fast, the streams running cold and fresh even in August, in falls and curves and rushes like the hills themselves. There in the lake valley where the countryside was going nowhere in particular, the water wasn't in a hurry either. Dead Creek meanders; even that is a mild word for what it does or doesn't do. It is made of loops of old river in the terminal stages of their riverness before becoming land. It is a thread of marsh more than a creek, a rich soup of water life.

Under the suddenly expanded valley sky I looked and looked into the marsh, and the more I looked the less there was to see, and, oddly, spookily, the more fascinated I became. In one place I spent an hour and a half sitting on a stone, watching a great blue up to his ankles in water (his ankles are where our knees are, in the middle of his legs, only they bend ankle-wise instead of knee-wise), and he was doing what passes for hunting: standing still with his eyes open and beak poised, his legs as inanimate as sticks. I watched the heron who watched the water. When he stretched his long neck it seemed to spread out from him smoothly, like a cat on the prowl. When he walked it was with a jerk-and-stop . . . jerk-and-stop motion that was tricky to watch. The eye catches the jerk and looks, and by the time one looks the bird is stopped and one sees nothing; and just as the attention falters and the eye wanders there is another jerk. They are big birds, after all, and may be hunted from behind while they are hunting below, so it makes perfect sense that their arts of invisibility have been honed, and honed.

When I looked up from my binoculars, the trees beyond the marsh and the mountains beyond them oozed and shrank, as if my eyes were zooming backward at the speed of sound. Vertigo — I held on to my stone and fastened my eyes to my binoculars again, and seemed to hang weightless over the water, scouting the horizon of the marsh world. After another hour of this I knew a few more things. I knew that in back of that gray stub there was a green heron padding around in the cattails. To the left of him was a muskrat tenement, to his right was a fat muskrat. Three species of dragonflies were mating and laying eggs on the cattail and rush stems within a yard of me. Goldfinches and field sparrows were foraging deep in the brush along the shore — and there were noises. There were clicks, coos, splashings, and fidgets in the rushes and the cattails, news of a vast invisible crowd: frogs, insects, fish, more birds — rails or bitterns — all only visible as shadows, ripples, whisks, jerks. I couldn't tear myself away. All these mysteries seemed about-to-be-revealed. It was like waiting in a theater in which the curtain was always just about to rise.

I have never acquired the good hard-nosed objectivity to media messages of all kinds that most people seem to have, or to drama, however gentle. I take what I see and hear almost too much to heart. For instance, after an hour of TV network news I am left with some unhappy, uncomfortable suspicions: that world leaders are vain and venal, that nothing is safe or sacred, that no one is to be trusted, and experts least of all; et cetera. All this exposure to the greatest of human dramas — international hanky-panky, love, murder, sex, violent death — the news, in short, delivered in a matter-of-fact monotone by a bland man in a TV studio — makes me uncomfortable. At least a wide-eyed street-corner gossip endows her tidbits with weight, with their proper horror. The effect of media news programs is to make me clutch at my material belongings, and throw up high-caliber emotional defenses, and peer at my surroundings down the steely barrel of suspicion: this fortress of the self is a burden on the soul.

Whatever it was that went on there behind the cattails, it was drama of a different kind altogether; as titillating and as unresolved as all true dramas seem to be. It made great news, in fact, and to my mind it is the only kind I benefit by watching (or by listening to); the hunting and hiding, the small-talk and big-talk, the sneaking and snapping, mating and eating and singing; all the unselfconscious noise of things alive. It isn't so much that wonderful things are happening there, but that wonderful things *are*.

By five in the afternoon, shaken by my vigil behind my

binoculars, I was struck with wonder at every turn; a crow rose chanting from the corn, his cries full of appetite and raw joy, and I felt the same chant, "Ah! — Ah! — Ah!" rising to my mouth. There was an oak by a bridge, vibrating with wind and nearly black in silhouette against a brilliant sky; my arms opened, and filled with moving leaves. I turned my cheek to the sun and the light was like the caress of a lover or mother, a hot touch on my skin, and I knew that nothing could be a greater gift than the simple touch of light. My watching in the marsh had turned me, like a sock, inside out to the world, and every nerve end burned with messages. I was suddenly, for a moment, all in touch.

Then it was gone; and I was left staring at the gravel road and rattling the map to find how far it was for the turn-off to the next bridge. I felt sated, awake, at peace, moved; it is so rare this turning, so much to be prized. The chrysalis that shields and restrains the spirit had split for a moment, and I had been winged! To stay winged longer might have been unwise. Who knows. I might have blundered ecstatic into the flame; run the car up a tree, dashed caroling into the muck. But I was tough side out again, and safe, and as I came to a stop in a clatter of gravel at the last bridge I heard the high keening cries of the birds that I had been looking for all day long.

The mudflats were covered with sandpipers, all busy — skibble-dab-dab-skibble-twirl-dab — their keening cries hauling out all my crumpled memories of long autumn beaches with their waves sighing up and down, followed by sandpipers; the running feet a constant stitching at the seam of sea and land. These are birds that breed on the northern edge of North America, on the wet tundra that fronts the polar ice pack. Walking off in the shallows were tall, graceful, lesser yellowlegs, which had come down from the Northwest Territories and James Bay on their way to the Gulf Coast. There were killdeer there too, and a semipalmated plover, but the greatest surprise of all was three northern phalaropes, flown down from their nesting grounds on Greenland, or Ellesmere

Island. They were quick, delicately made, with long dark pointed beaks; the females had molted the deep bib of red they wore in summer and were a plain black and white and gray in their wintering plumage. They were on their way to the tropical oceans where, all winter, they would be called sea snipe, a plain bird of open water. In August and September, in Dead Creek, they were both sea snipe and phalarope and neither: a bird between.

In the falling dusk the sandpipers rose from the shore, the flock folding and swelling over the mudflats and gathering birds as it went. The flock wheeled like a bomber squadron over the silky gleam of marsh water and then flew south. Whether they were going off to land at a sheltered spot two hundred yards away to safely spend the night, or at a sheltered cove two hundred miles away — two hundred miles closer to the Gulf or the Yucatan coast where they would safely spend the winter — I had no way of knowing.

With the sandpipers' flight, the air over my head was changed. I was suddenly and acutely aware that the air was full of birds; birds invisible, inaudible, purposeful, passing over.

Smoke

In late August the mornings here are empty of bird song. The rolling unmown pastures are tawny with seeding grasses, and are rumpled by the wind like the fur of an untidy animal. On the windiest days the fields toss like a surf, like a pale sea in which my sheep move belly-deep, drifting off here and there over a rise of ground, hull-down over the rim of their universe. The pastures and hedgerows are boiling with life; it is full summer. Wherever I walk, looking at the lambs, bringing salt and water, birds — groups of yellowthroats and chipping sparrows, whole cadres of barn swallows — scatter over the grass and through the underbrush, or toss wheeling over the grass. All of the young birds that were hatched and raised here this spring are fledged and hunting on their own; the sparrows are hunting seeds, and the warblers and swallows are hunting insects; there are plenty of both. The parent birds don't need to sing anymore to claim the boundaries of their freeholds. With all the young birds out and about there must be five or six times as many birds here now as there were in May, or as there will be next May — but they are not singing.

Many ornithologists believe that of all the hatching-year songbirds that fly away in September and October, between eighty and ninety percent will never come back. They will die on their migration route or on their wintering ground. They are a calculated loss, the price that their species pays for avoiding winter.

The yellowthroat that sang all early summer from the chokecherry thicket north of the house, and his neighbor yellowthroat to the west of the alfalfa field, will both be off to Mexico soon enough. A woodthrush has been singing in the red pines every May and June since I have lived here, and his song is welling, poignant, compassionate. It has the sound of rain in it, and harps. "Whenever a man hears it he is young, . . . and the gates of Heaven are not shut against him," said Thoreau. And when the bird himself leaves, quietly slipping off to Guatemala or Panama, he bears away with him the score and the instrument for this music that only May and lucky flying can conjure back.

The chipping sparrows will be off to the Carolinas or Florida. The song sparrow and the white-throated sparrow will go south too, perhaps no farther than a familiar bird feeder well stocked with millets and sunflower seeds, and I will have the generosity of a Connecticut housewife to thank for the songsparrow song that I will have to do without for these eight months. One morning a bird may be back in the high spire of the fir in the lower pasture, singing his "This-here-is-mine! —

see-I-made-it-back! — Alleluia! — come-hither-female-song-sparrows — hear-me!"

I will look out for these birds, I will be here.

If I have sometimes my doubts about one nation's unity of purpose with another nation, the bobolink — dancing clown of the hay meadow, with his white-gold cape and his nasal poetry — has no such doubts. The Argentine pampas and my hay meadow are equally home to him. If the ruby-throated hummingbird were asked which she valued more, my peach-colored lilies or the trumpet vines in a certain single Mexican garden, I don't think she could honestly say. They are both hers. And if her dual nationality gives her the duty of flying 500 miles nonstop and twice a year over the Gulf of Mexico, she has, handed down to her through (how many?) generations, the equipment to do it and the urge to do it too. Both gardens are her source and her destination.

I always seem to need reminding; the spherical singleness of the planet is hard to feel, and harder, in spite of all those satellite photographs, to see. We are told though, constantly told, unpleasantly reminded. The burning of high-sulfur fuels that run the industrial plants on which our economy depends can, through subtle atmospheric chemistries, bankrupt the economies of lakes, streams, whole soil systems, acidifying them to shadows. The cutting of the Brazilian rain forest may radically alter the amount of life-giving oxygen in our atmosphere, and/or the well-being of countless now landless Brazilians. Oil spills here kill fish and birds there. Our nuclear arsenal is, simultaneously, a tool for our survival and our obliteration. We too have our dual citizenships, our gulfs to cross.

So birds seem in their going and coming back to have solved something truly huge and worthwhile. They tow the bright threads of their existence like living shuttles, stitching seas, islands, continents, sewing us up into a whole. They weave live bright patterns which I imagine that I can see overhead in the warp of the winds themselves. In late July, and in

August, September, and October the birds are tapped by the hand of the master weaver and they are away, gone.

Have you had them? The dreams about flying? I read somewhere long ago that everyone does, that we have flight as a kind of universal longing, or as a memory of the womb before it cramped our style. I remember dreaming when I was very little that I crept in my pajamas to my mother's bathroom and then climbed up on the sink and launched like a balloon, and went swimming through the house, ducking the door frames, colliding with light fixtures, happy as a clam.

What is it then? Birds seem to tote some part of us in their wake; wild, unfettered, apparently free, they are a symbol of a lift and release from our clumsy earth-and-time–bounded selves, a release that is, above all things, our hearts' desire — is this it? If the truth be told, though, flight to birds is a massive effort; massive. Half of a dove's weight is pectoral muscle. Even the humble and more or less earthbound Thanksgiving turkey has twin hillocks of breast which so far outrank the feeble fans which shelter my own lungs and heart and haul my arms forward that they seem like another organ altogether. So. Why fly then? It is a handy skill for getting to food — insects, high fruit, an eagle's perspective — and it is a nice way to escape. Run. *Fly!* Evade! Skedaddle! Disappear! Go!

A sparrow flies away from the cat. He flies from one patch of seeding timothy to another. He flies to his nest. Then he flies to North Carolina: this isn't the same thing at all.

Sometime back when birds were just starting up (no pun intended), flight was useful, then it became necessary, then it became the earmark and primary survival tool of the species. In this way, yes, yes, it is like the human spirit. I fear, I tremble. If birds' migration is any measure of the thing, then the molt and fattening and flight of the spirit is the most painful and daring work we could ever garner the courage to do.

We have the option, often taken, not to try.

Migrant birds don't have the option not to migrate, to quit on the spot. They did once, perhaps, but took up the challenge bit by bit, like *Homo sapiens* bent on assembling a locomotive, starting off with nothing in his hand but a stone ax and the world. It took birds aeons longer to get migrations to their present state of greased intricate motion than it took us to make a locomotive; and it hasn't escaped notice that in the process of going from stone age to technological age we seem to have made ourselves. Migrant birds have assembled a mysterious and complex technology to escape cold, lightless, foodless winter, and in the process have made Bird a new and most marvelous beast. One assumes that they are still tinkering with a wheel or cog or valve in the machinery; the process goes forward, and not without pain.

Only about ten percent of the songbirds born here this spring will survive to return next spring. This is part of the deal. Evolution proceeds to feats as intricate as migration only by means of heavy selection pressure, and the selection here is made by all that keeps the birds from going or coming back: losing their way, leaving too late, or arriving too soon; flying too lean or too fat, or blundering into the attractive, deceptive lights of lighthouses, or into powerlines, radio stations, airplanes; striking out over oceans that are too wide to cross, or deserts too dry to find water in; weather that is suddenly too cold or too hot, too wet or too dry; trees with no fruit, and insects that do not hatch; hurricane, gale, simple thunderstorms; headwinds, crosswinds, no winds at all. There are also the hunters, human and otherwise, that haunt the beachheads of the great flyways, waiting for the marginal birds that plummet to safety and settle to earth on their breasts, wings dragging, mouths gaping, too exhausted to budge.

Migration isn't limited to birds. The closer I look at almost any plant or animal, the more it seems to tick, move, in an orderly or disorderly and oddly purposive way. Even the pasture thistle that, on dry days, lends its tuft-parachutes to any wind; and the juvenile great horned owls who just leave in October, and have been found, looking as aghast as always, in unsuitable places like downtown Detroit; even the young moose who have been known to wander into the suburbs of Boston, looming up behind mailboxes and decorative shrubs — even these random scatterings are migrations in truth. There may be a time when these places and ways work. They've worked before.

I read an article this winter, a scientific study about migrant rats. It seems that some families or clans of rats are highly migratory, and other clans are, just as highly, sedentary. Experiments were done with laboratory-raised rats from each sort of clan in order to try to find out what was going on. Why the difference. And it turned out that the only innate difference between migratory-type and sedentary-type rats was the degree of restlessness they had at puberty. Migratory-type rats become anxious and full of — curiosity? foolhardiness? — as they become sexual, as new hormones flush and transform them. Sedentary-type rats are calmer adolescents altogether; more content to stick with the status quo.

In late summer and early autumn a vast restlessness seems to spread and to catch everything; a conflagration. Gather and move! Watch; the globe has become a place of shifting things. In August the caribou begin to trickle south in twos and threes, moving off the Canadian tundra; by September the trickles will have gathered into caribou rivers that run south before the snows, into the shelter of the black spruce forest.

In September and October the bluefin tuna start to swim deeper, trending south and away from their summer feeding grounds off Nova Scotia and northern New England; they will spawn, in April, in the warm blue seas of Bermuda.

At nighttime in September, October, Indiana bats fly south out of Ohio and Indiana and Michigan; going hundreds of miles to ancestral hibernating caves in the hills of Kentucky.

In the cooling waters of the North Atlantic, fat young cope-pods — microscopic sea animals that are the feed for vast multitudes of fish — migrate down from the surface, some-times down deeper than three thousand feet, to spend their winter in the darkness. There they will be cool and safe and can drift, waiting for the rich spring bloom of their phyto-plankton food to beckon them upward again.

After the first autumn storms push their way along the Florida coast, the spiny lobsters that have spent all summer feeding in the shallows gather together. Lining up, feelers to tail — like a conga line of dancers, like elephants in a circus parade, as many as fifty lobsters at once — they traipse off to deep water where they can keep cool, nearly torpid, and safe, until by all signs of light and time and current lobster food is plentiful in the shallows again; and it is spring.

Look at it this way: picture a bird's summer breeding area as a color, an overlay on a map; yellow would be a good one. Then make the color of the wintering area blue. Play with the overlays. Push them around on the map. Keep them labile, in motion, open to invasions and excursions, expansion, contrac-tion. If you happen to make a place where winter and summer ranges overlap completely, then you have a green area where birds don't migrate at all. They may change territories (hill-tops to valleys? brushland to bird feeders? field to forest?) and strategies: these are your blue jays and black-capped chicka-dees and cardinals and so on. Another possible pattern: you could have the overlays overlap only a bit. The birds in the green spot switch strategies but don't migrate, but those birds of the same species who had spent their breeding season far-thest north would spend their winters farthest *south*, leap-frogging their more sedentary brothers altogether. This is what happens to many birds: meadowlarks, grackles, bluebirds, for example.

It is a clever plan, and a puzzling one. This odd malleable pattern reminds me most of the rats, those rats of the most-restless and least-restless adolescents. If stay-at-home-ness and restlessness are heritable traits (which is what the rat experiments are saying, at least as regards rats), then leapfrogging of wintering and breeding ranges allows for the gradual selection of one or the other; for sedentariness to become the rule, or for the yellow and blue overlays to shift apart, as climate shifts, as food supply shifts, as predator pressure shifts, as competition shifts, until they lie separated by mountains, seas, continents, millennia — joined by flying birds, and nothing else.

We go through a puberty once and a menopause once, but all of the birds who live here swing through these same sea-changes every year. I am staggered by the thought of this. It beggars description; it must be like being torn constantly to shreds, whirled like a lasso. There is a string of hormones in charge of this business, all commanded by the pituitary. Little larger than the head of a pin, set in brain-matter like a gray jewel, it is in turn keyed by changing day lengths, as though a clock were being punched. It can sense light through birds' thin skulls as if it were a third eye. Some day just past midsummer old hormones are phased out and birds' gonads begin to shrink to 1/2000 of their jubilant May weight; the birds are transistorizing payload, setting priorities.

Once mating and egg-laying are over with, birds begin molting, changing their feathers, as if plumage were a kind of carapace. Breeding, molt, migration; these three are expensive acts and take energy and care. They have to happen one at a time. So. In late summer the feathers drop away. But most birds can't afford to be flightless at all. Ever. A grounded sparrow is a sparrow without hope, and a grounded hawk is a hawk deprived of his livelihood. So the synchrony goes further. In July the marsh harrier dipping and hovering and butterfly-buoyant in her daily hunt over the lambs' pasture has twin slots of light in her wings. The feathers drop off in pairs, same feathers on opposite wings. Think of it. As each feather drops away, a new pair of pinfeathers pricks out, fills with blood, the new feather-vanes unfurl and twist out of their blood sheaths, lengthen; when the feathers are long enough, then the tip of each embedded quill pinches the nurturing blood vessels off and the feather is finished, and another pair falls away, and the hawk flies on. The hawk begins to look less and less simple; cogged and mysteriously windowed and doored, wheeling on invisible threads that reach from the sun to a mouse and tangle through half the breadth and length of the continent, each feather, each barb and barbule and barbicel and atom of each feather hauled and geared in, meshed in. It doesn't even purr. The hawk hunts, quiet as air.

In July and August I find signs, shards, every time I go to the woods. Here are splinters of blue-jay wing, the pinkie-finger-long flight feather of a warbler, a flicker's primary with its painted-looking shaft, the breast feather of an owl. I have them all in the big clamshell that I keep on my desk. The shell is a relic of a chowder made on the coast of Maine and in the company of friends, and made out of provisions found free in the sea (all but the milk, that is, and the butter and wine) to which the shell donated not only its contents but its services as dipper and bowl. It now holds memorabilia more recently come by — whatever my pockets are full of when they need emptying. From time to time I muck it out and it fills again, and in late summer it fills with feathers. But the owl breast feather won't stay put. In the morning I find it under my chair, stuck between two typewriter keys, halfway down the stairs. What has it seen, this peel of owl? What winds, what distances, what blood? It nestles in my palm, as clean and perfect as a shave of wood. One morning in late August when the trees have begun to color and the wind is blowing, the owl feather was gone without a trace. What trace could it leave?

What traces do I leave? I wonder about this. I shed candy wrappers, buttons, hairs from my head. An archaeologist might find wine bottles and cat-food cans, aeons hence, as signs of my tenure, and an owl feather. Let's say there were no birds for his reference; what would he make of the feather? Certainly that it was finely wrought, made by a different hand entirely than the one which turned out buttons or bottles. Was its use then sacred or secular? Sacred, without question; an effort of a priestess who worshiped through her craft, like a Chinese artist who dedicates a lifetime to the hollowing and carving of a single white jade bottle. A masterpiece, in short. The highest achievement of a culture dedicated to the discipline of the spirit, the flight of the soul. Is the truth more marvelous? What if I ghostily whispered in this archaeologist's listening ear that it was made in a cell-cluster in a barred owl who had been to Florida and back eight times? That I had picked it up from the ground where it had been tossed away as a kind of annual trash? That the highest work of my lifetime had been to collect the complex, the mazy, and subtle, and offer them like prayers: ah, God, this.

And then look: the hormones are doing their invisible dance, and molt is just the beginning. After they renew their feathers, birds fatten up. They have huge appetites suddenly and the hills are full of fruits. They layer on fat: fat is tanked under wings, across breastbones, frilling the gut, saturating the pectorals with golden oils. Then the birds gather, flock up, trading the security of private ownership and private space for the security of no ownership at all, and any space at all: restless armies massing for a march.

One evening in August, while I am off fishing at the river thigh-deep in dark water, trying to dab a fly out into a corner pool — a fly that looks like a gray-white moth which the grasses are full of, and that trout seem fond of — there are suddenly redwinged blackbirds, grackles, starlings, cowbirds, all flocking in the willows by the water. A few days later there are more blackbirds in the west hedgerow of the farm. The dark battalions dive and rise and fall for hours among the green oats, in the thick light of the August afternoon, like wind made manifest, visible; smoke before the fire.

Flocked, fattening, the birds wait for clear skies and a tailwind. One Sunday in early September it was cool, in the fifties and blustery. A front had moved through from the northwest and the woods were emptying. A kestrel tossed overhead in the wind, hunting. A phoebe ducked for flies by the barn, returning to a pine branch again and again; he wasn't there the day before, he would be gone by the morning. An almost insectlike ratcheting in the east hedgerow was only a black-throated blue warbler, alone there, rummaging in the spruce trees, hanging like an acrobat among the berries of the shadbush. Warblers, nuthatches, and a pair of white-throated sparrows hunted among the seeding grasses in the logging slash, as intent as they were in June when they had nestlings to feed. Now it was themselves they were fattening; packing it in, hustling to be off. The hedgerows were full of chips, whistles, rustlings, furtive scramblings; a few swallows tossed and swept through the air, filtering a last harvest of insects out of the rising breath of the meadow. The swallows were so buoyant, as if gravity had lost them!

In September the Canada geese began to come. I always seem to hear them first at night, coming over the hill, and I always catch myself wondering, shocked, what these lost high trumpetings are for. Are they a kind of taps for summer, or a battle cry? Neither one, O sleepy imagination, they are the chatter of geese, a chatter that binds them, a halloo along the swaying wedge to a mate or relative or traveling companion; a touch in the dark.

Later, the snow geese fly over in big glittering flocks that move slowly, high up, shimmering with whiteness. Then they are gone, the last of them gone, hull-down over the edge of their universe — and mine.

Flight

Sometimes I would like to get away. Not from the place, but from my own center of gravity; these eyes, these ears, these hands which show the wear of weather and doing, whose skin is loose from being flexed, soaked, cold or hot, hefting wood or hay. I would like to compress myself in a ball and be stretched all over again like clay. I would like another force to pin me down, another ether to breathe, another fresh set of senses; the world, then, would be another world. It would be a holiday, right here at home.

I have been reading about birds all fall, and watching birds, trying with all my might to get *inside* birds. This is an exhausting business; so one morning I took myself to the Montreal Aquarium to see, well, fish. How the other half lives, in fact; a new perspective.

I have always liked it there. All the display tanks are lit up from within so that the contents are brighter than life, on-stage, spot-lit. There is a smallish shark in a large tank and one has to line up with the schoolchildren to watch it; I am always as fascinated as they are by its bloodless skin, its steel eyes, its motionless motion. In other tanks there are schools of coral reef fish, each one a separate bolt of electric color. There are sea anemones as translucent as dreams, and live conchs trailing their billows of flesh, and sea turtles, their leathery shells overgrown with algae and polyps. There is an octopus, another favorite of the schoolchildren, a flayed horrific monster with its suckers stuck to the glass of the tank and its head/belly pulsing. There is even a stone enclosure for land tortoises, and another enclosure with a small alligator lying in it alone under a palm tree; and there are penguins.

The glass of the penguin enclosure extends up so that one can see air and water in one uninterrupted sweep. There are five kinds of penguins inside, and the little ones, the Adélies, are the most active. They shuffle to the edge of their authentic-looking floe and then tip their heads forward and go into the water, with the falling motion that a wave makes, curving over on itself.

Underwater, the stolid and shuffling birds are transformed into swift submarines with the sharp-eyed tilts of head and fish-eating beaks that sea birds have. The penguin's flight machinery isn't constructed for lift. A penguin's body is layered with buoyant fat, and with that and their lungs full of air they have their own built-in floatability here, and their wings are used for propulsion, for flash maneuvering after schools of fish. It is flight in a denser medium, but flight still.

The penguin wing has come the long way around the evolutionary barn. I can see this happening as if I had an imaginary time-lapse film of the thing, the camera clicking away over a few hundred million years. It all begins with the frilly webbing of a fish's fin. And then the fins become muscular and stumpy-paddle–like for forays onto shore, then the paddles stretch and articulate into an amphibian's legs, then into a reptile's horny claws; then the fun part. The reptile starts leaping, batting his arms for balance. The scales on those batting arms lengthen and thin into gliding planes, thin and fray into feathers. The whole reptile arm congeals into a proto-bird's glider-wing; then into the airfoil and propeller of a true-blue *wing*. Meanwhile the backbone is fusing into a rigid frame against which the flapping arms can work, the bones hollow out and lighten into thin girders, the vertebrae in the neck multiply to replace the flexibility lost in the fused back (a sparrow has twice as many neck vertebrae as a giraffe does); a great keel of a breastbone curves out to anchor the pectoral muscles; gradually the talent of maintaining a high, constant core heat develops — the dynamo ready to pump out the steady supercharge of energy needed to sustain a rocketing flight — and the lizard, belly in the dust, has become a flying machine. And then in the penguin this magnificently plastic appendage is back to being something like a fish's fin again, but vastly updated, possessed of a warm-blooded powerhouse and guided by a yeasty, whirling intelligence.

Watching them swim-fly there underwater, I am suddenly acutely aware of how unfinished each perfect thing is — each fin, stumpy-paddle, foot, claw, wing, flipper, hand. Let the time-lapse film run on into the future; it sparkles and leaps with possibilities.

Flight is such a complex, exhausting, engrossing achievement that birds have left it behind, or have left some of it behind, wherever possible. This makes a great example of the general laziness of evolution. Rule one: take it as easy as you can. If a bird finds itself in a situation where it doesn't need to catch or find its food on the wing or to escape predators or harsh weathers by flying away, it will slowly leave flight behind. The Rodrigues and Réunion solitaires are sad cases in point, each species so long isolated on its own cozy island in the Indian Ocean that they let their powers of flight lapse altogether. The solitaires, along with the dodo and the great auk, are extinct; chomped by rats and dogs, herded onto sailing ships for fresh provender like trusting cows. Of the solitaires only a few bones have survived as evidence. They were not only flightless, but highly edible and fatally naive.

Then there are birds that fly in a limited way; more for effect than for getting anywhere.

In early September the woods around the farm are full of ruffed grouse. People call them partridge here. They hunker in the leaves in the woods where they are invisible, their plumage leafily patterned in browns, grays, and cinnamons. When something or someone blunders within six feet of them, they explode up in a hurricane of wingbeats, and with lightning tilts and tilts again around branches and tree trunks, whistling like rockets, they disappear into the woods. The whole family of pale-breasted birds-that-burst — partridge, quail, grouse, turkeys, chickens, pheasants, ptarmigan — don't fly very far. They run and walk for their livings and they winter more or less in place. The rock ptarmigan spends its winter farther north than any other bird in North America, except for the odd snowy owl and a few ghostly ivory gulls that haunt the Arctic Ocean even in the wintertime. In some years the rock ptarmigan migrate a little bit, in flocks, moving down from their breeding grounds on the north coast of Greenland. Sometimes they come as far south as Churchill, halfway down the coast of Hudson's Bay. They are as white as snowballs; even the bottoms of their feet are feathered.

Of all bird things the wing is still the greatest wonder of all. In the six-day-old chick embryo, a hardly visible curl of forming flesh, the bud that will become the wing looks like a hand with four fingerlike digits and a complex constellation of hand bones. I fold my littlest finger into my palm and wriggle what's left; this is what four digits is like. Two days later the chick embryo's thumb has grown out into a small spine, which is all it will ever be. It will have its own little fan of feathers and be the *alula*, the winglet, on the leading edge of the wing; vital for balancing the aerodynamics of steep climbs and tricky maneuvers. The fourth finger remains a mere fleck of bone hidden in the wrist. But the middle two fingers, middle finger and forefinger (I put them up, give them an experimental wiggle; symbol of victory) grow out and join at their tips into a triangular girder. This is what has become of the bird's *hand*. From this hand the primary feathers grow, the propelling fan that will pull the bird through the air.

Leonardo da Vinci thought that flapping generated lift. He watched doves, and he dissected doves, and since half of the weight of a dove is pectoral muscle, he can be easily excused for thinking that they did all the work. So he designed a jointed system of pulleys and wooden limbs that were meant to be pedaled and pulled by the hands and feet of someone who was then supposed to be flapped up off the ground.

His study is a classic, but flight doesn't work that way.

Flapping is a kind of circular pulling motion, and it works like a propeller on the front of an airplane, giving the bird air speed, not lift.

Lift comes in such an unexpected and arbitrary-sounding way that it is worth the pondering. Flight works because of the principle of fluid motion, which sounds like an incantation or a recipe for levitation in a magic show. It is a respectable law of physics nonetheless, and states simply that the sum of the static and dynamic pressures on an object must remain constant. If the static pressure decreases, then the dynamic pressure must increase, and so on. If a wing is held out in still air, static air pressures are equal on upper and lower surfaces. (The downward pull is from *gravity*, which is something else altogether; something we're trying to get the best of here.) Anyway, if air begins to move over the wing, then dynamic pressure — the force of the air in motion — begins to play a part, and static pressures on the wing decrease steadily as air speed increases. Since the upper surface of the wing is convex (this is the important part), the air moves faster (more dynamic pressure, less static pressure) over the top of the wing than over its underside. As air speed increases, a point is reached when there is so much more static pressure on the undersurface than on the upper surface of the wing that the wing is literally pushed *up*. All that is needed for the magic to work is enough air speed — provided by flailing feet, churning propeller, jet-blast, flapping primaries, a nose into the wind — and you're off!

The expression "bird-brained" isn't a kind one, or rather it isn't kind when it is applied to one of us. It suggests something that stares, uncomprehending; something spindly, nervous, a slave of habit. A bird's head stripped of feathers and skull seems to be all eyes, each orb narrowing into a great cord of optic nerve.

It isn't enough to be endowed with wings, hollow bones, a supercharged metabolism; the brain is what flies, like the pilot in the cockpit of the plane, in his domed room filled with racing dials. The brains of mammals have evolved a certain way, by expansion of the cerebral cortex, a kind of gray blank slate capable of absorbing and collating vast amounts of information, of learning; of conducting "intelligent" behavior. Bird brains have their own elaborate strengths. They can, for one thing, fly. Their cerebral cortex is thin, the icing on the cake. In birds' brains it is the part called the corpus striatum that has developed into a mind. The corpus striatum is like prepackaged computer software; it contains a set of inborn behavior programs, each of which can be called into play by some particular "key": a sensory key — an event, noise, light, sound, motion; or an internal key — a certain lapse of time, an emotion, the completion of another program.

Another piece of the bird's brain — the cerebellum — is highly complex, too; fat, treelike, creased and folded like a fan. It is responsible for fancy physical coordination, for the twists and foldings of tail feathers, the slotting and waggling of primaries, the flits and tilts, bankings, soarings; the intricate maneuvering of flight.

Enter then another consciousness: a mind which has much of what we call the subconscious, muzzy and dreamish, translated to hard command. I try. One morning in early September I ran down the slope of the pasture, arm-wings out, trying to see as a bird sees: twice the field of vision, doubly deep focus, vision triply acute. I notice a leaf, far away; it is a black cherry leaf. I see the separate clustered petals of an aster, a spider on the aster; I bank, turn, with individual tilts of (how many?) feathers on my rump; I trip, roll down the slope, bruise my shoulder. I can't do this. I have to think too much.

Even a bird's hearing is different, skewed, tuned to a pitch that is lower than our ears can hear. As birds feel along their migration routes, they use their hearing as well as their sight to follow mountains, rivers, coasts. Waves pound against a shore, storms howl down a coastline, thunder drums, winds wail and groan, blowing between obstacles as if mountains were geological flutes, oboes, horns, as if every mountain massif, every ledge and hill, were a section of granitic woodwinds. Each of these things makes noise in very low frequencies, in the "infrasound" that birds can hear. These low sound waves travel thousands of miles without fading much. Some people believe that flocks of birds, drifting, gathering, restless, along the upper reaches of the Colorado River, can hear the surf on the Gulf Coast. The hisses and booms of infrasound give birds a reference to a landscape beyond reach of mere vision. It gives them a topography, the rough outlines of a map.

Then there is the weather. Most birds won't think of starting off without a tailwind. They have senses that help them to predict weather; most of us know rheumaticky persons whose sensitive fluid-filled joints of knee or elbow let them know ahead of time when a change for the worse is on its way, and the fluid-filled organ below a bird's inner ear is sensitive in this same way. Birds can sense a change in air pressure as slight as ten millimeters of mercury. They can sense storm, calm, change. Because it reacts to changes in pressure, this organ also functions as an altimeter and can feel a change as small as a thirty-foot rise or drop. Radar studies have shown that migrating birds keep a constant altitude, within twenty feet or so, even at night, through clouds, and over enormous distances. When a polar high-pressure system swings south, bringing cold clear skies, the flocks are restless; and when the wind begins to blow down out of the northwest at last, the flocks rise, like smoke released, and trail off down the clear moving river of the air.

My father has given me, as a reference, his 1958 edition of Bowditch's *American Practical Navigator*. The book weighs six pounds on the kitchen scale and contains, in highly concentrated form, a lot of what we have learned as a species from millennia of combings and homings across skies and seas and landscapes. There are chapters on Charts, on Piloting and

Navigation

G.V.T. Matthews's
*Theory of Solar
Navigation
by Birds* (1955)

The constellation
of Perseus in
the Milky Way,
from Johann Bayer's
Uranometria (1603)

Barn swallow

Summer and Winter
Ranges of the
Barn Swallow

from *Bird Migration*
by Donald R. Griffin (1964)

Dead Reckoning, on Weather, on Electronic and Celestial Navigation. There are hundreds of accompanying illustrations and dozens of appendices on such vital subjects as the Constellations, Navigational Coordinates, Latitude and Longitude Factors, Barometric Readings, Logarithms, Trigonometric Functions, and so on; there are 1457 pages in all. It is an indispensable work. For us.

Holding the old black tome closed and potent in my lap, I try to conjure up the load of things I would need in order to go, as birds do, across unknown spaces and arrive at my destination. Charts, sextant, compass, altimeter, radios, radar; my room fills with ghosts of gadgets trailing umbilical wires and needing grease and adjustments, maintenance manuals, spare parts, and months and years of training in order to begin to use them at all; the mind boggles.

I put my hand over the book, spreading my fingers; I want to pull the knowledge, soak it up, make it into *sense*. I have read in two books now that after birds fledge and leave the nest and before they fly south for their first winter they study the night sky. They watch the constellations, the movements of the stars, and most important of all they learn to know that part of the sky where the stars stay the stillest all night long: the northern sky, the quiet north star. Young birds that are brought into a planetarium will even learn to navigate by a totally bogus, made-up sky. In the autumn they want to move away from the stillest stars; they have learned their lessons.

They have solid-state equipment, too. They seem to be able to navigate with a magnetic compass that they can use anytime, even when the night sky is blotted by cloud or erased by daylight. On page sixty of my father's Bowditch is a rough illustration of the earth's magnetic field. It reminds me of the paper-plate-full-of-iron-filings-with-the-magnet-underneath game that we used to play in grade school; I liked the way that those filings would hiss in frantic curves, chasing the magnet that I was moving around under the plate. I sensed a hoax; I would always try to zip the magnet around faster and faster, zigzagging for all I was worth, trying to trick the filings and land them in a tangle. This plain lump of somehow-magicked metal, this "magnet," had a hold over those black bits — and over thumbtacks and paper clips — a hold that was coherent and predictable. Those curves of enslaved filings made visible a force that we are not equipped to sense any other way. We need tools to know that magnetism exists — compass needles, iron filings, obeying metals. Birds contain their tools.

The earth's magnetic field behaves as if there were a strong compact bar magnet at the earth's core. The poles of this magnet are oriented roughly north to south. Bowditch's illustration shows a spray of magnetic force bursting from each pole and then curving back over the face of the planet to meet the lines of force from the opposite pole. This force field is then bent and shifted by variations in the earth's crust and mantle as if it were a kind of wind that was continually being shunted around obstacles and funneled into others. Compass needles swing along the horizontal pull of this force, but they dip down a little bit as they point north, because the magnetic force is pulling them down. This downward pull is probably what birds feel.

The sun is the guide birds seem to like to use best, when it is there. But even in the daytime and under a clear sky, taking bearings from the sun isn't a simple business, because the sun's place in the sky varies according to season, latitude, and time of day, throwing masses of arcing variables into the solar equation.

A British ornithologist, G. V. T. Matthews, believes birds can memorize and project motion. He thinks birds can "see" the entire arc of the sun's path across the sky after having watched the sun for only minutes. And once a bird has projected this arc, he has access to two things — time and direction. In the northern hemisphere the highest point of the solar arc is to the *south* and when the sun is *at* the highest point, it is *noon*. The rest of this theory rests on the assumption that birds have an accurate internal clock — a clock that can be reset daily by the observed high noon — and an equally accurate calendar based on day length. Given these tools, and a navigation program capable of meshing them — of making the calculations and making sense of the results — then birds have a true bi-coordinate grid in which to fly, anywhere. Given the sun, they can figure out their place on this grid, just as accurately as I could figure out my latitude and longitude — if I had a sextant, grandfather's pocket watch, an almanac, and a patient mentor; a very patient mentor.

What this theory conjures up is a kind of consciousness of *place* that is so different from ours that we can only pick away at understanding it. I can describe the way it seems to work but I can't feel the senses that they have; that particular kind of knowing. Surety. If I were a Nashville warbler, perched on the Alice in Wonderland statue in Central Park, say, I would know where I was going and where *I was in relation to it,* even if one or both of these places were places that I had never been to before.

When my son was still less than a year old, I realized that he already listened to and made *sense* of words. It was as if his infant mind were full of blanks preset to absorb a verbal language; set to learn this language in great detail and wonderfully fast and to use it to meet all of his needs before he could coordinate his hands to wield a spoon, or his fingers to do up buttons or open a door. Long before he was tall enough to reach the doorknob of a door he knew the words *door, open, close,* and used and abused them often enough. A verbal language was his priority and his *modus operandi*, just as a navigational language must be the priority for birds. Perhaps the flocks of young swallows and song sparrows moving in the woods in August are learning these things; the syntax and vocabulary of darkness and light. Of magnetic dip and rise. Of stillness and motion.

There is more to it, though. I feel as though I were caught

in the absurd and wonderful position of the blind man who is trying to describe sight to the equally sightless; I can only say what miracles are there. What is there is this: many birds use different routes when they are going south in the fall from those they use coming north again in spring. Many routes have distinct bends in them, bends that are repeated year after year.

What is there is this: with few exceptions, the young, the hatching-year birds, leave before their parents do and make their first migration without any guides at all, except for those they carry. Often they use a route south in this first autumn that they will never use again. Young golden plovers' southward path is separated from their parents' path — and the path that they will use themselves for the rest of their lives — by more than 2000 miles. Young warblers often fly farther offshore than their parents, fetching up on islands, on ships, on beaches, whenever the wind backs on them; jetsam of a fickle sky.

All of this seems to mean that birds have maps — not like the maps we have, or will ever have. But maps all the same. With places on them.

Islands in the Sky

It must have been a puzzle since the dawn of time. Birds go, they come back; but where do they go? And how does one find out?

Olaus Magnus, who was the archbishop of Uppsala in the middle of the sixteenth century, claimed to have proof that swallows hibernated *en masse* under lakes and seas, lying packed mouth to mouth and foot to foot and wing to wing. He said that local fishermen sometimes pulled these torpid swallows up in their nets and when the fishermen took them home, the gelid birds would thaw and fly around. Pliny thought that birds hibernated in whirring balls like bees. Other people have believed that birds changed into animals or into other kinds of birds when winter comes, or that they slept through the winter months in hollow trees, or caves, or under stones, or wrapped in cocoons of dried mud.

A book about bird migration was published in a London printshop in 1703. It was one of the first treatises of its kind, the spearhead of a rapidly proliferating literature which, if gathered, would fill my house to the ceiling beams. The author was one Charles Morton. His rapt and humble spirit suffuses his work like a soft light. He collected anecdotes, watched birds, and read as much as he could get his hands on. He read Copernicus, and Copernicus had come to the conclusion, based on extensive observation, that the moon had seas, mountains, and an atmosphere just as the earth did. Based on hearsay, Copernican theory, and his own excellent observations, Morton decided that the birds that left Britain in the autumn spent their winters on the moon.

There are problems with this theory, and Morton, true to the spirit of science, struggles with them. The worst problem by far is that the moon is such a long way away. Morton calculated that it would take six weeks' flying time at 166⅓ miles per hour for a bird to reach its winter quarters there. He thought that this might be pushing it, even for a swallow.

Morton also wondered how they managed to navigate. He was the first to dare ask this question in print. After all, if birds flew off to the moon guided by sight alone, they would have to chase the moon in its orbit, wasting weeks of time and thousands of miles of flight. He thought that birds must fly up into the lunar orbit, guided by some innate faith, and then when the moon came close to them, they could simply turn and land on it.

Finally Morton puzzled over what birds did about sleeping and eating on the way. No one had puzzled over this before, either. He hazarded the guess that they might be able to fly in their sleep. He knew that they left in fat enough condition to be able to fly a long way, but he didn't think that they were fat enough to fly all the way. So Morton decided that there must be islands in the sky, conveniently placed so that birds could rest and feed awhile there before flying on. He knew that he was on thin ice with this idea of the atmospheric islands, and he made a convincing excuse at which it is impossible — after all these years and after all that people have discovered and have not discovered since — to laugh:

> *This I do suggest, because it is hard for me to persuade myself, that [the birds] come from any other part of the earth, as it is to persuade another, that they come from the Moon.*

It is still a struggle to believe that birds travel as far over the earth as they do. And besides, Charles Morton wasn't all wrong; because it turns out that there are islands in the sky, or what passes for islands from the point of view of birds. Bottlenecks, narrows, refuges, havens in the broad way south: an archipelago.

Cape May, New Jersey, is one of these islands. One of the best.

By the middle of October the leaves were falling fast. Leaves made pools of darkening color under the trees, and more showered down in every push of wind like sparks of a nearly extinguished fire. Flocks of blackbirds and starlings made soft, fluid smudges on the sky — birds on their way.

Yielding to a different impulse, and wanting to bear witness to the motion of this flight instead of seeing just the gradual emptying of my own fields and woods, I loaded up my quilt, notebook, binoculars, and a change of clothes, and drove south for ten hours at hummingbird speed, fifty miles per hour, down through the Green Mountains and the Connecticut River valley, and along the coast, past the big cities, and around the Pine Barrens to Cape May; a narrow sandy peninsula where the land ends and the Bay of Delaware begins.

In the summertime people come from the cities to the beaches and the hotels at Cape May. By the time the birds come through, most of the people have gone, and when I arrived there the village had the odd clockless feel of Emptied Resort, an off-season pallor. The sea in the evening was sprinkled with pale light, and the fishing boats were pulled up with their noses to the sky, at rest. The wind blew in against the black stone jetties, and gulls and scoters and a solitary male eider duck were rafted in their lee. A turnstone and a sandpiper poked among the rocks where the tide washed, and the marsh grasses were alive with the yellow rump-flashes of myrtle warblers: "butter-butts" in birder lingo. The far shore of the bay was invisible to me, and to the birds. Most birds don't like to cross water very much. When they come to lakes and oceans, they hug the coastline and follow the winding interface of solid and liquid, active and passive, surf and silence, light and darkness, like a track. So most of the moving flocks trend southeast and downwind across the continent, and then follow the coast and funnel down into Cape May. They often stay there for days, milling, getting their bearings, resting, feeding. Then they turn west and go around by the bay shore and cross the water inland, where it is narrower and they can see what they are going for: land ho, Delaware.

My old friend Larry Metcalf had been hired by the Cape May Bird Observatory to count hawks, and had invited me to stay with him there. The observatory is a research and education organization that operates under the aegis of the New Jersey Audubon Society, and in the autumn it makes an official count of the hawks and eagles that fly through. Every autumn a half-score of professional birders are hired to perch on a platform in the salt marsh and count the more than sixty, seventy, even eighty thousand raptors that fly over in a few autumn weeks — from mid-September through the end of November. By the time I arrived, the most massive flights of hawks and crowds of weekend birders had come and gone, and the season was at a gentle ebb. The numbers daze: one day in late September there had been more than sixteen hundred sparrow-hawks — kestrels — ruddy and scythe-winged, coming down over the marsh grasses in fives and sixes like squadrons of bombers on parade.

Then there were the sharp-shinned hawks, the "sharpies." More than four thousand of them a day had flown over the cape in the clear northwesterlies of early October. Sometimes fifty thousand of them are counted coming over in a single fall. There are Cooper's hawks, marsh harriers with their flexed-back wings, ospreys, goshawks, merlins, broad-wingeds and red-taileds and red-shouldereds, even a stray Swainson's or two blown in from the west.

And eagles: as many as three a day sometimes. On one memorable afternoon a bald and a golden had flown over together, dark, huge, wide-winged, steady in the gusting blow.

My friend Larry and the other hawk-watchers that had been hired for the season counted the hawks by using click-counters — like the ones used in theaters or in protest marches for keeping a count of the crowd. On top flying days, clear days with the wind in the northwest, they had to hold a clicker in each hand and wedge their binoculars in between.

No one even tries to count the songbirds this way. But one day when the hawk-counting was slower than usual, Larry counted cormorants, just for the heck of it. More than twenty thousand of them flew over in that one day within range of his binoculars, and arrowed out over the bay.

Aside from their value as sheer spectacle, the skiesful of raptors are like a vein of live juice — blood, flash-flood — that pulses through from the farthest fingerings of North America. Hawks come through the cape from as far away as Greenland, the Rocky Mountains, the Canadian Arctic. Raptors are at the top, the pinnacle, of the food chain: they eat the grouse and squirrels and mice and hare and shrews and lemmings and birds and fish, all of which have eaten crustaceans, worms, insects; and so on, down link by edible link to phytoplankton and algae, and the roots and stems and leaves of plants; the alchemists of light itself.

By counting the passing raptors (the "foules of ravyne," as Chaucer called them; birds of plunder, ravishment, seizure; of prey), the observatory keeps its fingertips on the pulse of a whole system composed of billions of individual living beings. The raptors are the crown of a food web that enmeshes half a continent, down even into the soil.

I had come to see birds. I was enchanted by wheeling, sharp-edged, chittering flocks of barn swallows flowing over the dunes, congealing on telephone wires; by a brown creeper beeping and spiraling up a tree outside my door; by the antics of a flock of butter-butts bouncing through a patch of clover; by the spectacle of hundreds of turkey vultures wheeling up a thermal on their way to the Carolinas. One morning there was suddenly the dark silhouette of a young golden eagle overhead. His dark soar made everyone fall silent: not just the little birds on the ground but the people, the trees, even the sea.

The run of the coast and the chance jut of the cape funneled the birds in, and the birds had brought a following of bird-watchers and bird-banders, hawk aficionados, and naturalists and researchers of every stripe. I stayed with a dozen of them in a gray house behind the dunes, our grocery bags arranged on the floor and our quilts airing on the line, as if we were only encamped there, as nomadic as our quarry.

They were an international crowd. Anat, an Israeli girl, had come to Cape May to learn to trap and band raptors. She had been banding songbirds for years in Elath, at the tip of the Gulf of Aqaba. Elath is an island in the sky for Asian and European migrants, the first spot of green after the sands of the Sinai. She had caught birds there that wore bands from as far away as England, Germany, Moscow.

Borja (Frank) Heredia had also come to band hawks. He

was from Spain, and was studying ornithology for a year at Cornell. He told us about watching the thousands of hawks that fly through the cols of the Pyrenees in the spring and fall, and the massive collections of European birds that cross the Straits of Gibraltar. There are these islands in the sky scattered all over the globe.

The questions sing and tease at the mind: where are the birds going, and how? In some people these questions sing and tease harder than in others. They are more aware than most of us are of the size and texture of our ignorance.

"You've got to see Sid's van!" people said, when I told them that I had come to see birds.

So that first evening I walked down the road by the sea and found a great humming lozenge of a vehicle looming out of the darkness and boom of surf. It was only barely recognizable as a camper van, so stippled was it with swinging dishes, portholes, antennae. It purred with energy as though it would lift off any minute and whir away. It was a state-of-the-art bird-migration laboratory, the creation of Dr. Sidney Gauthreaux, a professor of zoology at Clemson State University in Clemson, South Carolina. He was a large vital man with a deep drawl. Everyone called him Sid. He had put the van together two years before and had been on the road with it nearly ever since — to the everglades in January, to California, Washington, Oregon, Texas, New Mexico; anywhere and anytime there were birds moving.

"I'm developin' a standardized methodology for monitorin' bird movements," he said. "Come on in."

Inside the van it was as dim and comfortable as a bar. Two graduate students were sipping beer and sorting through a stack of clipboards thick with sheaves of data sheets. The rear of the van was a mass of equipment: coils of cable, video cameras, control panels, spotting scopes the size of bazookas. Sid sat me down in front of a television screen, threw a switch, twirled a knob, and the screen pulsed into life. Bright curving sparks suddenly eased across the dark. He had used an army-issue night-spotting scope with a camera and a vertical radar apparatus hooked up to it to take this videotape through a hole in the top of the van the night before. It looked like tracks in a cloud chamber; brief glows trailing briefer sparkles. The sparks were birds. Individual birds. Hawks and water birds fly in the daytime, but everything else, eager to keep out of the raptors' way, moves at night. Every night Sid would film twenty minutes' worth of a slice of sky: four degrees of arc out of the whole 180. When the sparks were counted and multiplied by the appropriate numbers, Sid could tell you how many birds were flying overhead every hour, what direction they were flying in, and how high they were flying. Fixed in space, counted in time, averaged over years, these were bird data that could be played with, used. Good data. Lots.

Sid flipped a switch and another screen tingled into greenish life, with the circular sweeping hand and subtle pingings of surveillance radar. Sid was using it to find out where birds were moving so that he could park his van in their flight paths. As the dish turned its circle overhead, the outlines of Cape May blipped into life, patchy and distorted. As I watched, I began to notice smudges, emanations, spreading southwestward off the coast.

"You want to see birds?" Sid whispered, his voice barely audible over the noise of the machinery, his finger tracing the gouts of greenish steam. "You've come to the right place, honey."

The next morning at a quarter to six I followed three of the bird-banders through the mist and across a field full of cattle toward the dunes and the sea. Near the edge of the pasture we came on a rickety plywood contraption that looked like the remains of a chicken coop chucked out to rot. It was a hawk blind, one of four scattered around the cape, and we were going to sit in it all day and trap hawks. In spite of — perhaps because of — its unlikely appearance, hundreds of hawks had been trapped and banded there in the last few weeks. It didn't look like the kind of place where people should be.

There were three kinds of nets surrounding the blind. There were bow nets, hoops with soft netting attached, that could be sprung by pulling a cord inside the blind. There was a triangle of mist nets made of nearly invisible black thread, each one six feet high and yards long, held up by slender poles. Then there was a dhogaza, an ingenious contraption from India. It was made of a semicircle of mist nets held up by bits of fishing line pinched in place with clothespegs. At the lightest touch the net would collapse and entangle a bird in its web. There was even a special bow net set up for peregrine falcons, who feed on birds and will take their prey only in the air. In front of the bow net a lure was attached to a length of bungie cord, and a string led back into the blind, so that it could be yanked on to bounce the lure into the air as though it were a sparrow in great distress. Since September, twenty-odd peregrines had been bagged by this ruse.

Inside, the blind was as cramped and complicated as the turret of a Sherman tank. All of the lure and trigger strings led into the blind through ceramic cable insulators that had been scavenged from a local utility company. The lines were hooked up to nails and pegs, and there was a crude bench where two of the banders could sit to pull on them. One person could stand, just barely, and peer through a slit window at the sky: the early warning system.

"Sharpie at three o'clock!" There was a spate of lure-wiggling, but the sharpie flew away.

"Hear that jay?" asked Chris. Chris Schultz was in charge of the banding in our blind. I could hear a jay screaming off to the east. "There's another sharpie up there, I betcha." A sharpie hove into view, angled, and dove. The banders wriggled the lures, hands on the trigger strings. Whoooomp. Bang! A bow net sprang, the sharpie leaping inside. Chris ran out and fetched her in, tucked under his arm, and went to work.

The stated purpose of bird-banding is to find out where

birds have come from, where they're going, how they get there, and what kind of condition they're in while they're on their way. While the birds are in hand they are measured — the lengths of their bones, feathers, beaks, wings. They are weighed, their feathers are checked for molt, and the down of their breasts and underwings is blown aside to see how much fat they are carrying. The fat glows yellow under their thin skin. The birds are aged, sexed, stroked, banded, and then let go.

Banding birds is a bit like throwing messages-in-bottles into a raging sea; not many are found, not many answers find their way back. To use money terminology: bird-banding has a very high cost/benefit ratio. Some of the hawks caught at Cape May had been banded in Greenland, or Maine, or Canada. Bands were returned from Central America. More fragments of hawks' travel patterns were traced, made sure; but for people who band birds it is very clear that the bird in the hand is its own reward.

"Female coop over the dunes, bring her in, bring her in! Pop that lure!" Whoomp . . . Bang! We had her. We rushed from the blind; by the time we were all out, Chris already had the big hawk held by her thighs, her wings pinioned under his arm. She stared out at us, through us, her crest raised in anger. She was all curved talons and golden eyes. Only hatching-year Cooper's hawks have golden eyes.

"And see . . . look, her primaries are frayed at the ends, and her tail feathers too, see? She's not much of a flyer yet. Bumps into things."

"Kestrel, kestrel!" Oooooo . . . bang. BANG we exploded from the blind in a practiced gang.

CRASH flopflopflop flop . . . "Hey! A merlin in the dhogaza, quick!" BANG.

Once they were caught, the hawks were put in cans. Pairs of coffee and juice cans of all sizes had been taped together end to end with duct tape, and holes had been punched into the bottom of the end can so that the bird, inserted headfirst, could breathe. The cans held the birds immobile and calm, like a hood on a falcon, but their talons stuck out where they were handy for banding. If more hawks were caught than could be weighed, measured, and banded at one time, they could be stacked up in their cans like cordwood. Once they had been banded and had their vital statistics written down on the chart, they were drawn from their cans like so many rabbits from hats, taken into the field, and let loose.

There were four hawk-banding stations scattered across the cape. At 7:30 A.M. they switched on their walkie-talkies and sounded more than ever like a squadron of tanks on the prowl:

"Calling north blind, north blind come in." (*crackle*) "Red-tail coming your way!" (*crackle*) "Five Coops and a kestrel and an adult female merlin so far." (*crackle*) "Yup." (*crackle*) "Yup!"

Autumn has a rhythm to it in the hawk blinds. The ac-cipiters — Cooper's and sharp-shinned hawks — come in first, from late September well into October.

In October the accipiters begin to ease off and the buteos come; the red-taileds and red-shouldereds and rough-leggeds, all big soaring hawks that stay up high, watching, hanging in a slow circling glide, waiting to plummet on unwary rodents and birds in a close-winged bomblike stoop.

The falcons, the peregrine and the little kestrel, come through in bursts all autumn long, drawn or pushed by forces other than mere time.

Each day in the blind has a rhythm to it, too. From dawn to 10:00 A.M. is always busy; the birds are just up from their nighttime roosts and are hungry. At midday the buteos come down to feed. At 3:00 P.M. there is another flurry of activity, a kind of suppertime rush. From 4:30 to dark it is merlin time.

At dusk the hawks went to roost. The hawk-banders gathered their data sheets and we went back to the gray house behind the dunes to shower, drink beer, eat supper, and to gather around Bill Clark, a raptor biologist who was in charge of the hawk-banding project at Cape May. Bill towered over everyone, blond, tall, quiet and unassuming. In spite of our eager questioning it was nearly impossible to get any straight answers out of him about his subject; perhaps because he was too aware of the gaps in the data, and of the limitations of data in particular, and the futility of straight answers in general. He hedged, hemmed, and hawed. He had very likely spent more hours watching and touching hawks and eagles than any man alive. The raptor-banding project was his baby; the result of his experience, experiments, and tinkering.

One evening Bill showed some slides of young bald eagles that he had been watching for much of the summer. The young eagles liked to gather at a particular farm pond and Bill had set up a blind there. The young eagles didn't fly very well yet, but they practiced a lot, grabbing branches in midair and dangling from them like acrobats. The farmer who owned the pond left toys out for his avian guests — empty Clorox bottles were popular — and the eagles spent hours rolling them, pouncing on them, picking at them, like kittens with a ball of wool.

At dusk another banding project swung into motion at Cape May. Owls, of all birds, have kept a shroud of mystery around themselves, simply because they are difficult to see. They hunt at night when it is too dark to watch them; in the daytime they hide. When they migrate, they move at night, hunting as they go, like the hawks whose niche they take over at dusk and give back at dawn. Katy Duffy has been banding owls on Cape May for years.

"We don't have a lot of answers," said Katy. "Mostly we have questions."

Katy is dark-haired, handsome, and she walked along the forest paths quickly in the dark, her flashlight bobbing. I had to run to keep up with her. She patrolled her line of nets and traps every two hours, all night long. She used the same mist nets that the hawk-banders had used during the day, and she set out special traps on poles for the owls that liked to hunt from perches instead of on the wing. When an owl landed on a pole, the trap would spring, wrapping a soft string noose around its ankles.

When I went out with Katy at midnight, all of the nets were empty, but as we waded through the tall grasses of the marsh a flopping thing materialized ahead of us: a barn owl, tethered to the foot of a pole by the loop of a sprung trap. He stared into Katy's flashlight beam. He was the color of milky coffee, with long narrow wings, and his eyes in their heart-shaped facial disk gleamed like plums in a saucer. The facial disk was a bowl of stiff, scalelike feathers that could focus sensory input like a dish antenna; he could turn his head through 360 degrees of arc, sweeping his world for the faintest of rustles, the smallest shiver of mouse-moved grass.

Katy released the owl and reset the trap on its pole with one deft hand, her flashlight clamped between her knees. She held the bird by its legs and tucked its wing-tips and tail feathers into her fist so that it made a sleek immobile handful, its eye staring into hers.

"You've got to watch it with the working end," she said, pointing at the talons with her flashlight; there was a mass of tangled hooks below her fist.

Bird in hand, we hurried to the nearest blind, a luxurious roomy place in comparison with the slanting box in the cow pasture. Katy canned the owl by feel and lit a Coleman lantern. In the hissing, contrasty light she looked like a conspirator, a spy, a resistance fighter, a baggy-jacketed general of some guerrilla army. Owl talons and tail feathers protruded from the Maxwell House and Mellow Roast cans, the harvest of a stygian, invisible world; ammunition to be tossed, braceleted, return-addressed, weighed, measured, out into the darkness of our ignorance. Amen!

Once the lamp was lit Katy opened a tackle box full of the tools of her trade: pliers, coils of bands of different sizes, wires, and tapes. She drew the owl from his cans, talking to him and stroking his soft nape, and then measured his wings and checked him for molt. No molt; a hatching-year bird then. She measured his leg for a band. She told me about owls, rapid-fire, as if she were talking to herself. This one's breast was creamy with flecks on it like poppyseeds; the creamy-breasted barn owls are males, the cinnamony-breasted ones are females. The older the bird of either sex is, the paler it gets.

In the autumn of 1981, Katy had banded 212 owls; 115 saw-whets, 48 barn owls, 48 long-eareds — big dark birds with a look of perpetual catatonic shock — and one great horned. "The Big One," Katy called him. She has trapped one Big One almost every year. A pair of taped-together three-pound Maxwell House cans were reserved in a place of honor in case of a great horned.

The best nights for trapping are the calm nights following several days of northwest blow. Calm nights are good for hunting in — there is no wind to confuse sound or motion — and the northwesterlies have brought a fresh crop of hungry owls down the coast.

On our last check before dawn, there were six at once in the traps and nets, saw-whets and barn owls and one long-eared. I carried one barn owl myself, like a bouquet, its facial disk a double-centered flower. As we hurried through the woods, the branches of the trees were sketched against a suddenly paler and bluer star-filled sky. We trotted along on winding paths through thickets of plume grasses more than fourteen feet tall, their long stems looming and arcing overhead like bamboo. By the time the birds were banded and measured, the sky showed bright purple through the watchwindow of the blind, and as we set them loose the horizon was orange, paling to lemon. The loosed owls flew away, one at a time, slowly, soundlessly, over the tops of the bending grass.

I spent the morning of my last day on Cape May in the north blind, where the banders were hoping to catch an eagle. The stubble field nearby had been a favorite hunting ground for eagles all autumn long. While I was there we had a visitor, a young man named Robert Grubh, a visiting dignitary from the Bombay Natural History Society. It was a cold morning and his borrowed hat and jacket were too big for him. He giggled with recognition at the dhogaza, pointing. He stood on the upturned wooden box next to me and we looked together through the long slit window at the top of the blind, watching the sky. When I asked him why he had come to the cape, he said that he was studying vultures in India and that he wanted to find a way to trap them.

"In the fall, you see, the birds come all together like this down the sea" — he held his slim brown hands, their heels together, their fingers apart, in a V — "like this. And the vultures, they follow. And here —" He tapped the heels of his hands together, the fundus of the V, the arrow-point, Cape Comorin and the Palk Strait; "here they come, oh very many, and there we will trap!"

An archipelago.

WHITE-FOOTED MOUSE

II ❧ The Bartering of Leaves

I ween that I hung on the windy tree,
Hung there for nights full nine;
With the spear I was wounded, and offered I was
To Othin, myself to myself,
On the tree that none may ever know
What root beneath it runs.
— HOVAMOL, *in the*
Elder Edda, c. 1270
(translated by H. A. Bellows)

Make me thy lyre, even as the forest is:
What if my leaves are falling like its own!
— PERCY BYSSHE SHELLEY,
"Ode to the West Wind"

Space Ships

In the September wind half of the plant world seems to be flying off, and the other half has either already flown or is busy assembling its gear. The fields and the pastures and the slopes of the hills are full of seeds and spores, all of them being hurled away. The leaves will go too, and soon. First the birds disappear, then the seeds, then the leaves; by November we will be left with a world stripped, uncolored and unmuscled. It is as though we were hoisting ourselves, all these hills, into the cold and dark between the moon and Mars. These are all preparations for a journey through space, and time.

One afternoon in the third week of September my son and I went on an explore through the fields and found a patch of milkweed in the pasture, tufted with white. At first we found the ripest pods and tore out fistfuls of fluff and threw them up. Then we discovered that if you held the wide case bottoms open and just blew, the seeds, which are layered in there like the scales of a fish, would come free one after the other, roaring up around one's head like a swarm of silky bubbles. The point of the exercise was to empty a pod at one blow. The pods were splitting and flexing their opened cases up to the wind; we were only hurrying the wind's job.

Afterward we found puffball mushrooms under the pines. The ripe ones had holes burst in their middles. We picked them and puffed the spores at each other, running and laughing and trying to woosh each other in the face. Each mushroom was only the size of a modest chicken's egg but took ages to run out of ammunition; each bout of our spore war went on for at least ten minutes before we had to search about and reload. I remember reading somewhere that giant puffballs, which are the size of ostrich eggs and weigh several pounds, have enough spores in them so that if each one hatched and grew to maturity the puffball crop would outweigh the planet. . . . We were toying under the pines with minor sprayings of fungal fecundity, puffing mere continents in each other's ears.

Down in the rough pasture tall sedges held up brown pompoms that scraped off easily into our hands, sifts of brown chaff and white deltoid seed which it was fun to fling; chaff and seeds blew off, scattering among the grasses. Some plant seeds, the seeds of orchids, for instance, are so tiny that they blow about in the highest winds of the atmosphere, riding down who-knows-where as the nuclei in drops of rain. Farther down the pasture there were black raspberry canes rising five feet in the air, armed with hard, serious thorns. Each cane held up wide panicles of berries — the inmost ones pale green, the higher ones rose, the tipmost ones a deep blue black with silver lights. These last ripe berries pulled off easily into our hands. They were sweet and heavy flavored, and each bobble of fruit had a hard single seed that gritted in our teeth.

Later that afternoon it occurred to me, quite suddenly, while I was arranging the last of the red summer apples in a black bowl on my table, and draping an impulsively purchased bunch of purple grapes across them — a luxury because it was September, after all, the last and richest month of summer —

that most live things move through wild transformations in a roundish form; streamlined against the rushing of the here and now. Winter above all things is a time to hole up, play dumb, to go congealed and small. It is also an excuse to launch oneself off, to try something new in the world: this is what plants seem to be doing.

Look at it this way. You want to colonize the universe, and you could never make the trip yourself. Let's say you spent a few hundred million years perfecting a design. It might be something like this: you take one of your embryos when it is as small as a grain of sand and put it into nearly suspended animation. You give it a good big food supply, very rich; full of fats and proteins. You equip it with sensory scoops and programmed biological software that can test surrounding temperature, chemistry, light intensity, and so on, and that will give the embryo the A-OK only when all environmental systems are go. You give it a timer, which will activate the sensory scoops only after the cold and dark of space have been left behind and a new planet has been reached. Then you wrap the whole business in a series of thin flexible laminations to protect the embryo and its attendant marvels against meteor showers, radiation belts, unpleasant chemical oceans, et cetera. The final coat has been carefully devised to make the whole thing look like an innocent pebble. Then you take a few dozen of these and around them you pack a large quantity of desirable stuff: some form of concentrated energy, say, something which is always in short supply in the universe and which nearly all of the Other Aliens (you are not alone in this place, after all) want and need. Over this you wrap a final lamination that is colorful, bright, and very attractive. (You have never actually seen these Aliens, but you know from years of experimentation what it is that they like.) Then you suspend the whole business where they can find it easily, and you wait for one of them to take it away, consume the concentrated energy stuff, and leave the unwanted pebblelike bits on some

Space Ships

convenient planet. You are a tree; you have just invented the apple.

In September the forage in the woods gets tough and pale and makes poor eating, and at night the deer come up into the fields, which have been mown in midsummer and are green with tender new growth. In the mornings I find cloven hoof-prints under the apple trees, the fruit from the lower branches and the windfalls gone. I rage. I put my black dog, Dunbar, out at night, forgetting that what he does at night is sleep. (Which is what he does in the day, too, it seems, a fault of canine middle age.) In the morning the deer move off into the fringe of woods and the rough pasture. The apples are digested. The seeds move through the deer's digestive acid baths un-scathed. They are deposited among pellets of fertilizer. The snow falls, after a while. The time clock is running, the tem-perature gauges are measuring the cold. Like most local seeds they won't sprout in Indian summer or a February thaw; they need a certain length of time in cold of a certain depth before they *can* sprout. Before they are primed. A seed's defenses are complex, cautious; perhaps because a newborn tree is both immobile and defenseless. In April the dials will click, the sensory scoops nod their approval; warmth, oxygen, water, light; all systems go. The embryo wakes, a root pops through casings, seed leaves unfurl in a patch of light. Takeoff, flight, touchdown: a new apple tree steps into the air.

If you were a Kentucky coffee tree, a chestnut tree, a white clover, a willow, a mustard, or any other plant that one might care to mention, you would have done things differently. The willow fluff that escapes from the hedgerows in June carries a seed which has a food supply that will last at most a few days, but the poverty of its supplies means that it can travel light — far, in other words. A chestnut on the other hand travels heavy with a purpose. The chestnut trees by my parents' house in Connecticut open their spiny cases all at once, over the space

The Bartering of Leaves　　ꞏ　　53

of a week at most, releasing a shower of plenty that drives the local squirrels into a frenzy of maniacal grabbiness. Given the hysterical pace of the harvest, even the most level-headed squirrel can't possibly remember where he put all his nuts, and the sprouting of young chestnut trees every spring, along the hedgerows and in the old fields, bears fine witness to the ingenuity of the trees.

Consider the Kentucky coffee tree: a nine-days'-wonder if there ever was one. I was introduced to it for the first time in the office of a botany professor in Boston. I was completing a botanical research paper of some kind, and I had gone to see this professor for a reason which was important at the time but which I have since forgotten. All I remember now is the Kentucky coffee tree. At some time during our interview the professor scraped back his chair and went over to a corner of his office where there was a glass bowl full of water and brown things. He picked one of the brown things out and handed it to me.

"Ever see one of these?" he said.

It looked like a flattened chestnut, mahogany brown, as smooth as wood. No, I hadn't.

"It's the seed of a Kentucky coffee tree. It's been sitting in this bowl of water for ten years," he said. "Sometimes I change the water." He looked at the bowl with a crooked smile, as if he were talking about his goldfish or budgie: clean, good company. No trouble at all.

The year before, he had taken three seeds out, had rubbed them hard with coarse sandpaper, and had put them back in the bowl. A week after that, two of these seeds had sprouted. He took me out to the greenhouse and showed me two sturdy seedlings in pots.

Kentucky coffee-tree seeds have the most waterproof coat of any seed in North America. The world, maybe. Unless the seed is physically damaged it can't sprout. Ever. The trees grow in fertile river valleys through western New York, Nebraska, Kansas, Kentucky, Tennessee. They aren't common. Some lucky seeds may be bounced down a river in the spring flood, ground against rocks, and tossed up on a drying bank, having had just enough roughing up to let water in to the embryo so that it can sprout and grow. That's the tree's destination: plenty of spring rain and a rich bottomland far from home.

Some seeds can wait a very long time. Some books claim that, under the right conditions, lotus seeds can wait more than a thousand years for things to be just so. The record-holder, though, seems to be an alpine vetch, a small plant of the pea family that is adapted to tundra living. A seed of this vetch lay in a fossil rodent burrow deep in permafrost for more than ten thousand years. Some scientists who were interested in climatic change in the high Arctic exhumed the burrow and carbon-dated its contents and analyzed the plant seeds and stems that the rodent had gathered for his winter store. Alpine vetches didn't grow anywhere near there, hadn't for a long time. According to an oft-quoted botanical legend, one of the scientists took the vetch seed back to the lab and planted it. It grew.

Closer to home, the large measure of patience some seeds have can be a nuisance. When we first plowed the field behind the barn, it had lain fallow for more than fifteen years, but there were clots of yellow mustard in the new oats, and under the timothy hay the next summer was a heavy surf of white clover. I had planted neither, and neither one had been there in the field before. I suspected my seed company of gross negligence until I read in one of my agricultural manuals that clover and mustard seed can live for more than five decades in the soil, waiting for the field to be plowed. Plowing means less competition from other plants — plenty of growing room, in other words. Clover and mustard seeds have their sensory program: this much cold, this much warmth, this much moisture, this much light, and a whole lot of oxygen: then they may sprout! Unless all of the requirements are met, the seed won't. Plows and harrows not only kill the competition but fluff in the oxygen, lots of it. That is what does it; the final key. Every time the fields are tilled now I can rely on the mustard's being there; its yellow flowers in July are a declaration of faith.

As seeds, plants lose their conservative phlegmatic character and become alarmingly high-tech and athletic, capable of withstanding space-time warps, the pummeling of frost, the fiddles of decay, heat and pressure, acid baths, even ionizing radiation, with near-impunity. They manage a lot of this by being dehydrated; what has no water cannot freeze, is uninteresting to bacteria, has a very slow metabolism (food supplies last a long time this way), and ionizing radiation has a much less disastrous effect in dry tissue than in wet because water molecules vastly magnify its damage. I wonder, if given several millions of years, we could invent an apple.

By October my orchard was bare. I had snatched what I could under the noses of the deer, and the trees rustled their drying leaves at me. At me? No. I am invisible to them, one of those aliens they have conspired to seduce. Like the burdocks and tickseeds that nab my pants, the plant world is after any motion at all; mine, the dog's, the birds going south with blackberry seeds stuck to their beaks. The wind, a child's breath, a game.

Light, Years

Tree form is a function of light and years, which seems obvious enough until one wonders how it's been done. If, like me, you want to do a little forestry, then you are always wondering how it can be done better — "better" being a subjective judgment in this case — because the trees do their part of the job well enough. Most of the trees worth looking at in my woods are a great deal older than I am, and are sensible about light, space, water, soil chemistry, and time, in ways that I'm not. Besides, the whole above-ground part of them winters in the wind, which I could never do; which no animal that I know of could do. I have respect for them. Respect is too small a word here. Awe would be better. I have awe. The more so because I have cut a lot of trees down every year. This is my part of the job. No matter that I must seem as small and skittery and quick-lived to them as a mouse would be to me.

One morning at the end of September I walked through my woods with Rich Carbonetti, a forester who works free-lance and who helps me to decide which of my trees needs cutting next.

Walking in the woods is what Rich likes to do with his time. He is sturdy, and wears logger's boots of the same blunt sturdiness so that he looks as if he had been born with them on. His truck is full of a comfortable litter of tanks, spray-cans, and hard hats, and the back of it houses two golden Labrador retrievers who walk everywhere with him, slipping through the trees like happy scouts with their tongues lolling and their eyes full of pleasure. The three of them are good company in the woods, I always learn more than I bargain for, and the woods improve.

We started by walking up Glen's field into the woodlot where the maples were beginning to color. A few fallen leaves were scattered in the ferns like scissored chips of colored paper, yellow and rose. Twenty cords of firewood had been cut in there by my neighbors and all out of trees that Rich had marked in yellow paint two years before. He was pleased, and I was. The brush piles were neat. There were pale roads made by pickup trucks in the mashed ferns. The woods were opened and lightened. There were patches of sky. The mashed ferns were part of the woodcutters' good deed because ferns put out a toxic chemical that discourages the new trees beginning their long ride up: my first tidbit of new knowledge for the day. Rich stopped to yank an evergreen seedling up by its roots and throw it over his shoulder. I didn't want evergreens in there. He ran his hands through the waist-high leaves of a young ash as though he were stroking the head of one of his yellow dogs.

We went on through the pastures and into the sugar woods. Some of the young maples were as round as my thumb and others were as thick as my arm; I remembered when they had been brushy deer-gnawed seedlings whose top tips had barely poked above the January snow. Now they were too crowded and needed thinning, releasing, more room. By the time any of them grew large enough to give anyone syrup we would both be very old, but that didn't seem to matter; we hung onto them, pointed at them, chose between them, held and shook their boles as if we were swinging children by the hands.

We covered a lot of ground and at eleven o'clock when the sun puffed away the clouds the woods warmed with bright unhurried color. The ferns were a yellowing green, maple branch ends were slabbed with corals and pinks, in the open spots there were clumps of electric-purple asters. We looked through the evergreens where logs and pulpwood needed to be cut, and I gathered a shirtful of orange chanterelle mushrooms for my lunch.

Everywhere that we went Rich gestured at trees and talked about them. One old maple was bent to one side, its branches warped in its eighteenth-century youth by overcrowding; another one had branch tips that traced the full shape of an egg in the air, and so was reaching its full potential. This one had a canker, this one a bad frost-crack, this one a handsome burl. He liked what he called my "wildlife" trees, the dead stubs pocked with holes, tenements for insect-eating birds.

I began to think about this as we went along: if light and time are the shaping forces here, then they must be sensed by the trees, sensed and used.

I sense light with my eyes; light that is nerve-shunted and brain-processed into what I see as color, form, and distance: the pale furrowed bark of sugar maples, the darker smoother bark of red maples, the olivy green of spruce against darker firs; the tilt of needled ground where I am setting my foot. This is what I need from light. The marsh hawk scouting the pasture edges, and the goldfinches darting from the thistles to the trees, see things differently. For one thing, their color sense is skewed toward the yellows; for another, they resolve shapes better, which gives them the necessary gifts of seeing tiny movements, minute detail. On the other hand, the trees not only need to see where light is coming *from* so that they can send their twig ends that way and their root tips the other way, but they also need to use each day's light as marks in a solar calendar, the rising and waning of light making up a kind of annual clockface so that they can tell their place in the year. They use light to tell time. So that they can change, and change mightily, and survive; also mightily.

What trees use to see with turns out to be almost nothing. I picture a fantasy laboratory in which a team of white-jacketed technicians shove an entire fully leaved maple into a massive machine, which grinds, whirs, sloshes, into which chemicals are poured, in which thunderstorms'-worth of electric energies sizzle; finally a tiny spigot is turned and eureka, a miniature test tube, well corked, is held up to the light: the technicians gather. It is a quarter full of a greenish protein. If you dabbed a bit of it on your forehead, you could move blindfold through four dimensions. If you were a tree.

This stuff is called phytochrome. It is a Jekyll-Hyde pigment in that it can exist in two different forms: one is blue green, one is light green. If the blue-green one (called Pr) absorbs red light, it turns into the light-green one (called Pfr). If Pfr absorbs far-red light, light of longer wavelengths, some of which are so long as to be invisible to us — infrared — it turns back into the Pr form again. It switches.

Whenever you have something that switches you have the potential for, well, if not intelligence then at least the ordering of information. A computer memory is made up of nothing but switches. Our nerve networks work the same way: along any one nerve thread at any one time a current either is or isn't running. A green plant then is a skyful of chemical switches that can be thrown by light.

It turns out that almost any plant part contains phytochrome. Leaves, buds, seeds, even young bark. All day long as sunlight shines on the leaves, the two phytochrome forms exist in a kind of equilibrium, but because of cogs and shunts in the switching process there is always a lot more Pfr than Pr, as long as the sun shines. At dusk things change. No more light. In the dark the Pfr begins to shift, gradually, into Pr, running down into it like sand through an hourglass all night long. As the sun comes up at dawn, the hourglass is almost instantly turned over. Most of the Pr zaps back into Pfr again.

So the nights can be measured, and the nights change.

Plants have their own coded programs hitched to levels of Pfr and Pr, alarm bells that signal the start of germination, growth, flowering, fruiting, dormancy, even death. When I plant spinach in the spring, it bolts for the sky almost instantly, flowering, its leaves gone inedible. When I plant spinach in September, it doesn't bolt at all and I can eat its leaves until the snow covers them up. According to built-in spinach wisdom, bloom time is when the days are long. The big Christmas cactus in the house has its own brand of flowering judgment and blooms at Thanksgiving, because, sometime in late October, it judges the nights long enough to bud, and hasn't been informed that the days grow shorter here faster than they do in its native home.

At some critical night just past midsummer the trees in the woods get their messages, each species in its own time; and their getting-ready-for-winter program begins. First twig growth stops, then no more new leaves are made. Then buds begin to form at twig ends and at the protected joints of leaf and stem. By the time Rich and I took our walk in the woods all of the maple twigs had gone a chestnut brown and winter buds lay along them, pointed and scaled like the bodies of slim finless fish. I split one bud with a fingernail and looked; it held a compact green fishbone, an embryonic twig with bumps of leaf along it like ribs, all contained in the bud's flame-shape. The old leaves were still there, still green, still measuring. The leaf-stems were still green too, but there was a distinct border between green leaf-stem and brown twig. I yanked a leaf and it broke, there, just on the color border, leaving a smile-shaped scar on the twig. The border is part of the plan, too. It is a layer of tissue, and as the nights grow shorter still, the cells that make it up will weaken and dissolve, letting the leaves fall away by their own weight.

Autumn is a good time to work in the woods. When the leaves are gone, you can see what you're getting, where you're going, what else there is. By the time that the leaves have fallen off, the deer will be as gray as the bark on the trees, and the frost will be gray on the ground in the mornings, and you will be able to see your breath as if you were the spout of a boiling kettle.

By the end of the morning Rich and I and the dogs had covered a lot of ground. There were logs, pulpwood, maple thinnings to be burned to boil syrup, and firewood marked for many years ahead. When we were coming down the hill on our way home, I suddenly remembered another forester whom I had met on my brother's farm. A friend and I were with him deep in the woods, looking over young maple and beech that we wanted for firewood. The forester had bent to the ground and picked up a handful of dead dried twigs. He had arranged them in his hand in a little bundle, like a fan.

"In most of the world," he said, "this is firewood enough to cook a meal. Women walk miles to carry a bundle of this home on their backs." He looked at me, pointedly, I thought. He threw the twigs away. "Here we can afford to let them lie and replenish the soil. We can afford to be good to the trees here."

We walked on, my friend and I silent, like lectured school-children. My lust for hefty dry firewood has always bordered on the intemperate, and I have been joined in this love of wood-cutting recently by my brother; when he and I get together now we talk about trees. I remember that fistful of twigs, though, and I sometimes look askance at green leaves as if they could measure my shadow and know my lustful thoughts.

The trees transform themselves. We change the woods; for better or for worse. For better or for worse, then? I puzzle over this question like a worried husband. I haven't taken any vows, I slipped into this woodsy relationship because I liked the look of the place, and wasn't quite aware that I would have to deal with the presence of so many individuals who had staked a prior claim. Nobody told me ten years ago that good husbandry meant cutting trees. When a big tree is cut, it falls with a sound like a heavy sigh, and settles to the ground with creakings and rushings like the prow of a boat meeting a wave; a confluence of light and time that can be put to another use.

In the Green Room

This is the slope of the world; I feel the tug down and brace my feet in the grass. In my lap I have my notebook and garnerings of plant "roots" spilling from a paper bag. In front of me is a tree. The contents of the bag and the tree are my morning's work; I want to find out where plants are going to, now that the leaves are yellowing and winter is on its way, and the slope seemed a good place to do it at the time, but in looking out I feel suddenly assaulted by the hills. This morning the hills demanded my attention in a new way and now they make me unsure, even a little scared. When I sat down here, I held onto the grass as if it could keep me from slipping off.

This morning an earthquake woke me up. The house rumbled and rattled around me and the bed swayed, and my first thought was that the furnace had exploded and that the house was on fire. I had visions of struggling through the smoke and flames with my son in my arms and squeezing out with him through the back window and sliding down the shed roof, already mourning the loss of the old cedar bed in which I have slept most of my life, the wooden animals that I bought from a little boy at a waterhole in Kenya for three sharpened pencils, and all my books. I was awake then, sitting up, staring, but the house was quiet. My son slept on in his bed. When I tiptoed downstairs to the cellar, the furnace sat as furnaces do, and I began to suspect that forces were in motion that were greater than mere furnaces could supply.

A friend of mine who lives sixty miles away told me this morning, when he called me on the phone, that the quake had woken him up, too, with the thought that his wife and child had fallen down the stairs. We began our days with visions of calamity only to find that nothing much had changed. When I looked out of the window, the fences were no more crooked than usual, there were no smoking calderas among the oats.

The quake had registered 5.2 on the Richter scale. The Richter scale runs from 0 to 10 — a zero being the subtlest terran quiver recordable on a decent seismograph. (Minus Richter fractions have been recorded on the best ones, jiggles that are hardly of concern to common mortals.) An 8.9 is the highest that any quake has bounced a recording needle to date; a 10 would be the epicenter of Doomsday — an Armageddon.

It was a clear October morning; the fields were like emerald carpets and the maples in the hedgerows were opulent billows of color. I set off with my bag and trowel and notebook to plumb at firsthand some of the wintering secrets of plants, and came here to this slope of pasture acknowledging — in some backwash of my morning scare — the bedrock itself, its layered anatomy heaved beneath my seat.

All I need to do is to look at where I am; the evidence is all here. At my back the ground rises and to my left it slopes west, riven by the V-shaped chop of the ravine in which the

Tamarack runs. Over one shoulder is the wide bowl of the swamp and the hills that form its watershed and the Tamarack's source. Below me and to the west the land slithers down into a scoop of valley and then rolls up to the south and west and drops away again, turbulent as a sea. The blue-purple line of the Green Mountains rises beyond like a tidal wave, a *tsunami*, rushing in. Where one can see the rock underpinnings of all this, in the cuts where the highway goes, they are layered like a pile of rugs. They are tilted, mashed, shoved into rolls and wrinkles by the heave of continents; by Europe ramming into us, pulling away, ramming and pulling away again; by the tread of glaciers pressing down and letting rebound; by hot shoulderings of magmas underneath. The land rose, fell, rose. Still rises, falls. The tree and I are perched on the flank of a geologic wave. We hang on for dear life.

Three years ago I had a new well drilled to water the sheep at lambing time, and 120 feet down the spittings of rock dust from the drill turned a sudden floury white. I held my hand in the shower of it and collected a palmful of limestone, the skeletons of tiny animals that had whirled and drifted through their short lives in some ancient sea. This height of land on which I brace my back was once the seafloor, and the hill has — deep inside itself — the color and chemistry of bone.

Suddenly everything that I am exploring — live, surface things — seems fragmentary, insecurely perched, hardly worth the ticket. I am seated on miles of living rock.

I think that the bones of things say a lot about the lives they frame. A man's skeleton has a weak and vulnerable back, but the skull confronts one from the top like a holed white ball radiating power; and those tinkling intricate showers of finger bones want to fondle, twist, and speak! The skeletons of trees are always reaching through their whole bulk to the sun. The maple in front of me is the biggest tree on the farm, in girth, anyway, and is well along in a rich middle age. There are holes in its bole where branches fell off. Its base is split, twisted, hollowed by rot into a room with two doors, opposite each other, one heart-shaped and the other curved over in a Gothic arch. Its crown, which was once as oval as an egg, has flattened, and in a few years its center will be gone altogether, leaving a low mendicant's tonsure of leaves. It is busy healing its wounds, achieving a nearly human character, enduring the tunnelings of beetles, the webbings of fungi, the hollowings of birds. Soon, even in my lifetime, only a barkless stub will stand, a doored and windowed tenement but no longer a living tree.

I have brought my sack of earth-crumbed treasures here, because it is a good place to sit in the sun and the grass and look them through. I pull out a trillium bulb, like an inch-wide miniature of a tulip bulb, trailing rootlets from one end and sprouting a flaccid dead stem from the other. In those starchy bulb-layers made up of fattened and hugely modified leaves the trillium will keep itself until April. Next there is a plump, scambled object which looks more than anything else like a wildly schizophrenic french fry. At its tips it holds pale cones, and from each of these a single leafed stalk will push up in May, subtended by the little rosy bells of Solomon's seal. This plump crisp "root," which is as fryable and edible as any french fry, is an underground stem that has specialized in winter storage. Then there are three little spring-beauty bulbs, tear-shaped and pale. In the center of each bulb are flowers already formed for next spring. Next I pull out a dirty tangle of clover roots, all gathering to a bunched crown, like a waist, a thickened dollop full of stored food and the live growing clusters of cells from which all of its new roots and leaves will grow. The roots themselves are pricked all over with collections of pale globules the size of radish seeds, convenient houses for the clover's private colonies of nitrogen-fixing bacteria. The bacteria feed some of the nitrogen that they fix from the air in the soil to the clover as a kind of rent. Next there is a cattail corm that I got from the pond, soaking my shirt cuffs and muddying my boots; a larger version of the Solomon's-seal tangle and also a stem of underground persuasions armed with the greenish conelike tips from which next year's cattails will come. I wipe one of these tips in the grass and take a bite; it is crisp and tastes of sweetish cucumber. All of these roots, corms, and bulbs store starch for winter food and as the raw material to push new leaves and flowers up with after the winter is gone. From the oats in the field I got nothing but a handful of seeds, which are all they have to winter with. Happily for me, the oats like other annual grasses are generous with seeds, spending up to sixty percent of their whole year's energy budget on them. The oats are still soft, and they taste slightly floury, and still sweet.

The burrowing in that plants are doing, the retreat to the ground and storing up of wealth there, has all been set in motion by that touchy green protein, phytochrome. The retreat is hurried by the cooling nights and by the light frosts that have already come, singeing the tops of the pumpkin vines, and by the simple orderly completion of the plant programs begun last spring: leaf time, flower time, fruit, and then, now, wintering.

The slope is filling with the eddies and blown spume of change; I am seated in fiery goings-on. Even the little ground pines by my hands, which creep bristling across soil too acid to grow grass, have lifted candlelike strobili that have gone pale gold; when I tap them puffs of spores blow away. These spores are so oily and fine that they have been used to make explosives. Below on the slope the docks and buckwheats are still in bloom, white and pink and green, full of brownish seed like flecks of coal. Under the pines where I walked this noon there were suddenly mushrooms everywhere — yellow dead-man's fingers, tiny red umbrellas, fat taupe and brown and purplish cones, their undersides charred with spores. The air fills; in and under the fabric of the soil, roots, corms, bulbs fatten. I don't think that the earthquake has shaken them as it has me. Winter is a predictable kind of Armageddon, a calamity calmly weathered, an end of a world that they understand and are preparing for; caught between the forces of darkness and light.

I am still sitting here, confronting the tree now, which of all things looks most unmoved by wind or heaved slope. I know it holds on with the weave of its roots as wide as the reach of its twigs. Its outer leaves rustle, the color of red coral. Inside there are yellow leaves and green leaves. It looks as though it were hung with incendiary pigment which one could grind and mix with oil and make a painting with, a Veronese–sized melange of fiery angels with swords in their mouths and their feet aflame. It would be glorious enough, but it wouldn't last very long because the pigments are alive. Yellow-orange carotenes, they are part of the light-trapping machinery of the leaves and are revealed, like vivid petticoats, only when the heavier dress of green chlorophyll has died away. They will die away, too. The tree is pulling its resources inward.

To where, then? A maple has no starch-storing tubers or buried bulbs. If one stripped away the skeleton of the tree, which is all of the wood and bark, one would have an odd apparition here, a tree as translucent as a veil. There is a thin layer of live tree flesh wrapped around the outside of the column of wood, and a second tissue-thin layer just under the bark. The pointed buds are also alive.

These veils of tissue and the sparklike buds are all of the tree that is alive, except for the leaves, which are going soon, some of them falling off now, rattling away in an orange gust. If once could collapse this tissue of live tree, one would have a bushel-basket full of greenish film like a monstrous silk stocking, another basket full of buds like pointy peas. The bulk of what we think of as Tree is skeleton; exuded, hardened, layered inward and outward, but as dead as hair or nails.

I have left something out. Assemble and hoist the filmy tree again: look, there are spokes that project inward from the cylindrical films of flesh, vascular rays that angle through the sapwood. They are the maple's live cellars where it assembles its sunmade sugars into starch for wintering rations (not that there is much tree left to winter; perhaps this is part of the strategy of shedding one's leaves), but the starch is also banked capital for a May reinvestment in flowers, twigs, new leaves.

The tissue-thin fabric of live tree will stand out in the cold this winter as it has done for several centuries already. It will be chilled to more than thirty degrees below zero F for days on end, under its carapace of bark, wrapped around its skeleton of wood. There is an intriguing mystery here. Ice crystals formed in live tissue, whether plant or animal, kill. That is a law, a given; it can't be tampered with. It isn't cold that kills things here, it's the slashing and puncturing of crystal arms of ice.

I wanted to see this filmy tree flesh for myself, so yesterday I cut and peeled a maple twig with a kitchen knife and put peels and live twigs under the dissecting microscope and had a look. I'd seen drawings of all of this in books, but this was the real thing, flayed open. The bark of the twig was as brown and shiny as bread crust and full of bubbles, streaks, and yeasty imperfections. Under the bark there was a layer of pale green as thick as a strip of dandelion stalk, and made of concentric laminations that I could see poking out at the crudely knifed edges like layers at the edge of a piece of smashed plywood. One of these layers, which poked out farther than the others, had the texture of the gridlike glass walls of a city office building. The centers of the "windowpanes" were translucent, the "windowframes" a solid green. Each was a single live plant cell, with the green walls of tough flexible cellulose made up of layers of tiny webbed fibers. Inside these walls lay a skin-like film (I couldn't see it, but I know that it was there, thanks to those schematics in my biology book), and inside this membrane was the nearly clear cytoplasm, the living stuff, milky with tiny organs; the part of the tree that mustn't be allowed to freeze.

It is water that freezes; I have to struggle with myself

sometimes to remember this. Water with anything dissolved in it — salts, proteins, sugars, alcohols — freezes at a lower temperature than water pure. The more solutes there are in it, the lower the freezing temperature of the solution.

It turns out that the tree's method of winter survival is a lot like the way we used to make applejack. We would take a keg of raw hard cider, as dark and yeasty as stout ale, and put it outdoors in the deepest January freeze. At the end of a week or two we would hammer the lid off and make a hole (I chipped away once for an hour with an icepick to get in there) to the middle. There, lo and behold, alleluia, was a gallon or so of applejack; as clear as a bell and ninety proof. It was the water that froze in the keg, and as the ice put together its strict lattices it "kicked out" most of the solutes in its way — air, alcohol, sugar, flavors — until all that was left at the core was the magic mead.

Part of the wintering program of the tree is that each cell's membrane changes its strategy. The membrane is like a border guard and lets into and out of the live contents of the cell whatever it is that the cell needs, or needs to dispose of. The membrane breathes, eats, defecates. It selects. A semipermeable enclosing membrane is the first precondition of cellular life.

What happens in September and October and November is that the tree's cell membranes become more and more permeable to water. By the deep locking-time of November frosts (we are coming to these fast, too fast!), the membrane can let water flush in and out of the cells at will.

Outside of the membranes, in the weblike walls of these green rooms, there is some pure water; this is where ice crystals will form first when its gets cold enough. Water then flows easily out of the cells and adds to the growing crystals. The colder it gets, the more water moves out of the cell and turns into ice — outside. The membrane collapses around what is left like a deflated balloon. The vital cell stuff concentrates itself like applejack; all of its organelles and interior membranes and saps will be there still, viscous but undamaged: alive.

Every plant has its limits: tropical ones can't do this trick at all. Maples can do it for longer and at colder temperatures than, say, oaks can. Often a plant's preformed flower buds are killed at higher temperatures than the hardier leaf buds are; any of my forsythia twigs that poke above the snow are flower-less in April. Most of the plants here can't survive for long at much below −40°F.

There are other, more sneaking dangers. On a cold winter evening hard sharp noises snap in the woods like rifle fire: trees crack open as their outer wood freezes and shrinks faster than their core. Waving and clattering branches can rub each other raw. Up in the mountains, snow blown hard by the wind will wear away bark and needle leaves as if it were sandpaper. And there are porcupines, who eat tree flesh for their winter food.

The machinery whirs. All of the tree's molecular juggling adds up to endurance. All I can *see* is that the leaves are going. I look out again from my slope to see — just to see. The forest cover over the hills is lumpy and nubbly, suffused with color. The lime green and yellow of the turning birches up in the mountaintops finger into the high darkness of spruce and fir. Lower down there are islands of coral-and-gold sugar maple and beech; damp hollows hold red maples like a ruby velvet. A few roads gleam like snail tracks. There are lozenges of fields; dull buff of unmown grass, the mown fields very green, the lakes like bits of wind-tarnished mirror. If this were an alien planet and I had just landed here, I would see the nap of this forest as a single live fabric, jazzed with life, woven warp and woof over the planetary bones. The bones move, the fabric flexes like the skin on a hand. The forest grows like a complex membrane at the interface of solid rock and gaseous atmosphere, drawing from and contributing to both. Only when one gets close in to it, armed with a field guide, perhaps, can one pick out each biological stitch and give it a name, a spurious separateness, which — in its intricately threaded life — it doesn't have and never has had. The fabric can be raveled, worn, and made dull; here whole slopes of the higher mountains are gray with dead trees, rusty in summertime with dying needles, the roots and foliage pickled by air pollution and acid rain. We can crush, snip, and wear it away.

I find this all very impressive. We can crush and snip and get away with it. Why not? It's fun, it has its advantages. The fabric slips a knot here and there with every species pushed to extinction, every ton of hydrogen sulfide pumped into the air, every acre paved. I wonder sometimes if this isn't a form of jolly suicide. Won't our supporting fabric collapse under our weight if we keep this up? Well, yes. Everyone knows this. But it isn't a subject that one mentions in polite company, just as one doesn't graphically describe a degenerative disease, the lesions of leprosy, the violence and incontinence of the gaga. The avoidance seems to make the problem of our use of our power even more visible, as if you saw people streaming around a rock in their path. I avoid because it would be painful, inconvenient, and terribly lonely, to climb. By avoiding, I cut myself off. Most of the time I manage to see these hills as a fabric that I can bounce on, that I am free to tamper with, even smash and stain at will like a spoiled and unloved child. This avoidance of the issue can be wonderfully subtle: for instance, you cannot, after all, lightheartedly bulldoze a friend. So it is convenient to make of trees things that are no longer our friends but manipulable objects. I was convinced, for a long time, that trees were not really alive; not *really alive*. Sometimes I still manage to convince myself of this, but it is not as easy.

And I don't, when I kill an animal to eat, ask its permission and then thank it for giving its life. The northeastern woodland Indians did this all the time, but it has, like other kinds of politesse, gone out of fashion. When I eat spring lamb, chicken, beef raised on corn and grass, its life is passed on to me in the form of another hour or day or month of my life lived. The thread is passed, I am become the shuttle. Given that I may have some choice in the matter, what then shall I weave?

This morning I thought that I was going to be houseless, barefoot in my nightgown, as collapsed as a tree without its wood, but I was wrong. There was no calamity. None. Not yet. I will shrink in there and live gratefully in my wooden house, and put up the only resistance to winter, and doubt, that I think might work; and that might also in its simplicity distill the soul. I will stay there, burn my wood, love my child, go out no farther than the grocery store, the swamp, the ravine, and the pond; and watch.

Falling Off

On the tenth of October we had our first hard frost. At dawn the ground was as white as bone and the valleys were muffled in banks of fog. The lawn was crisp and every leaf on the birch by the door wore a white crystalline frill, and every grass stem in the hedgerow was a panicle of hoar. When the sun touched the grass, it thawed to its emerald green again, spangled with moisture, but in the shadows of the maples it stayed white until midmorning and was sprinkled with freshly curled and fallen leaves, which were cinnamon and coral and yellow. In the afternoon the air smelled of earth and apples. I looked at my woodpile and I thought — as I think after every October first-frost — that it looked too small.

I went to the woodlot and cut dry limbwood for my cookstove and made a deal with a neighbor to cut another cord for me in exchange for several cords for him. From the garden I rescued the last of my onions and cucumbers. I dug a bushel of potatoes and brought in three wheelbarrowsful of pine twigs for kindling, and one wheelbarrowful of pumpkins that had been growing wild all summer on the old manure heap below the barn. There seemed to be a thousand things which needed doing, and all at once, though I thought that I had been harvesting and bringing things in for weeks.

The hurry and bustle is infectious; plants' summer sun-harvest has been packed away in roots, seeds, wood, and suddenly everything wants a piece of it. The next night when I was lying awake in the dark I heard a crunching below me from the garden. Kneeling on the bed, I eased the screen away and opened the window wide so that I could lean out. The moon was full, the air as cool as a wash of water. A full-grown and heavily furred raccoon, as round as a drum, came through the path between the cabbages and the corn. He moved along the rows as softly as a shadow. I thought again of how much I have lost this habit of moving well; I make noise, I tromp and slouch; except when I move in the steps of a practiced dance I have little or no awareness of how I move or of what I am moving through or against; or of what might be watching.

I watched the raccoon for half an hour as he did his acrobatics in my corn. He would choose a stalk and climb up it and ride it down, and then tear off a cob with a lush ripping sound, and peel and eat, making sucking noises that were as juicy and rude as a child chewing a wad of gum with his mouth open.

The next morning a squirrel got into the garden. The red squirrels had been nipping off pine twigs for weeks to get at the swollen cones, which they had packed into little hollows in the ground between the trees, presumably for winter consumption. Red squirrels are nervous at the best of times; in October they are paranoid, defensive, wired high on some autumnal amphetamines. This one chirred and chuk-uk-uk-ukked from the garden fence, his tail jerking in rhythm, his paws tucked at his belly as if he were holding up his pants. He leaped among the corn stalks, throwing himself from one

Falling Off

to another, the tassels wagging over his head. Two blue jays flew in and out of the garden like mosaic chips of sky, picking holes in the tomatoes that had been left there and had been blackened by the frost, and they leaped off the pea fence into the bowed face of a sunflower, pulling away the pale seeds.

The garden is too close to the house now for the deer to come up into it. When I had a big garden at the edge of the field, the deer would raid it in October after the frost; they would dig up carrots and potatoes and gnaw holes in the pumpkins and winter squash; I had a race with the deer to the harvest there every fall.

Three nights after the first frost we had another, but this time it was only the valleys that were filled with hoar because — since they were unprotected by fog this time — the cooling air had run down into them, sparing the hills; in the morning the fields there were as gray as the fur of a wolf. I called a logging friend to ask him to cut me two truckloads of hardwood logs — wood for next winter and for the winter after. My shed was filled with pails full of tomatoes and apples and onions, there was a second bushel of newly dug potatoes against one wall, there were tubs and baskets full of pine cones and twigs for kindling and two heaps of winter squash; so that I could barely walk through to the door. I dusted and sorted my canning-closet shelves — jars of peaches and pears and applesauce, raspberry and strawberry and rhubarb jam, chutneys and pickles. I took a lamb and one ewe to the slaughterhouse and put the roasts and mutton sausage away in my freezer; it seemed to be more than I could possibly consume, but every time that I picked my way through the shed I was like a miser feeling of his gold.

When we had our third hard frost and even the stones went a hoary white, I thought of Rosie's story about the mouse. Rosie and I have known each other now for a long time and she is well aware of what my shed looks like in October. Hers, if anything, looks worse. She lives two townships north of me, has more and better sheep than I do, a bigger garden, and three more children. We have made expeditions together either in her battered pickup or mine to sell our wool, buy rams, or show our lambs at fairs. Sometimes we get together in the evenings and drink wine and eat late and talk about sheep and other things, and one night last year she told me about a jumping mouse that had moved into her house the winter before.

The mouse had been interested in hoarding food and had found a bonanza in the bag of kibbles Rosie keeps for her dogs in one corner of her kitchen. There was a large vaselike terrarium in her shed, its contents long defunct, and in a matter of days it was filled to the brim with a pyramid of dogfood. The mouse must have clawed its way up the sides and dropped the bits in one by one. Because of the terrarium's curved-in rim there was no way that, if the mouse ever got in, it could get either itself or its goodies out. Someone sitting down to play the piano found that the piano had been filled with dogfood tumbled all anyhow among the strings. When Rosie opened the bottom drawer of her desk, she discovered that her ledger-books had been entombed in more than twenty-five pounds of dogfood. There were little ventilation holes at the back of her gas stove, and one evening after the oven had been lit the house suddenly filled with the smell of scorching dogfood, and nothing short of mass destruction with a blowtorch could get the stuff out.

A mouse has no sense of judgment in these things. Once his hoarding program had been switched on — switched on by hormones loosed in him by the short autumn days — there was nothing but the passage of time that could turn it off. What patience he must have had to build his stores and pyramids! Armed with food enough for fifty mice, did he think himself wealthy? Was he satisfied? Arrogant? If he hadn't spent his nights scurrying with ever more redundant kibbles, what would he have done instead? Studied the cello? Loved? Lain about dreaming in the warmth under the stove? No. He would have been prospecting for birdseed, or peanuts, or cheese doodles. "Enough" isn't in a mouse's autumnal vocabulary. Perhaps, in matters of stored food and cut wood, it isn't in mine, either.

In October and November I watched the hills change, their color emptying as if it were being poured away. When I worked in the woodlot in the third week of October, the leaves were falling singly everywhere so that the ground was patched with circles of strewn color, with the same speckled yellows as were overhead. Every day the circles of fallen color were renewed, and every day they were thinner, sparse, finally gone. By the end of the month whole streaks of forest were gray as mist, lit by a few late-turning trees whose crowns stood out like single billows of flame. The top branches in the hedgerow still held a few last leaves that glowed against the fading hills like yellow lights.

The glimmers of a pattern show up here: it seems obvious enough that the mouse and the squirrel and I are hoarding against the prospect of winter hunger, but it turns out — and this is unexpected, a marvel — that the trees are trading their leaves against a winter thirst. Winter isn't only too lightless and too cold for most plant's chemical machinery; it is a drought of momentous proportions. Any maple fully leaved in January would be mummified, withered, seared. Winter winds are as arid as desert wind is, and blow a fog of ice crystals as sharp as sand. The tissue-thin fabric of a broad leaf, holed to let in air, veined with water, would freeze-dry in one sunny December day; hung out over the reflected snow-light, it would heat in the dry air and would lose water faster than any roots could draw water from rainless ground. So hardwood trees shed their frills and become almost cactuslike, first dispensing with all possible dryable surface and then stocking their living flesh with extra sugars to ward off their dehydration — just what they do in a summer drought — and then the twigs seal themselves in, patching their leaf scars with corky cells.

The Bartering of Leaves ꞏ 77

The levels of "enoughness" vary here; a maple loses all of its leaves in October, pines or spruce or fir will drop only a third of theirs; but by November the buds of the evergreens will be coated with resins as if they had been dipped in paraffin and the needles will have the white sheen of exuded wax; the evergreens seal themselves in, too.

By November the grass in the fields has gone dull, first fading to yellow and then to a juiceless sand color, so that I can believe that we have entered a kind of desert.

The hills have a new pattern to them, a somber underweave; a pointed pelt of spruce and fir darkens the mountaintops and the rockiest sloping ground, and the frost pockets — the swamp, for one — where cold air flows and sits, and the north slopes; anywhere that the soils are thin, cool, slow to recycle nutrients. On these patches of impoverished ground trees can't afford the luxury of putting on a whole new crown of leaves every year — so they don't. But the evergreens pay the price of living on poor soil by wintering hard. The waxes and resins that they layer on themselves, even the construction of their wood, whose cells are pocked with rubbery valves, are all defenses against extremes of thirst. On the highest mountaintops where winter wind and sun are both far worse than they are in the woods down here, the evergreens are battered into low hedges of dwarf forest, huddled in the lee of boulders and sheltering slopes; places where they will be protected from both wind and light by drifted snow. From these low forests some branches reach up, and are as gray and scoured as bone, as though they had been soaked in salt.

The evergreens have some advantages, though. With two-thirds of their summer needles they can and do go on making what light there is into food for themselves even into November, and can begin again in March, six weeks or more before maples have leaves at all. They can choose not to push out their own new growth until late May or early June when the weather is warm and settled, and then they can make their investment in new needle leaves directly from the yield of the old. These are "decisions" of forest economy; of a system of trade and barter in which the currency is energy — energy of light, heat; ready energy held captive in the molecular structure of stored sugars and starch; and potential energies fluxed in the chemical forge of the soil, in which trillions of small and smaller dwarves beat discarded leaves and whole trees into nutrient gold.

In November the falling larch needles sprinkle the ground like slivers of gold in truth. They are the last of the leaves to fall. All of the trees here, simply by being what they are and where they are, speak a language of private profit and loss.

The swamp that lies in its hollow just to the east and borders my land there holds acres of black spruce, each tree with the starved tufted look of taiga, "spruce-moose." They are natives of the vast muskeg of central Canada, of the forests that push to the borders of the barren ground. Under the black spruce are sphagnum mosses and tough-leaved shrubs and creeping flowers that also belong, by rights, to the far north. Just four miles south and west of all this and downhill, where the big river runs in its wide valley, and where I go in the summer to fish for trout, there are linden trees and patches of red oak. Both the oaks and the lindens grow as far south as Kentucky and survive north of here only in the valleys where winter cold and drought are buffered by water — next to the big rivers, or the Great Lakes, or the sea. Like the black spruce they let me know just by being here that these hills are part of the pattern of arboreal trade that feeds and clothes half a continent. In late October the oaks are as red as fire; but the black spruce are as impassive as they were in June or January, their branches short and their foliage dense; as if winter were their true element, which they have learned to endure by being conservative and darkly dressed.

One afternoon in the middle of November it began to snow. The air filled with a shiver of tiny bits, a swarm, a mere disturbance in the air that blotted the mountains out, then the hills; and then ghosted the trees away so that the house was surrounded by shadows, like an unfinished sketch. I lit the furnace fire for the first time, knowing that from now on we were on our own here, afloat, like a lighted ark. It was dark already at half-past four. The fences and trees were lined with snow in the morning, as if they had become abstract, rough, scribbled on, slashed with spangled white, no longer fences or trees at all.

It is, I thought, the end of a world. Now why did I think of that? I thought; and then I remembered Carmen's story, and rooted it out of my notes so that I could remember what she had said, what I had written down.

Carmen came to stay with my family when I was very young. She was a Colombian friend of my older sister's and when she emigrated to the United States she spent her first winter in our house. She could neither speak nor write English very well then, but all of us spoke enough Spanish to manage. No language could have been enough, though, for her to communicate her concern, and then her terror.

When the trees began to turn color, she wondered what was wrong with them and thought that they might have been poisoned. When their leaves shriveled and dropped off, she wondered why we didn't have the trees cut down and carted away, they were so ugly, and so dead! She was always cold; even in the house there always seemed to be drafts, especially when she looked out of the windows at the dead vegetation; after a while she stopped looking and kept her face turned away. She noticed, too, that it was getting very dark, that the days seemed to be shrinking in and the clocks always seemed wrong; it was dark when she got up and dark again before it was time to eat supper. When we had our first howling blizzard and the morning came and a foot of snow covered everything up, she thought that the end of the world had come, and was amazed that we were all so unconcerned, grouped around the fire, drinking soup and roasting chestnuts. She couldn't believe it when I went out and threw pieces of this snow at my friends, and rolled it up to make a bulgy figure with a broom in its hand. She thought that we were all mad.

She only told me this story last year, laughing at herself in hindsight, shrugging her slim shoulders, which were collared in fur, though she made it clear that she had been very frightened, then.

Nothing could prepare you for winter if you had never seen it, or never known that it would end. Even now, with my cellar and shed stocked and my freezer full I feel the stir of fear; of niggling doubt. Will it end then? Won't it just *keep getting dark?*

I have just read about a study that has been done on the effects of a global nuclear war, one which would explode less than half of the thermonuclear megatonnage now extant on the planet. According to this study clouds of dust would be blasted into the upper atmosphere by the force of the explosions and would hide the sun to such an extent that, even if it were summer, average air temperatures in the northern hemisphere would be lower than $-13°F$. Bacteria would survive, I am sure, and would have a ripe old time of it, too, since not much else would, except perhaps for some seeds. Seeds in general seem to have a profound mistrust of the world, and to have adjusted to most of its horrors.

It is December. There has been snow, two blizzards; one windy, one calm. The world of the ground has been gradually muffled and blocked from view. It is a month of darkness filled with busy preparations for the birth of Light; in the midst of this, the solstice on the twenty-first passes almost unnoticed. The nadir. The turning point, after all, of a mere orbit.

My son is in bed by seven, and the evenings are long, and now that the harvest has been coped with and the sheep have been bred and brought into the barn I am free for a while to enjoy my riches; I choose a jar of sweet pears and keep the fire up in the cookstove, and my feet up on the fender, and read. What? I come slap into it again; here I thought I was going to be comfortable all evening with some nice Norse myths and I'm shanghaied, jolted; forgive me, Odin, old friend, but I'd forgotten what you'd been up to all this time.

It seems that Odin as chief of the gods had a mission to stave off Ragnarok, the Norse equivalent of Armageddon. On the day of Ragnarok the Frost Giants would descend and wreak a mighty havoc, destroying heaven and earth in the process. Odin's job was to put this all off as long as possible. He did this by giving things to mankind, which was generous of him, since he often did so against the wishes of the rest of his pantheon. He gave us fire, for which I am exceedingly grateful. He fought and won the skaldic mead from the race of the giants, a drink that made anyone who drank of it a poet. He bought wisdom at the Well of Mimir and paid for it with one of his eyes. Finally he hung himself on Yggdrasil, the great ash, the Tree of Life, and at the end of nine nights he saw something lying at his feet; and it was Runes. Runes, which had both a common and an uncommon use; they could be used to keep accounts and name names but also had their sacred patterns, "words," perhaps, enchantments, magics, truths.

After Ragnarok life would rise again, from Yggdrasil, from the Tree.

From a chink in the side of the stove — and it is an old stove, twice as old as I, old enough to have earned its chinks — comes a yellow, hot, wavering light; sunlight made captive and now made free. It must be winter; the chickadees dash and dive around the bird feeder in the morning, and a red squirrel has found a way to leap into it, into the bowl of what was touted as a squirrel-proof device; is anything anything-proof? Life will out, it will! I take an unreasonable joy in this, rubbing my hands together: see, even a squirrel isn't fooled by that Plexiglas umbrella, the strength of the squirrel is in his leap; leap then! We too have been given gifts: wherefore shall we leap?

The world appears to be gone, but is not gone. It is all here. The trees are self-flayed bones, and to the uninitiated they look as dead as doornails, but they too have their gifts, and will survive anything that is coming to them now except a sharp saw. A trillion seeds have been launched here and are traveling. The light on the snow makes me shine and waver, as though I had been kindled; light for its own sake, spangled and reflected; when I put on my boots and run down the slope the snow crackles under my feet and it is a sound which says *run* then and *run* there are no paths here anymore and there is a way between every stick and tree and stone and fence — a world undressed, secretive, and filled.

PORCUPINE

III ✹ *Hieroglyphics*

Tom looked, but he could see nothing in the middle of the pool but one peaked iceberg.

"I see only a great iceberg," he said.

"That is mother Carey," said the whale, "as you will find when you get to her. There she sits making old beasts into new all the year round."

— CHARLES KINGSLEY,
The Water Babies

Problems of Navigation

There was no sun at all, only a low whitish New England winter sky, and it was dark soon after four. Quite dark. No moon, no stars, no wind. For early January it was not even very cold. And once it was dark, the world outside seemed to have dissolved entirely, leaving me captive in the floating window-prismed ship of my house, navigating a multispiraled track — a track strewn like a mass of bedsprings — bearing me across the known universe at a brisk 600 million miles an hour.

I made a good supper; there was roast lamb from a November slaughter, snow peas from a June pick, baked potatoes from a sack cellared in October, a pot of chutney made on a rainy September afternoon. While I cooked and ate I trusted to autopilot all the while. I have no gauges here, no radio to base, no altimeter to let me in on the high-flying whirl of this patch of planet. If I were a physicist and could map my springing course, would I know any better then where I am off to?

It does me good, when I go outside for a walk, to trace the tracks and trajectories of other lives. I like to know what it is that came this way, its path crossing mine. I like to follow other animals' direction through the woods, reading where I can the reasons for their choosing to zig, zag, hunker, dig, or chew. Some paths are only partial, even single glyphs, which need much reading between the lines to make any sense of. Other passages — even whole animals — are vanished altogether, their absence a message in itself, which intrigues me all the more.

I make my own way here, my wandering path to shelter and food, and faith, too, to those things that hold me alive, keep me awhirl against the chill of winter within and without. It happens, when I trace this passage, that I find that what I have come to depend on is no simple thing. The potatoes I peeled for my dinner had a tan dust on them, all that was left of the rich loam that I dug them out of; a loam made of sands and gravels ground up by glaciers, and of a thousand dead bodies of grass, all enriched more recently by sheep dung and wood ash. It is soil that grows good potatoes. The tubers are oval and mealy, they tumbled out like nuggets when I dug them up. They are where the potato plants have invested all of their summer gleanings from earth and air, laying their harvest of sugars into granules of starch. Each single granule is layered like a pearl. In two months or so, by March, the starch will begin to mobilize, and the potatoes in their sacks in the cellar will begin to sprout white fingerlike shoots from their eyes. They are alive, these potatoes; collections of food and sprout-buds wrapped carefully, immobile, on autopilot too.

My neighbor Glen lived here on the hill literally all of his life, and he was as well adjusted to its winters as any person could be. He dreamed dreams, cursed his beloved cows, and kept a good garden, and when I began to farm here myself I admired him very much; because, among other things, he managed to eat his own potatoes all year long. In March he would inspect his cellared sacks and when the eyes began to grow he would empty the potatoes onto the cellar floor and pull the eyes out, and put the potatoes back again. Blinded, disbudded, hopeless, the potatoes lasted on through June; increasingly sticky and yellow and less interesting to eat. In July Glen would go out and rummage under the new potato hills, plucking any round marble-sized potatolings he came to; infant potatoes, one of the most ambrosial of earthly delights. Glen always had potatoes and he was a fine gardener and knew his stuff — but what sort of life is it that we lead here, blinding our food, robbing the cradle? That each harvest should be taken in its own time sounds self-evident and sensible, but harvest time is short, and what of us, animals whose lives are long? We cheat, that's all. Like everything else. The squirrels have their heaps of cached cones, the beavers have their underwater store of alder and birch. I have my canning closet and my sacks downstairs, and the grocery store, whose plenty never ceases to amaze: Californian lettuces, Florida pink grapefruits, crabs from Alaska, and strawberries from Australia; a planetworth of goodies eight miles away. Glen didn't go to the store much.

Each to his own, then. Even birds and squirrels have their individual style. There is one squirrel who robs my birdseed, the other squirrels don't. The porcupine in the maple woods eats maples only, the porcupine on the farm below ours eats hemlocks all winter, though there are plenty of maples nearby. It is good to watch the passages of the other live things here, to explore with them their problems of navigation in a hard time. All of them need to eat. What pluckings and robbings are they up to?

My house flew on all night, off on its own bound course. The next morning it was January the sixth, and when I roused myself to light the furnace it was still dark, and we were still flying through space; and it was Three Kings' Day. Three kings arrived at a manger side in Bethlehem nineteen hundred and eighty-some-odd winters ago, and we remember this, a milestone in our journey. The crèche on the sideboard was finally complete. The three porcelain kings who had spent the last weeks wandering among the dishes and the salt and pepper shakers and the newspapers and toy cars had finally, day by day, been coming close to the manger itself. After the furnace was lit and the kettle set to boil, I moved them very close. They too had their own style in their hard time. I watched them there while I made breakfast and while the light leaked back into the world, until I saw that we had come to land among pine trees and surrounded by mountains and wildly sloping fields of snow. I thought about the tromp of camels outside the door, the jingling of harness, the strange voices, the star which came to rest low in the east there. By what star does anything navigate here, to find what it is that it needs the most — food for the body or for the soul?

A walk in the woods is always good for the latter, anyway, so in the afternoon I went out, over the fields and around one fence and over another, and past the crumbling stone foundation walls of the barn that stood here sixty years ago at the slope of the hill. Beyond the ruins of the old barn is the foundation of the house that accompanied it, the original farm on this place, its cellar-hole closing, as Robert Frost said, "Like a dent in dough." How malleable the earth is, I think, and how accepting; and how finally healed.

Where the west wall of the house stood is a hedge of knotty lilacs with limbs as large as my thighs. Under the lilacs a groundhog has made a burrow. Last summer he would whistle and dive home when I came to give salt to the sheep. In summertime the grass is deep and green under the lilacs and from the entrance to his burrow the groundhog can see clear to the mountains. In the winter light the lilac branches are a bunched ripple, like uncombed hair.

I went on through the old Christmas trees, which have grown too tall to harvest now. I cut one anyway every December and chop the top off for the living room, and the rest of the tree rots, building a crisscross of softening fir bones in the shadows.

We take our harvests; all that I ask when I go to the woods is that I be granted a sign. One more glimpse, one more gift, however small. The signs of life are nearly always small. They are always in code. Send me one.

It was quiet by the woods and beginning to snow. Flakes of fine stuff drifted out of the windless sky and the silence was as absolute as if the air had been wadded and insulated against all input, all molecular disturbance, all smell, all color, all noise. The colors of woods and hills were vague washes of gray and buff and olive gray. I began to think as I crossed the field without having seen any sign of life anywhere that I was wrong; that this world is as truly lifeless now and as eventless as it appears, as sterile as glacier ice, high desert, the sea-floor at 3000 feet, the air above the ozone, the souls of the damned, the dustless holes of space. The trees were tatters, bones. The mountains were disappearing. The light was diffuse, colorless, browning out, as if any moment the power were going to fail us altogether, the mainline downed in some accident in the whirling works of compounded orbit, leaving us tumbling here, sucked of heat and air, in the dark.

The light was still fading as I crossed the shoulder of Glen's field, but there was a little track in the snow: Hieroglyph One. A meadow vole had scuttled by there this morning. There he crossed the snow surface, burrowed into a bunch of grass, emerged again, ran on the crusted surface again and into another hole in the grass stubble; he swerved and zigged and dove, looking for food, frightened perhaps, keeping to safe clumps of grasses as much as he could. In the hollow beyond, where it was too weedy and wet to mow hay and where the weed-tips poke up, there were more little holes and tracks, tiny stitchings. An ermine had been there too, laying his twin-dot track, sniffing at every hole. No sign of chaos here. Only business.

I wrote it down. So much for a half a mile.

Then at the edge of the woods, with a brief warning of

whistles, I was surrounded suddenly by a flock of chickadees. "Seet! Seeeet! Seeeet!" they called. There were more than a dozen of them; one landed a foot away to peer at me from black eyes and then he was off with a loud fanning rattle of wings. The birds flirted, tipped, dodged, whirled over my head branch to branch; "Seet! Seeet!" calling all the time, hanging upside down to hunt in the nooks of twig and bud and bark for insect larvae, pupae webbed in, spiders' eggs, beetles in hiding, dormant aphids, seeds blown and lodged. A faint high whistle from a fir gave another bird away. I watched carefully; she was shy, this one. There was a shaking in the fir twigs, more shaking, more high whistling, then a flash of a golden head, a tubby gray-olive body; a golden-crowned kinglet. Then another bird appeared, one whose nasal beeping had given him away before I saw him; a red-breasted nuthatch poised upside down and as suddenly flown from the trunk of a maple. It is a common gang, these three: chickadee, nuthatch, kinglet. They are all tree scavengers and are all oddly similar to the eye, but their methods are different. The chickadees hunt in the outer branches and pick at the cones of the evergreens. The kinglets hunt in the deeper cover of the firs and spruce. The nuthatches spiral the high crannies of the tree trunks themselves. But how — I am agog at them again as I have been so many dozens of times by these same whirling flocks — how do they keep warm?

If birds couldn't keep themselves warm, they would have to be muddy quiescent skin-breathers like frogs. They have a brain-controlled thermostat which holds their body core at 104°F, and to keep it there they burn rich food: sugary larvae, oily protein-rich seeds, and lots of all of these. Light time is hunting time and hunting time is short now. At dusk they take themselves off, each bird to its own tree-hole or bark-curl, and then they hunker over those toothpick-sized legs and keep burning. To maintain this pace birds are endowed with a curious arrangement; they can shunt energy in and out of their fat stores with ease. A warbler may tack on another twenty-five percent to his summer weight to take him to Connecticut in the fall, but a chickadee can add ten percent to his body weight in a single day of winter foraging. And whether this fat fuel is burned to move a migrating warbler three hundred miles south in one October night, or to move a chickadee through sixteen sub-zero hours of a January night, it makes little difference. These are both problems of navigation: space and time.

The chickadee zips around; he needs to zip around. One of them landed on my hat (five chickadees this winter have landed on my hat) and he has learned somewhere about chainsaws and about how they open the carpenter ants' nests at the bottoms of the firs, and how grubs are exposed under the saw-ripped bark, and how the cones come down with the cut trees and scatter their seeds in piles, and how the birches bow and bring their catkins within reach. Whenever we begin cutting wood in the winter, the chickadees are there in minutes, calling back and forth, waiting for a chance to inspect the damage. The nuthatches and kinglets ride in their wake. If a pileated woodpecker drills a rectangular quarry in a spruce, the chickadees hear, and the hammering warns them of the possibility of table scraps. They hear my porch door open and by the time I am there at the feeder with my quart jar of seeds and peanut-butter sandwich rinds they are there too, perched inches from my hands. The kinglet never comes to the feeder. The nuthatch spirals and beeps nearby but rarely approaches. But the chickadees know no fear, or perhaps they know a greater fear; they dash in among the jays like jackals among lions.

At last the chickadees went off down the hedgerow, convinced that nothing about me was edible today. One of them left something behind; a single down feather that drifted in the air like a flake of snow. A hieroglyph of a different kind from tracks or songs! I chased it, grabbed it, gray white and tiny as a willow-fluff, flinging its feather-barbs wildly so that it was nearly round, each barbicel a hookless fur. Down is the finest, lightest insulation invented by anything anywhere. Birds have a stake in keeping things light. Their down keeps them warm and their outer feathers are like oiled shingles that shed water and wind. When it is very cold the down is fluffed out, each featherlet hoisted by its own tiny muscle to hold more air.

The flock was gone, but not gone far. I always seemed to run onto it in this same patch of woods, and I wondered about that until I read somewhere that a chickadee flock has a territory that it keeps to all winter long; twenty-some acres of woodland and brush. The chickadee flock is a gang of relatives and neighbors and hangers-on with a distinct pecking order within itself, like a flock of hens has, or robins, or flamingos; capped by one top female and one top male. Then there are "floaters," too, drifters, the lone birds I sometimes come on in these woods, each as silent and secretive as the flock is loud and full of bravado. They are the low birds on the chickadee totem pole, each one caught between the safety of the mob and his own put-upon status in it. They have made a choice of solitude in which they have no one to count on or peck on but themselves: their private problem of navigation here. Our own anywhere.

I went on up the border of the wood, and right away, sign piled on sign now, a grouse burst up with a thunder and whistle of wings from the snow and brush and disappeared. I tracked her backward, pushing under branches, laying my own deep and big-footed trail beside her delicate three-toed one. In one place she had eaten raspberry buds, ringing the cane with green spots where she had plucked them away. Then she had pecked at a tuft of sedge looking for seeds. She had scratched beside a stone and among the old cones under a fir. Grouse don't often forage on the ground in winter. On the snow crust she could, for once, walk without floundering on her small feet. In autumn the grouse grow horny projections on their foot soles, hobnails for walking in the tops of trees. I have seen grouse walking in the networks of fine twigs in the aspens and plucking off buds there, as comfortable as if they were on solid ground instead of thirty feet above it.

Then there was nothing. The woods were empty again, the fine snow was closing in like a drawn scrim, and I began to lose my bearings, finally picking out a familiar tree and then the homeward line of the pasture fence. Suddenly there was a clear high whistle — a single bright tone — and a brown creeper flew down like a leaf and disappeared against the rough bole of the big cottonwood which broods over the old farm place. She went around the tree upward and sideways and reappeared again. From fifteen feet up she flew down to the base of a big aspen and started up, jerkily, probing in and behind bark nubs and ridges with her scimitar-shaped beak. She is another tree-hunter, with a specialty in large crevassed tree-trunk bottoms.

Farther up the pasture road there was a sudden loud squeak and a flash of color, and a male hairy woodpecker arrived overhead and began pecking away at a maple limb not five feet off, his pecks mechanical as a jackhammer. He pried up a bit of bark, picked out and ate something pale, and then squeaked again, looking at me sideways out of a single glittering eye: the last sign of the day, the bird-who-hunts-beneath-the-visible.

This is the pattern that stands revealed; if trees are good hunting in winter, then the trees will be hunted elaborately, each age and kind of tree for its own sake, each layer and level of the tree world with its own form. I can't help but think that from season to season or year to year the pattern changes, too. Last September the gray birches were infested with leaf-rollers. The leaf-roller larva furls a birch leaf around itself and webs itself in, thinks itself safe. A chickadee flock had discovered this ruse somehow and were hunting from one birch to the next, hanging upside down on the fine twigs to rip open the rolled leaves and pluck the larvae out. Some winters here are good cone years in the spruce and some years aren't. Sometimes the aphids are on the boom, or the bust. In a thaw there may be a freak hatch of mosquitoes. The pattern shifts, the birds with it.

My bird feeder is a kind of mecca for the opportunists among birds. Thirteen blue jays have visited it all winter, their flock as constant and predictable as the flock of chickadees that hunts Glen's woods. They wait in the pines, I see them there (Ha! I see you there!) when I go out in my boots carrying my quart jar. With screams and loud fannings of wings they descend before I am back at the porch door. They leap in the air, crouch, and raise their crests, and threaten each other with beaks wide and wings open; one leaves, two stay, obeying the order of dominance they have set among themselves. Sometimes as many as five crowd in together and at other times one — Boss Jay? — feeds alone and makes the others wait. All day long the jays are around, they steal the dogfood from the dog's bowl in the shed, rob the chickens at the barn, and hop, scavenging, among the hay leavings in the sheep yard, and they let it be known: "Jaaaaay!" Here comes the barn cat! "Jaaaay!" Here she comes again with the quart jar! In the mornings before breakfast I see them together pecking up gravel from the bare spot by the mailbox, grist for their crops. They do their rounds.

In midmorning a flock of evening grosbeaks sometimes comes in, descending and decorating the little tree by the feeder like ripe bright fruit. The males are the colors of winter sunset; golden yellow, fierce black and white; the females a dull olivy echo. They perch all together, there are no fights here, no noises; they come down and sit shoulder to shoulder cracking seeds and spitting sunflower hulls like seed-eating machines. Then they are off. It is a good cone year now as these things go, and seeds are what they are good at, so they don't have much need of me.

There are other birds here that I see less often. On the way down the hill road to town there is one place where the road tips south and where the snow melts away even in midwinter. Often a flock of pine grosbeaks is there in the dark gravelly patch, picking up grit. Sometimes in the swamp I see them flying and scattering overhead, big dark olive birds, the males liberally rinsed in a deep rose tint as if they had been dunked in raspberry sherbet. They rob the fir and spruce cones and nip off the buds of maples and evergreens. Where would they find the gravel to grind up this tough stuff if it weren't for the road, I wonder?

Four miles farther along the valley road is Benny's farm, with the biggest herd of dairy Holsteins in the whole township. There are rambling brown barns perched on the valley rim, three huge silos, and miles of enviable flat cornfields along the road and river, each one decorated with brown daubs — dumptruck-loads of manure — in carefully landscaped rows. The silos wear a flock of city pigeons, rock doves, who make their livings from the drizzles of fodder that leak from the silo bottoms. They also strut in among the cows and peck, as pompous and iridescent as ever even there, and when they wheel over the valley each ascending bird has the heart-grabbing silhouette of the Dove of Peace.

The manure piles in the corn stubbles have their share of visitors. A crow or two can almost always be found there, en route to or from the sanitary landfill up the gulf road. The crows, and the family of ravens that lives on the mountain at the head of the swamp, both visit the sanitary landfill every day all winter, to the despair of the man who bulldozes our daily trash. They scrape away the sand which he so carefully 'dozes over the evidence and pick, pull, yank, tear, and unearth miscellaneous goodies and then consume some and scatter the rest. They have a good time. They are in the same business he is in: disposing of anything deemed inedible by anyone else; but they make life difficult. They make a mess. And when they aren't subverting the sanitary landfill they spend some time at Benny's piles.

They are worth a visit, these piles. Sometimes there is a surprise. On my way to town I often pull off and stop there, reaching for my binoculars, and scan the humped rows: crow here, crow there, then, yes, a flash of white, a glitter of rising wings — snow buntings. Plump white birds washed with russet, their wings and tails tipped with black; ambassadors from a far place. Snow buntings breed in the coastal tundras of western Greenland, Ellesmere Island, coastal Alaska. In the autumn some of them find their way here.

They find their way. Sometimes I find them. The deception is strong but this landscape isn't empty. We whirl here, the birds whirl with us, each on our private orbits. *If I were a physicist and could map my springing course, would I know better then where I am off to?* The intricacy astounds, boggles, mystifies; each bird found on the pale face of the winter landscape is like a rune traced on the lip of a grail. All I can ask is that I see.

Hall of Darkness

It is an amazing trick. The magician hides his white rabbit for an hour or half an hour under the false bottom of his black hat or in some recess of his draped table, but the groundhog hides himself. I know where he is, he is down in the rootiest recesses of the lilac hedge, and he will keep himself there for five months or more before the wand waves and he is hoisted by his small ears into the world.

He leaves no sign of himself, no tracks, nothing bitten or

dug up. His hill of earth by his burrow door pushes the snow into a mound as small as any drifting wind would; his total absence is a sign of nothing less than genius. He knows, inside himself, where he is going, and when.

His conjuring trick begins late in the summer with fattening up. Keyed by shrinking daylight and a slew of hormones, he fattens himself until by October he is richly furred and stout, and ready. No one is sure what it is that gives him the final push. What is the brink of winter to him? Groundhogs kept in a comfortable well-lit laboratory still get fat in the autumn, but they never manage to hibernate. Hibernation means a lowering of body temperature and you can't lower your body temperature if the environment isn't cold. And fat has something to do with it, too, because older and savvier groundhogs go into hibernation sooner in the fall than younger slimmer ones. These are pieces of the puzzle; the whole eludes. We can't define, exactly, the world he is caught up in, meshed between the workings of his body and the world around him, his own world of lilac hedge, tumbled stone, sheep, wind, his private hunger; the leaves scattering under a gray sky.

It turns out that not many animals do truly hibernate, let go of that hard-won skill of keeping themselves warm from the inside out, because like all risky private lettings-go it is not easy to find a place safe enough to do it in. Hibernators need a hidey-hole and the complex series of behaviors to find a good hole, or to make one. They need a place that is safe against frost and predators. A tall order. So there are not many hibernators here, or anywhere, for that matter. Groundhogs, jumping mice, bats. That's all we have. Farther north where the frost runs deep in the ground there are no hibernators at all; Arctic mammals have to keep themselves warm, keep the inner fires burning. They have no choice. There is no safe place there to let go *in*.

The groundhog's solitary digs can be found wherever there is grass, clover, and burrowable soil, from Newfoundland to

Alaska and south to Tennessee. He is a success story of sorts, having solved the problem of there being nothing for him to eat for three to six months of the year by eating nothing for those three to six months. In January the groundhog is curled, cold, in his burrow, his body temperature fallen from 98.6°F to 36°F. He takes one light sighing breath every six minutes. He conserves energy by spending almost none. If the house of the body is unheated, there is no heating bill: simple. A biologist once took a hibernating groundhog and rolled the stiff, cold, furry ball back and forth on his living room rug, and a stiff, cold, furry ball he remained. It takes hours to emerge from such a deathlike trance. He will keep his own appointment with the year, his metabolic clock set for sometime in March or April. When I pass the lilac hedge on my way to the woods, I send him my blessing.

Enough energy to live with is the groundhog's goal, the aim of everything that lives here; the quintessential brass ring. Food, and warmth, and the energy to find or make more of either one; none of these is easy to find in wintertime. The signs I discover, the signs that are absent, even the passages of my own days, speak of the volatile and latent flow of energy, here now, spent tomorrow, gusting away.

Before I go to the woods I have a big breakfast — oatmeal with syrup, toast with jam and butter, boiled eggs, and coffee. When the work with the ax has warmed me up, I feel the great burst of energy that comes from working through such a breakfast in such a cold. I take off my mittens and hang my vest on a branch and work with my hands warm and bare on the smooth wood of the ax handle, turning my breakfast into columns of heat that rise from my shirt collar and wrists and from the planes of my face, and into noise, too: the soft whuffs of the branches springing into the snow, the whocks of the ax on wood; and into the heat the ax head gains by the friction of its swift passages through the wood. When I stop and prop my ax against a tree and pour coffee from my thermos and sip from my red cup, the heat my hands have given to the ash handle of the ax vanishes into the air and is gone, outward bound.

The trees, the groundhogs, are in a sense nothing more or less than energy transformers, switches in the flow. A water-wheel turns the potential energy of the pull-of-gravity-on-water into a wild resonating noise of meshing gears and spin-ning shafts and ends by grinding corn into meal. Live machin-ery is less loud, better meshed and greased; the tree makes no noise that I can hear, however many summers' worth of sun it turns to wood. My joints hardly creak, the thump and rumble of my gut is inaudible unless someone puts an ear to my belly; but I turn oatmeal to heat and eggs to sound, and — in a small way and for a small time — I can change the woods.

When I go there in the morning, I see that the track of a fox crosses the homeward track that I made the night before. The intricate journeyings of energy here astound: in June the selected wavelengths of sunlight are trapped in the machinery of a grass leaf and are forced to the labor of making sugar out of air and water; in July the sugars pack into the starch of a grass seed; in January the seed is found and eaten by a meadow vole; in February the vole is pounced on and swallowed by the fox, and unspliced bits of vole move through into the belly and blood of the fox; and now, through the running of the fox, the contracting of his muscles and the racing of nerve pulses that bring him the news of the woods at dusk, the June sun goes back into life heat, which is dissipated slowly through the fox's skin and heavy pelt and through the panting of his breath into the air; and is out, and gone again.

When I think of this image of live things as series upon series of interlinked wheels, I am astounded that they manage to grind at all. Now. For these midwinter weeks — how many? six, eight, ten, it depends on just where you are — more heat is lost, more light reflected back, more calories burned, than the sun now gives us. If the earth didn't tilt and run round in its orbit, within months the system would begin to collapse;

the rivers would stop running, the ponds would freeze-dry to stony bowls, the trees and animals would run through their stores and starve; and soon enough this piece of planet would become a frozen desert as lifeless as the moons of Jupiter, a gyrating wasteland. We live here now only through the intercession of June sun. We are spinning on momentum.

At noon in January the shadows are as long as the shadows of a summer evening. By four there is too little light to work in; behind little fiery tufts of cloud the sky is as yellow and opaque as milk-glass. A soft gray cloud mass hovers over the mountains and curves into soft hummocks like a bright silver velvet, as gray as ash in its shadows.

By the time I am out of the woods it is sunset time and the milk-glass sky has gone ochre, the yellow stained with an orange wash. The clouds are charcoal, the mountains a luminous purple as though they were made of a heavy glass behind which a light was shining, and the snow on the trees and meadows is lit with this purpled light. The branches and forests are black. The mountain-broken line of ochre sky is the only solid thing left, the only thing not drawing films of darkness over itself. From the brow of the hill at the edge of the darkened woods the sky looks strangely solid, like a piece of crockery, a shard lit up on a dark museum wall to be looked and wondered at, studied: Shard of Sky, Winter Dynasty, January Period, 1983. Courtesy: The Sun.

One day, in the trees below the maple woods, I found something else. A limb of a tree had fallen and part of it stuck up through the snow. Under this protecting limb, which had collected snow like a roof, a natural tunnel ran down to the ground. I reached in and found dry leaves, a fir cone, a collection of maple seeds pasted together with hoarfrost. A foot away another branch projected in the same way, and between the two there was a line made by a dragging tail between stitchlike hop marks; the signature of a deer mouse.

I looked there every day, and every day there were tracks.

Then when we had a spell of deep cold there were no new tracks. When it stayed below zero for a week, I looked nearly every day but the slate was wiped clean by fine falls of snow. Perhaps, I thought, the deer mouse has been eaten. By the fox, the horned owl, an ermine, a weasel. Then it was suddenly warm and nearly thawing and the deer-mouse tracks were there again between the branch tunnels; no, she was not eaten. But she was somewhere. Else.

She has her budget, this mouse; an energy wheel spinning faster than most. When it is very cold the energy expense of hunting is greater than the expected profits; she stays home in her nest then and sleeps.

Exactly where these profits and expenses are rung up and recorded no one is sure. It isn't just "sleep" that she falls into, either, in the cold days. Between hibernation proper and plain sleep there are a lot of choices, a hall of darkness with many doors. "Torpor" is the name for them; a slight but controlled lowering of core temperature, drowses deeper than most, useful for the short haul, and the long haul, too. Bears torpor, so do skunks, and chipmunks. Unlike bears the chipmunks are too small to put up all their fuel stores as fat. They make complicated burrows with a nest room at the center in which they pile a hoard of seeds, nuts, and other dormant edibles, and then they make a dry grass and leaf nest on top. The chipmunks curl up there even on autumn days when it is too wet or cold to be out harvesting and as the winter deepens the time that they spend in torpor there grows. The chipmunk wakes up every so often to visit his toilet room and dig under his bed for a snack; foxes are no concern of his, nor weather.

Live things seem to have been formed most by those pressures which have threatened them most, which push them the hardest. A piece of clay has no shape until the potter's hands challenge the lump revolving on the wheel. With a press of thumbs and the restraint of a palm a rim rises and thins to a fine curve. Fingertips smooth the bowl, fashion a spout. Clay teased out between the palms makes a handle. The pot has a form now and a behavior; a use. Winter has perhaps the firmest hand on all of the malleable life forms here. In the forms of the finished pots we can sometimes glimpse the mind of the potter.

The watching of *shape* and the reading of snow tracks are good ways to catch the patterns, and the reasons behind them. Not just the reading of one day's work but the reading of many days, because the days — and the tracks — change. In watching the movements of animals, the forms they take up, one notices after a while that roundness is one good form that cold encourages; when the chipmunk goes down into his torpor he curls up, laying his tail around his feet and nose. Ants and bees hibernate in spherical creeping balls. Deer mice pack in together in a communal nest, each one squirming toward the center in turn and elbowed out to the cooler rim again in jerky convection currents. When I am chilled I hunch my shoulders and pull my knees to my chest, approaching — within the limits of the way I'm made — a perfect sphere. I wrap up my vital core as the chipmunk wraps his. The pattern is everywhere; the dog curled on the hearth, my son knee-to-nose under his quilt, the fox curled asleep in his den. Each square inch of warm exposed surface loses heat, and each cubic inch of live tissue makes heat; these are the only heats we can lay claim to. A sphere is the shape that has the minimum heat-losing surface for any given volume; a soap bubble, a sun, a sleeping bear. Roundness is an Ideal.

So is largeness. Large animals lose less of their heat because they have more heat-making volume in proportion to their heat-losing surface of skin or fur. So they have lower energy budgets to begin with. A deer mouse burns eight times more oxygen (and food) per gram of her body-weight than I do, and I burn three times as much per gram of me as an elephant does per gram of him; it makes good sense, in the cold, to be large.

Deer mice make themselves bigger by bringing in more mice to share the huddle in their nest, and the colder it is the more important it is that the huddle be large. A classic study of mice, huddles, food, and cold came to the conclusion that five mice huddled together each need about thirty percent less food in order to survive than a lone mouse. Lone mice don't last long.

Here is another pattern that can be traced in the array of forms; in the coldest weather the deer mouse is torporing, gone; the meadow vole is not gone. On the coldest day of the year, –10°F at midday, I found meadow-vole tracks fresh in the light snow of the day before. He had come up from some burrowed and thatched recess under a huge boulder by the brook and had crossed the brook on the ice, and had scavenged around in the meadow on the other side, in and out and under the snow, and then gone home again.

A meadow vole looks like a brown scuttling sausage. He has small, moon-shaped ears half-hidden in his fur, and a very short tail. The deer mouse has large fine ears in which one can see the little veins, and long white feet, and a long tail; they all cost her heat. The meadow vole can afford to be busy; his extremities are conservative, they have been rounded off by a firm potter's hand. The brown lemming of the high Arctic has no visible ears at all, his tail has been abbreviated to a nub, even the bottom of his feet are furred, and he is as close to Round as an animal can be.

One can pick this pattern up across the continent: the kit fox of southwestern deserts has great ears like a bat, the red fox has generous pointed ears, the arctic fox has round teddy-bear ears, and even these are almost invisible in his thick fur ruff.

There are mysterious things that go on, beyond the forms of sleep and shape, the technologies of insulation. There are energy demands which seem impossible to meet, but they *are* met. For instance, there's the problem of the pika. A pika is a rat-sized relative of rabbits, and it lives in the high boulder slopes of the Rocky Mountains. As one might expect, it has very small ears. It dries piles of grass leaves and stems for its winter feed, it doesn't hibernate, and it makes its nest in a burrow in the stones. Before snow falls to insulate the burrows it gets very cold there, and it is impossible for the pika to eat enough of her hay to keep herself warm. It turns out that she survives these autumn weeks by burning up all of her brown fat: a special tissue that is fat (full of fuel) and brown, with tiny organelles called mitochondria. Mitochondria are vital, and spooky. It turns out that they were, probably, and *long* ago, separate tiny creatures that crawled into one of our one-celled, microscopic, and remote ancestors and made themselves at home, specializing in transforming food into usable energy. There they still are, in every cell of every animal, sprinkled like lucky stars. Brown fat has more than its fair share of mitochondria. When in need, the pika can turn on these after-burners and they push her through.

When there is a week of deep midwinter cold, or a five-day blizzard in January, and another in February, I often wonder, immobilized in my chair by the fire, how many patches of brown fat are turning on out there, like live fires in the woods.

We all have it; the super-heat machine, the rocket engines couched in a sea of fuel. Some people believe that true emergencies, terror, life-and-death matters, all have the power to turn our brown fat on, to give us the supercharge which has the uncanny property of stretching time out and giving us lightning-fast reactions and an almost superhuman strength; we are left shaken, shaking, shocked at our own power.

Brown fat seems to live, like a patchy mantle, in between the shoulderblades. Thinking of its poised brute power, I feel a subtle hoist from there, an itch, an impatience; it is as if, folded in the formed and fired clay, even the most solid pot had *wings*.

Deer Spring

It was the end of January; an inch of new loose snow lay over the tough sun-crust. The low sun flirted behind an icy veil of fog. The snow was like a new white paper rolled in between the soil and sky, a thin crisp sheet awaiting print.

The trees stood stiff and still on the brow of the field against the curve on curve of shades-of-gray hills. I kept a lookout all the way down the slope for any sign of footprints, but there were none there, and I felt as I have often felt before — a captive in my limited senses. This captivity is intentional, use-full, well reasoned; because we came into our species-hood at the edge of some wide plain in which we were meant to see, as a lion sees — when we stood up to peer across the grass — herds of animals in the distance. And our ape-nature left us its gift of seeing the play of light and shadow in the deep woods and the colors of ripe fruit in the branches. We see well at a distance; we see form, and color. But our nose has one-sixtieth the power of a dog's nose. A bee can smell his mate two miles away. A fly can see motion in all directions from hundreds of spiraling lenses. A mosquito can assay the chemistries of water with her hind leg to see if it is good for laying eggs in. A bat knows about the jut of a twig and the flight of a moth by shouting into the void and listening for echos. But an insect-eating bat doesn't hear very well in the low frequencies inhabited by the human voice, the bark of a dog, the pines shushing in the night wind. If those noises interfered, she wouldn't be able to focus in on the echo-shape of a certain mosquito, and mosquitoes are her business. So all of our focuses are narrowed; and our myopic view is the only view — according to the great selecting wisdoms of survival — that makes *sense*. But I still envy the dog his nose. What wonders could I find out here if I had his nose?

I looked for footprints. Suddenly down by the deer spring

there had been a flurry of activity. The hares had been dashing around and around the bushes, leaping in great leaps, and then just hopping, hopping, and nibbling there, in no rush. One had run out in a big loop out and back — playing? They had been eating the meadowsweet bushes, slicing the twigs off with their razor teeth in a slick efficient cut, which is so different from the ragged edges of the twigs that deer have fed on; deer have to grind their browse off with their cud-chewing molars. Where the snow had hoisted the hares up among the branches they had been eating the needles of the pines. The snow was packed down there and strewn with their droppings, like collections of neat tan nuts.

The deer spring is the only place on my land that has a sacred quality, a nature deeper than itself, and anyone I know who has been there has felt this, too. Where the pasture slopes steeply through a growth of young trees a spring of water comes to the surface, following some outcropping layer of impermeable rock. Fifty or sixty years ago the farmer who lived in the old farm place and let his cows graze this woods laid a circle of stones to hold the spring-water. The circle is the size of a washtub, the water is black, overhung on two sides with the branches of spruce trees which half-enclose it, like arms. The spring never ices over, it runs even in the driest summers, sending its overflow trickling into a little meadow. The deer come there to drink all year and the sheep come to it in the summer when they are living off the rough forage in the woods. For years my instinct has been to make a stone bench beside the spring and erect a stone — a menhir, a lingam — to stand among the watery grasses and beside the dark font. Having not yet given my life over to contemplation, I have never built either, and I come there instead to see what the hare and the deer are doing, or if the sheep have water in August; and I always lean over and drink myself, following Robert Frost's "Directive": "Here are your waters and your watering place./Drink and be whole again beyond confusion."

Many years ago, in January, I found all that a fox or a

weasel had left of his winter meal, a single white hare's foot. It was furred top and bottom like a mitten, and when I spread the furry webbed toes they covered an area as large as the palm of my hand. In order to bear his weight over this soft snow as easily as a hare's hind feet bear his three-pound self, a 160-pound man would have to have feet more than twelve inches broad and thirty inches long. When the snow is deep and soft and has no crust on it, nothing can move on it easily except these snowshoe hares. And even then they move on paths, ancestral trails, one following another. Everything else moves *over* the snow, either by leaping through the trees, or by flying, or by burrowing *under* and through the drifts like the weasels and otters do, who swim in the snow as easily as if it were water. Or, if they have to move at all, they move only at enormous cost; like the deer, whose sharp slim feet are not good for traveling in deep snow at all.

Hares are also wonderfully collapsible. Look; here one went off in a dash from the pines. Something must have smelled him out or a branch crashed in the night, sending him shooting off, dodging, side to side in a dizzying zig and zag, and then he stopped dead just over a mound into a hollow: optical illusion . . . no hare. And the fox, if there was a fox, ran past following the course that the hare was on and wasn't. Then the hare dashed again, doubling back, stopped still again in mid-run, nose quivering. While the hare runs he is all angular length of long leg, long neck, long ears up; all dissipating that burst of body heat which he makes by running hard. When he rests in the pine hollows he hunkers between his hind legs, draws his neck in, flattens his ears to his back, and becomes — round.

The snowshoe hares are also called varying hares because they turn brown in the spring and white again in the autumn; all but the tips of their ears, which stay black all year, just as the ermine's tail-tip stays black, both dipped in a wintery inkpot. Snowshoe and arctic hares, white-tail jackrabbits, snowy owls, arctic foxes, polar bears, willow ptarmigan, mountain goats — the idea seems to be for large animals who are exposed on the snow surface in the cold to be white. White isn't good only for camouflage; white hairs and feathers, which have no channels of color stuff in them, contain more dead-air spaces to keep their bearers warm. Each of a deer's outer hairs is also hollow, which makes them good, if brittle, insulation. The winter fur of the hares, minks, otters, and bobcats conserves heat because it is double-layered, with an outer coat of long shining water-shedding guard hairs and an inner batting of fine soft fluff, which traps body-warmed air like a bird's down.

I live and move here in borrowed trappings; sheep's wool and deer skin on my hands and caribou skin and sheep's wool on my feet. Sheep's wool is nothing more than hollow-shafted underfluff with all of the guard hairs bred out, over the years of our knowing what we need from sheep. Only the Scottish blackface sheep still have lots of long tough hairs left in their wool as protection against the Scottish rains; which is why a real tweed jacket prickles and wears like iron and is all but waterproof. My vest is filled with goose down, plucked from the descendants of geese who once flew many thousands of miles to nest in a tundra marsh, and line their nests with breast feathers, and nestle their eggs in against their skin.

No man-made fabric holds in heat and breathes out moisture as well as these, nor are man-made fabrics as comfortable to wear moving or working in the woods as these animal-made things are. How long has it taken the animals to make them up? The art and science of his fur — multilayered, adjustable, easy-to-maintain, winter-white — is all coiled precise information that lives in every cell of the hare's self. When it is very cold under the trees at night, he fluffs his hairs to contain more air, and when I am chilled, the muscles at the bases of my hairs — which may be ineffectual but are all over me — hoist the hairs in a vain effort to fluff me out too. All I get from this archaic process is goose bumps, an innocuous rash. The goose, hoisting her down feathers, would get warm.

The geese have given us other things, too, with which we

have protected ourselves against greater threats even than the cold of January. Thomas Jefferson wrote and signed the Declaration of Independence with a quill pen, the long primary feather that had once been the leading edge of a goose's wing. The word *pen* comes from the Latin *pinna* — feather. The word *write* comes from the Anglo-Saxon *writan* — scratch. This sharp mouselike scratching must have kept many a light-sleeping companion awake while the scratcher penned his way into immortality by the light of a tallow candle. The goose feather has thus sent our thoughts and desires farther through space and time than any goose has flown himself. The geese still write their own messages here in the skies of October and March; but they are about freedom from winter, and their own freedom from want.

As for the writing of hares, that is another thing. I have followed hare trails for years and have discovered that they usually fade off after a while, their makers going their separate ways; into the alders or young maples or pines to feed, or into the depths of the young spruces to hide, or somewhere else for no apparent reason. Sometimes these trails are intersected by the dotted-line hunting trail of a fox, the wider loping tread of a dog or coyote, the wandering double-dot trail of a weasel or an ermine. Sometimes they end in a flurry and the footnote of a horned owl's wing-tips. Once I found blood and fur in the snow and drag-marks where a fox had made a kill. I often make the mistake of believing that a hare's world is utterly sandwiched between feeding and being fed upon; and then I am wrong.

Because once, in midwinter, on a morning after a fresh snow and a full moon, I came to a circle of big spruce trees where five fresh and well-used hare trails converged, and there where they came together a circle a yard broad had been trampled into the snow by many hares all leaping on their hind feet. It was a circle like a wheel; the hub was unmarked snow. I think the hares had been dancing there. What was written there was an enclosing circle, like the deer spring, or a planetary orbit. Are hares ". . . endowed by their Creator with certain unalienable Rights," among them the pursuit of what, under the moon?

Ravine and River

At the edge of the ravine there was a yellow tree which was, from a distance, as bright as a light among the gray trunks. Coming up to it, I saw that the bark was completely gone, both the bark and the live tissue that is under the bark; the flesh of the tree itself. What was left were runic brown markings and scratches in the flayed wood, saying much about a porcupine's hunger and thorough work.

Because their arsenal is so good, porcupines are portly and slow-going, a lesson to us all: defend thyself and take it easy. Defend, that is, not arm. The porcupine isn't an aggressor to anything but trees. His tracks in the snow are a hybrid of a peculiar tractor tire and a heavy dragged broom. It is easy to see porcupines once the leaves are gone, perched up in some comfortable branch-elbow and going about their eating business there without any rush. Their black faces are strangely apelike, they have the delicate stiff fingers of an old woman. They peer down at one with a thoughtful, serious look, the sober glance of a judge.

One of them lives in the rubble of the big barn on the deserted farm that lies below ours. Another lives just above our sugar woods in an old den tree, a five-foot-thick hollow beech, riven by a great frost crack that a porcupine once widened eight feet up to make a door. All eight feet are now well filled with compacted porcupine droppings. Last year, out of urgent necessity, the present tenant made another door three feet above the first. But the tree is old and rotting now and the roof must be getting leaky, so I wonder how long he will stay.

Another one winters in the woodshed of our sugarhouse, nesting up on twenty cords of free lunch and under a good roof. When I oust him in March, he retires to a hollow under a rusted sugar pan that was discarded by the former farmer, and he shows me his spined and speckled backside, like a monstrous sea urchin's, when I pass. The porcupine of the ravine must live somewhere nearby; he can't go far from home in wintertime. Usually porcupines will haul themselves through the snow to some favored tree, often a hemlock, or a maple, and then squat in it until the food is gone and tree ruined.

They don't de-bark the hemlocks so much as graze on them, lopping off small branches that end up by falling to the ground; a bonus much appreciated by deer and hares, and by the little birds who come to pick open the cones. But porcupines are no respecters of forestry, and one of them can lay waste acres of good trees. Many foresters shoot them on sight, and my neighbor — who loves his woods and every tree in it with a vengeance — has shot 127 porcupines in fifteen years on his own land. As for the Indians who once lived here, they had a different view of things, and made a kind of deal with the porcupine; sparing his life in times of plenty so that he would appear when he was needed. Porcupines make good eating, and they are the only animal which an unarmed man can kill with a stick.

Thinking of these things, I went down the ravine hand over hand from tree to tree. It was very steep and I suddenly slipped and let go my grasp and slid down twenty feet before fetching up against a birch in a cloud of snow. Most foresters think of gray birches as worthless trees, best cut and left to rot to make room for maples and ash and spruce. Perhaps I will take a lesson from the Indians, the ghosts in my woods, and spare my birches, make a deal here; be there when I need you.

Farther on, at the level spot where we had cut our firewood the year before, piles of severed treetops lay everywhere and the deer had been busy in them. I chose one of the deer tracks at random and followed it, stepping where the deer had stepped.

Hieroglyphics   ◂   *115*

She seemed to wander almost aimlessly like a sheep in a lot, a victim of random motion. She stood awhile by a big spruce, just lifting one foot several times and setting it down again. She went on and grazed awhile in the needles of a fir, biting the tiniest branch tips off and nibbling the needles on the larger twigs as though they were kernels on a cob of corn. She stopped at a sort of mini-ravine, a cleft that holds a brook in spring; apparently it looked too wide to jump across, but she paused there, considering. Her toe marks were sunk deep in the snow. Then she turned and wandered off again to a huge dead tree under which were the tramplings of many deer. Odd. There was a sweetish smell in the air, a little like licorice, a little like the boiled-milk candy that Mexicans make, *dulce de leche,* a toffyish puddingy sweet which you can eat with a spoon. If you dare. Once begun it's hard to stop. The other side of the dead tree held the source of the good smell; it was covered with the jutting shelves of a caramel-colored bracket fungus. The brackets had been gnawed and chewed by the deer and the lower ones showed many tiny bite-marks of small rodents. The brackets had the texture of halvah; crisp and soft at once.

I didn't know which outward track belonged to my original deer, so I chose one at random and followed it to the river. She stood there awhile, chewing cud again, perhaps, or just waiting; deer are sluggish in winter, yarded, in a conservative semidrowse. I sat on a log nearby, waiting too through some allotted time. The Tamarack river made a faint liquid ticking under the ice; in another place the water swirled ice-free and swift, and there was a deep swallowing noise as it was sucked back under a mass of frozen rubble. The river had frozen, broken and burst, floed and refrozen many times; the ice itself was layered in stripes of dark and light. The autumn had been rainy and very cold by turns and had made the river into a rugged toothy place. I think I began to join the deer there, to *think* deer; to look around me warily, sniff, burp a cud, and chew again. Rub my nose on the inside of my front leg. Look up. Scratch an itch on my haunch with my lower teeth. Then it was time (whose time?) to move off. I followed the deer up the river, wandering but purposeful now to the place where she had slept the night before. The deer bed — oval, dark, deep in the snow — was at the base of a great hemlock tree at the foot of the ravine, just where the forest began to shelve gently toward the river. I sat in it. It was surprisingly small. With my legs heels to buttocks I barely fit. I could see the imprint of her (why was I so sure it was *her*?) sharp toes and the angle of her bent wrists pressed into the snow. It had a smell; vaguely beefy, doggy, goaty, musky; not at all unpleasant. The bottom of the bed was ice and had a few long blue-gray hairs stuck in it. With the hemlock at my back I could see out to the river, and far in both directions along the shelving shore and north up the ravine. It was a good place to lie, keep watch, sleep. There were spatters around the bed where she had stood and shaken the light night-fall of snow off her coat in the morning.

I sat there a long while. I had been the deer for a moment, for a flash. Perhaps in following and following one can sometimes find, stumble on, a chink, and walk in as a guest. A friend of mine who is a historian at a university says that sometimes, when he has been decoding some manuscript for hours, ancient Sumer has become more real to him than the Boston that he inhabits. He sees the women walking with their silks draped over their shoulders and hears the fruit-sellers calling in the streets of 4500 years ago. Something like that had happened to me: the inscription become life.

I emptied my pockets there. I am an inveterate treasure collector and my pockets are big. I took out a piece of porcupine-chewed twig collected from the morning's tree, and a palm-sized piece of maple bark inscribed with the exquisite wriggling glyph of a bark-beetle larva, and a six-inch-long bevel-ended piece of an alder branch, gnawed barkless, stolen from one of the beaver lodges in the swamp the week before. Then a sliver of fir wood rasped into pale Matisse-like curvatures by carpenter ants, a piece which I had picked from an ant's nest that had been quarried and raided by a pileated woodpecker. Then a chunk of the sweetish fungus with the marks of deer and mouse teeth on it, and two goldenrod galls as firm and round as brown marbles, and a twisted handkerchief that held a jewel-like sift of fish scales — all that a winter rain had left of a bit of otter dung on a rock by the river. "Eye of newt, toe of frog . . ." No, no incantations here, please! These are not magics, only the simple inscriptions of hunger and bodily functions; what brew would they have made anyway but forest dust? They were a sheaf of stumbled-on scribblings from which one could dare to read lives; let these lives abound, let them abidingly chew, gnaw, squat, dance, rasp!

Chickadee

IV ❧ *Secret Worlds*

*Hast thou entered into the springs of the sea?
Or hast thou walked in search of the depth? . . .
Hast thou entered into the treasures of the
snow? Or hast thou seen the treasures of the
hail . . . ?
Out of whose womb came the ice? And the
hoary frost of heaven, who hath gendered it?
The waters are hid as with a stone, and the
face of the deep is frozen.*

— BOOK OF JOB,
Chapter 38

*To be in any form, what is that?
(Round and round we go, all of us, and ever
 come back thither,)
If nothing lay more develop'd the quahaug in
 its callous shell were enough.*

— WALT WHITMAN,
"Song of Myself," 27

Hast thou?

"AAAAAARRRRRRR . . ."

The alarm clock wakes me up. Time. Noise. It is dark and time to move. I roll over and turn the horrible thing off and lie a moment staring into the dusky shapes of bed and room, surfacing; the crude reverberations of alarm sealing off that barrier between my waking self and whatever worlds I keep to when I am not awake. What was it I dreamed? What was I there, how many strange, elaborate, ancient shapes have I laid claim to, and forgotten?

Noise . . . is air molecules bumping together in response to a disturbance in their midst. It is a kind of traveling energy, like the ripple-ring that spreads from a water droplet which has fallen into a pool. When I clap my hands to rouse the cat off my legs where he is sleeping, curled in a heavy ball, noise spreads from my hands in a sphere; the sphere meets the cat. The clap-bumped air is collected by his outer ear and guided down his auditory canal to his eardrum, which in turn shakes the chain of three amplifying bones, the hammer, the anvil, and the stirrup, whose footplate is embedded in a window of the snail-like cochlea, where the vibrations are sorted and turned into nerve impulses that are transmitted inward by the eighth cranial nerve; the cat leaps, there is a patting of paws on the floorboards, and he is gone.

I turn on the light . . . why am I surrounded by miracles? Perhaps in being so rudely rooted out of whatever filled world I inhabited five minutes ago some tendril or hem of that world still intrudes into this one, and so I am made suddenly conscious of the vibrating bulk of the air, earbones, the curve of the retina, cleansing eye-blinks, all the hidden machinery; all the intermediaries that propel me into being. I am propelled into this form, which I inhabit, complete with strict limitations, the worst of which is that I have only one among the trillions of possible live shapes, sets of skills, arrays of sense.

This light is another form of traveling energy, radiating from the lightbulb and then reflecting from bedposts and walls in that narrow selection of wavelengths which I happen to be able to sense with my eyes. My bed is warm, I don't want to get out of it. Heat is infrared "light," another longer wave-lengthed form of electromagnetic energy, in motion just as a river is — by definition — in motion. It turns out that what I perceive is only transition itself; and I turn and turn in these flows, feeling and seeing and hearing, emitting my own heat and noise. I make a supreme effort and get up and go downstairs, shivering.

I am a wheel: I turn in my own ways. Everything that is alive is spinning. An energy blows here and turns us: life is the whir of the spokes. But the world outside my window, and I am looking out there as I put my checkered coat on over my pajamas, looks sucked dry of any energies I could trust. It is cold, it is dark, it is bare. For the three deep winter months this part of the world functions at a net energy deficit. More units of heat and light are reflected and radiated away than are collected anywhere. How then do the wheels spin, and where?

The snow covers the fields and woods as my quilts covered me. The farm pond is as sealed as if someone had poured a dozen cement trucks full of liquid paraffin over it all. What energies flow there of heat or light are invisible to me, I am shut out, insensible to them, left on the surface here. Soil and water are clamped, shuttered, barred, still. No wonder we can think that everything alive out there is sleeping, rolled immobile in clean white, like comatose patients in sterile, soft beds. Rubbish! NO! Why do I persist in *thinking* that behind a closed door lies nothing at all? Well, simply because I do not yet know what is there.

I need a key. Many keys. I need to enter the secret rooms of winter with the same curious urgency with which I enter dreams.

Zero

Cold is the absence of heat. That's all it comes down to. At zero a winter day is a gaping maw, a swallower of heats, a round sucking, depleting, exhausting empty vessel into which — when I open the door and step out into the woodshed — my own meager warmth disappears at a crazy rate. Heat like water pours downhill and pours the faster the steeper the gradient it goes down. At zero it runs from me in a waterfall, a resounding white-water; I have armed myself with double mittens, double socks, boots, and wrapped scarves, damming the flow. The cold air bites my eyes as if it were acid, or dust.

The business of measuring heat flow/change is new enough. Yesterday I read in my encyclopedia that, in 100 B.C., one Philon of Byzantium made a gadget for demonstrating the expansion of air, which was, quite by accident, the first thermometer. In 1592 Galileo Galilei improved the model by using a container of alcohol that could rise through a glass tube as it warmed and expanded, and in 1611 his colleague Sanctorius marked Galileo's thermometer with a scale of "degrees" — scratches on the glass? By Fahrenheit's time thermometers had caught on in a big way and more than thirty-five temperature scales had come into use, though I am sure that most people still functioned well enough by sticking their noses out-of-doors in the morning and deciding whether it was hot or cold. (A three-layers-of-socks day? Two? None? My three-year-old son asks, every morning, with his bear under his arm: "Is it shorts or jeans?") Now there are thermometers which can measure heat flow over a hugely wide range, by measuring changes in electromagnetic radiation and electrical resistance; this is what today is about, why I am up early in a dark house, tiptoeing in my, pajamas and boots. I am going to measure.

There is a limit to cold, a temperature at which no lower temperature is possible; an absolute zero. I am as pleased by this as if someone had told me that there was a limit to greed, or evil. The Kelvin temperature scale in which absolute zero is *the* zero is used by physicists whose work makes Fahrenheit or Celsius unwieldy. No one has been there yet, but in closing in to zero Kelvin (K) strange things begin to happen: ordinary things become superconductors, helium liquefies and flows uphill. Zero K is *minus* 460°F. At zero K no heat flows anywhere, even molecular motion nearly quits, chemical reactions cease, every*thing* is completely still.

I think of a violent thing I saw once at a university seminar on thermodynamics: a physicist took a rubber ball, bounced it twice, smiling, and then dunked it in a vat of liquid nitrogen (−371°F) and then fished it out with a scoop and threw it at a wall, and it shattered like glass, shards plinking to the floor.

Every thing above absolute zero radiates heat.

At five in the morning I try hard to remember this. It has been below familiar, prosaic zero F for a week, below freezing for five weeks; I was up at 1:00 A.M. to feed the furnace and the fire is out again now. I bunch newspapers in a hurry, hack at a chunk of board to split off kindling. The cellar is dark, lit by a bulb; the sky outside is dark, lit by a knifeblade of a moon. I toss in kindling, small sticks, large sticks, a wooden match; air sucks up the chimney into the void and a white-gold shiver of fire curls into the wood. I run upstairs and switch the electric burner on under a kettle of water. The indoor-outdoor thermometer over the kitchen sink says that it is 54°F in my kitchen, and 15°F outside, nine inches away. Not a cold day as things go, here.

I get out of my pajamas and struggle into my underlayers while the kettle creaks and hums, the water molecules bumping faster and faster as they soak energy from the red coils of the stove, and roll finally into vapor — ah, coffee!

I pull on wool pants and shirt, and heat-damming layers full of dead-air pores put in by sheep and weavers, and while I drink my coffee I load my pack with my black measuring box — a microvolt meter — and extra mittens, and pull on a thin faded-blue cowl which my uncle wore in World War II, when he was an ace pilot in the RAF, wrenching his Spitfire through hairpin horrors and shooting down the enemy. Thus well-armed, I add sweater, boots, mittens, and step out into the morning.

We are near the height of land here, and to the east the ground slopes into the bowl of the swamp, a bowl dark with black spruce like a swatch of central Canada left behind in the glacier's last fast retreat; a gift. Because cold air drains into it, making a temperature inversion in clear weather, there is a frost down there nearly every month of the year. Through all of this last clear windless night all things above absolute zero have been radiating heat unimpeded to space, and the cooled air has slid down between the tree trunks, night breath, into the swamp.

My friend and mentor Dr. Peter Marchand earned his scientific stripes by climbing Mount Washington weekly all through one winter, toting his microvolt meter and plugging hair-fine thermocouples into spruce needles to see what temperatures the trees were feeling. Now he has set up a series of thermocouples in the swamp, tied to a stake. The first and deepest rests four inches into the swamp soil, among the roots of swamp grasses and blue iris. Another rests at ground level, a third four inches above that, and five more at equal intervals upward, and more again at three-foot intervals until the last hangs twelve feet above the ground. This time he wants to find out what is happening in the ground, snow, and air. Each thermocouple's working end is a soldered joint of copper and constantan wire, the wire then runs through insulated cable to a plug that fits the meter, and the meter will say what the temperature is at the working end. I also have one of Peter's long probes with a thermocouple tip, like a fencing sword, topped at the hilt end with a coil of gray coated wire and a plug for the black box. Thus equipped, I feel removed, scientific, official; after all what fool would be out at this hour of the day unless he had cows to milk, lambs being born? I am a watcher by morning now, my flock a curve of numbers and a red meter-hand.

I go into the swamp by the winding way I call the rabbit path, following game trails along marsh-margins and cutover forest and along a logging trail bordered with naked, bristling tamaracks. The mountains are washed with rose, the color-trumpeting of the sun, a color as audible as blood or the heart of a flower.

The rabbit path opens into a wide field, the heart of the swamp, the flat beaver meadow with the Tamarack river running through it like a high road. The snow is shallowest over the ice and I can stride upriver easily into the sunlight. How many hundreds or thousands of beavers have lived here no one knows; the meadow is theirs, made by the silting-up of generations of dammed ponds. There are two new dams and several old ones here now, the old dams dark and overgrown, tumbled remains of beavers that have been trapped out, ottered out, that have lapsed into death, or have eaten everything eatable and gypsied on, leaving their ponds to silt in and add another layer to the layered meadow. Under the beaver work which overlaps like shingles, might there be the compacted ooze, full of lichen flakes, pollens, the skeletons of tiny fishes, of a Pleistocene lake that once reflected mountaintops still covered in glacial ice? What lies on the bedrock here, the bottom line, the Chapter One of the swamp's history? I often wonder. I am walking on a tome.

While I am going east into the winter sun out of sight of all houses and flanked by old dark trees, thinking of the layered meadow beneath me, a memory almost as old as I am appears like a flash, reeled off some bright buried spool. I am not quite two, it is autumn, I am sitting on the long stone at the bottom of my mothers' garden, peeling an onion. I peel and peel, each layer coming away crisp and satisfying, revealing another layer; suddenly the alarm! *Look* what this child has been doing, just *look!* They hold their noses. Pah. I am frightened and cry, and am stripped and bathed, still crying. The onion doesn't wash off easily. I smell it for days in my hair, under my nails, in my skull. Yes, dear, someone says; I know you were trying to help Mummy peel the onion. No, I wasn't trying to help anyone. I was *peeling*.

How do I get to the center here? The live center of the wintering world, the ground? The birds have flown away, the animals have gone somewhere, the black spruce trees are like sticks wearing futile gray tufts. Where do I dig my fingernails in here? The thermocouples and the microvolt meter are supposed to be a key of sorts; a way into a world that I can't enter myself.

My river stops in a confusion of alders, an overgrown dam. I scramble up and through a haywire crisscross of branches to the level plain of the old frozen pool, and next to the pool is Peter's stake. The taped cluster of wire leads wears hoarfrost, an armor of shattered light, as if it were a species of metallic branch. I hump out of my pack, pull out the black box and calibrate it, twiddling the hairlike red line to zero, and then begin plugging the leads in one by one, scraping the frost off each plug with my mitten.

The air temperature over my head is 9°F, and rises slowly until at the snow surface it is 11°F, and once into the snow itself the temperature rises faster until, eight inches above the ground, it is 25°F. Four inches farther it is 30°F. At the soil surface it is 34°F, and four inches into the ground it is 36°F. The red line on the black box tracks its numbers and I write them down. Even though Peter has warned me about what to expect I don't believe the numbers. I take off a mitten, and slap the black box with the flat of my hand. Come on now, make sense for me. I run the series again. The numbers don't change. In a two-and-a-half-foot interval there is a twenty-seven-degree difference in temperature. It is less than thirty degrees cooler down there, in the muck, four inches into the swamp, than it was over my kitchen sink an hour ago.

Peter has told me that no matter how cold it gets — twenty, thirty, forty below zero — and no matter how the wind hurls itself along the river and over the beaver meadows, the temperatures of the unfrozen soil surface, and of the soil itself, do not change more than a degree or two all winter long. Providing there is snow. The snow is an air-trapping insulating stuff like wool, pelts, goose down, Styrofoam, rock wool, quilts. The poet in us may have seen the snow as a coverlet that winter draws up over the bare November bones of the hills; and it happens that the poet in us has glimpsed a truth.

I pack the notebook up and the black box, and unpack the long thermocouple probe and hold it between my hands; a fencer testing his metal. All right, I'm ready. I go on upriver. There is a new dam and a new beaver lodge there.

On the way I stop three times to push the probe through to the soil, down through the snow and swamp grasses. Within a degree or two the answer is always the same: zero or just above — zero Celsius. Freezing. I suspect the black box of cheating, of being stuck at zero C, at 32°F (it wavers a bit, 34° or 31°), but when I point my probe to the sky the box tells me that it is still 9°F up here; the box is not stuck. It has, in fact, made sense, perfect sense. It has touched the soil for me. Another world.

In northern Canada, where it is still beaver country, the best time to make a census of beavers is midwinter. Flying in a little plane over the meandering rivers and black spruce muskeg — and this is muskeg here — one can easily see which lodges are full of beavers: they have a black hole at the top like the smoke-hole in a wigwam, a dark circle where the warmth of the beavers inside has risen and melted away the snow.

The lodge upstream is taller than I am and I have to clamber up, gripping with my knees, and then press the probe down gently through the sticks and mud. It slides in as if it were greased through the bull's-eye center of the dark melted circle. The black box says that it is 45°F in there, eleven degrees shy of my own morning kitchen. And the probe isn't down to beaver level either; how warm are they, fat, furred, on their bed of dry shavings? Beavers breed in January. Perhaps the female is in heat now, perhaps the big male is pushing her with his nose, pressing his cheek along her flank, putting one paw, in an encouraging way, on her back. Perhaps she is letting her belly down in the shavings and looking at him out of the sides of her eyes.

The sun is high now and a wind is coming up along the river, and I am hungry. There is a sound of tearing, a stink of onion in my skull; what is at the center when all the layers — the crisp layers of the sheltering snow — lie around my feet like so many shavings, peelings of a bulb? Perhaps only a pale shoot, eager, naked, patient, blind. Perhaps deep within the zones of fat waiting leaves is the vortex of a flowerbud, past and future clasped together and held, folded in concentric hands, like a prayer.

Layers

"Hast thou entered into the treasures of the snow?" asked God of Job. I ask myself of myself; I want to know the pieces here, the peels of the bulb, the coverings under which so much of this January world is curled or moving. Each snowfall and even each minute of snowfall and every hour of weather, and time passing, changes the layered being of the snow.

Early in the winter, schoolchildren take tissue paper and scissors and fold the paper over several times before they begin to cut, and then they clip out loops and triangles, large and small, crude and delicate, and then — the moment of unfolding! As each fold opens, stiffly, the matched intricacy astounds everyone. See? And then the crystals are pasted up in the schoolroom windows where we can all see them.

Sometimes the snow is not so warm that the crystals clump, or so cold that the snow is only powders and shards, and it is not so windy that the crystals have bumped and shattered, and I can see them whole against the darkness of my wool coat for a moment only. They lodge, then clump and break and melt from my breath; intricacy to be glued up in the windows of the soul.

Snow is everywhere. Cirrus clouds are high wisps of snow that drift even to the equator, 15,000 feet up and higher, edging in at the brink of warm fronts as faint high sifts — the stuff of moon rings. The anvil-shaped tops of summer thunderheads are filled with crystalline snow like pillows full of feathers, and as the crystals grow they fall, sweep up water, melt, and hard rain falls that lodges the late hay and gathers the scattered sheep into knots under the trees.

Each shape of crystal falls from different warmths and densities of cloud, and one single storm can deliver many shapes of snow, each spun from its own patch of sky. All but the coldest crystals grow from seeds, nuclei: chips of ice, air-borne bacteria, mica specks, volcanic ash, rabbit hair, the dust of meteors.

Most snowflakes are six-sided like the packed cells of a bee-hive, their shape delivered direct from the triangular template of the water molecule. The central oxygen and its two bound hydrogens inhabit a bulbous triangle; the basic unit of all shapes of frozen water. Some crystals are hexagonal planes, spoked and edged with ornament like a Spode dinnerplate; others are six-pointed stars, lacy or fernlike or formal or lobed like flowers. Sometimes the flakes are six-side columns, either hollow or filled, capped with hexagonal plates, or plain. Some-times the crystals are odd, broken and then regrown like twisted trees; and sometimes the snow is only formless powder, or icy needles, or the fuzzy separate flecks of graupel, soft hail, its small crystals covered with a fuzz of rime. When it is very cold and still and clear, moisture condenses out of the air itself and falls as a sequined wind, spangling the shoulders of the drifts.

Here where the wind comes straight from the mountains January's fine powder snow comes in hung on the bias, its warp driven at a slant. At the ground it whirls up and is snatched and carried in great clouds like smoke, hissing and drifting to a stop in the backwaters of the air; behind fence-posts, the screen of orchard trees, the stone shoulder of the ledge jutting here, the house walls, the barn walls, the wood-pile, downwind of a clump of brush, a stone, a broomlike tuft of grass. One blown, bent grass stem scribes a wild circle on the snow, a small sketch of the galaxy, an expanding sphere.

The stuff gets everywhere. I remember vividly my first autumn on this hill when I was living on a farm down the road, in a house in mid-process of being gutted and "fixed up." Old houses here tend to get stuck in mid-process for a while because of the chanciness of weather and budget, and mine was no exception; and with the first windy December storm the snow came in. It came in all night while we were asleep, through cracks and pinholes around windows, between beams and joists, along the floor; and by morning long knife-edged mini-drifts were everywhere — in the dog's bowl, draped across an armchair, quietly enveloping flowerpots, bathtubs, broomhandles. A friend of mine once left his window open "a crack" and by morning his bed with him in it was buried in a perfect pristine snowdrift that was *two feet deep*. An elderly friend who has lived all his life up here tells of visiting a neighboring family during a snowstorm many years ago. The children were sitting on the stove, the mother was perched on a case of canned peaches with her feet in the oven and reading them a fairy tale while the wind blew snow through chinks in the clapboards. The children were protecting their faces from the driving snow with folded newspapers. I don't know. It doesn't sound impossible to me.

It's a gigantic sandbox out there. Snow is light, easy to pile and push. Trees make it into a kind of fanciful architecture. The pines catch the snow, their needles sieving out each flake of aggregate crystal, and in minutes their outer branches grow a fur of white. In the spruce woods of the swamp the wind is confused and slowed to a full stop, and the snow sifts in undisturbed and gathers in the needled branches that are held out to it like hands. The wood of needle-leafed trees is flexible on purpose, light, tough, fibrous. Caught there, the snow hauls the lowest branches to the ground and pegs them like the struts of a tent, and more snow falls, thatching the roof.

We have no words for these things and need to hold their images in our minds without the benefit of simple loosening sounds, words, to give us access. The Eskimo have words: *qanit* is falling-snow; *aput* is snow-lying-on-the-ground; *qali* is snow-caught-in-trees; *qamaniq* is the-shadow-under-trees-where-little-snow-lies; *siqoq* is snow-moving-over-the-ground. Even "How many *snows-there-is-none* have you seen?" the Eskimo asks, wanting to know how old you are.

As the snow itself ages each crystal changes, knits, making a fabric. Weighted by newly fallen snow above, the fine points of the crystals break. Blown by wind, the crystals shatter into an icy dust that packs into a firm, toastlike layer. As the snow lies, the finest needle shapes vaporize and the vapor recondenses between the crystal arms, and these larger rounding crystals grow until the snowpack is made up of irregular ice grains; with thaw and pressure this metamorphosis speeds up until the pack is a heap of ice marbles. Layered and compressed year after year, this once-snow can become, at last, glacier ice.

New, light, fresh snow holds so much air between its flakes that it is as good an insulating material as dry peat or dry wood, and the Earth under it — rock, soil, water — is such a slow absorber and spender of solar heat that twelve feet down it is even warmer in January than it is in June. Added to the stored solar heat is geothermal heat conducted out through rock and soil from the molten nickel-iron core of the planet, and this heat is enough all by itself to vaporize an inch of snow a year. These trapped, protected heats make the bottom of the snowpack warm. As the snow deepens this warmer moist air in the bottom rises up, shedding moisture as it cools, the vapor recondensing around the colder crystal cores above. The bottom of the pack disappears, vaporized, leaving hollow cuplike and tree-shaped crystals called depth hoar. The whole pack becomes unstable on its feet, the stuff of avalanche.

There are no avalanches here, and the depth hoar makes a delicate space in which small animals live. The hills are not tilted enough to shrug off their snow. The fabric of the pack is knitted up around the trees with little wind-made rucks around the tree bases, and fancy frill-work downwind of the stones, and crisp ruffles across the meadows: tiny *sastrugi*, wind-ridges-of-snow.

Among the weed tips and stones at the edge of the meadow are bluish holes the size of a quarter, and scuttle marks, and more holes. The snow is a clear boundary like the wall of a house, excluding some and protecting others. There are many lives at home there, moving, behind the snow.

A coarse sedge grows in the damper hollows of the sheep pasture and the sheep won't eat it; "swale grass" is what people call it here, because it grows in the swales, the damp dips of the fields. In the summer it is a brighter paler green than grass, a waste of a farmer's time, space, fertilizer. After snowmelt in April these places are full of round swale-grass tunnels and collapsed thatched nests, all looking like the ruins of some Amazonian Indian village seen from the air: no good, they've moved on. (Upriver for fishing? Into the trees to hunt? Downriver to trade?) They are the winter warrens of the meadow voles.

The meadow voles are not the only animals who live in the snow. One January day three years ago I found an odd thing, a whirling tunnel excavated just under the snow like the humped track left by an oversized mole in soft soil. There was a tough melted-and-refrozen layer in the middle of the snow-pack, an artifact of an old thaw buried by storms long since, and the ruffed grouse who had made the tunnel couldn't get through it. Grouse will dive from the trees at dusk deep into the snow and then fly through it with their wings, like diving ducks through water. I have found the little snow-caves that they sleep in many times. They are oval and deep like the impression of a heavy loaf of rye bread, with a heap of orange semicircles — grouse droppings — at one end. Sometimes there are the brush marks of flailing wings in the snow to each side, made as the bird burst from her sleeping place. Grouse will hide from night, cold, and bad weather in caves like this, covered and surrounded by snow, until their cropful of aspen buds is gone and they are hungry again.

One notices things, patterns in tracks, patterns of use. Every animal that moves on the snow — hare, deer, porcupines, foxes, ermine, weasels — all like to travel in the shallower snow of the *qamaniqs*. The hares, who also do much of their foraging at night, spend their days in the deep almost subterranean caves of the *qamaniqs* under the young firs. In very cold weather the red squirrels disappear under the snow altogether, burrowing in to their stashes of cones.

Some of the users of snow are nearly invisible. In the high dry meadow by the house, short-tailed shrews spend their winters foraging for seeds, insects, worms, buds; they are busy tiny animals like velvety torpedoes. In the woods there are the pretty white-bellied nocturnal deer mice, and rough-coated boreal red-backed voles, and minuscule masked shrews — thimblefuls of energy. All these small rodents and insectivores have such huge energy appetites and lost heat so easily from their small selves that they couldn't survive long cold winters if they didn't live under the snow, which insulates their warrens and protects them from shifts of weather and the view of owls.

The soil itself is covered without effort. When there are twenty centimeters — less than nine inches — of snow on the ground, one December skyful, then true winter begins underneath. Nine inches of light new snow is the winter threshold, and then the underworld begins a time of sheltered calm and darkness, protected from the pitches and yaws of cold and wind.

It must be dark and damp and monotonous down there, but the snow still offers enviable shelter. We live on the surface only, the outside, the face of a desert planet which is stitched with scant tracks and flown over by paltry dozens of birds, and a screaming wind.

There is a different way of seeing something when it is used, necessary, not just watched. The hunter sees the hunted animal as a part of himself. When trees are cut for wood to burn the trees change, and the change is irreversible, there is no going back. How can I enter the snow, then? I watch, read, study, examine, dig, build snowmen and snow dinosaurs and snow forts with my son, but even my vocabulary is borrowed. No one has ever *seen* the small rodents, under the snow. One can trap them, study them, read the signs of passage, but we are not there. I can see things only from the place I am. When the snowman has been topped by a straw hat and provided with an old sprung shepherd's crook and a wig made of sprigs of dry meadowsweet flowers, I go into my own house, entering outside the snow again, leaving a bulgy effigy. I stamp my feet clear, drape our sodden mittens by the stove, and light the wood fire; and at night the *siqoq* brushes against the window like the fur of an animal.

Hast thou entered . . . ?

There are, must be, ways in. The Eskimo not only had the vocabulary, but they made use of snow, and most of these skills have lapsed into anachronism now as so many of the technologies of our species have; largely unmourned, happily left. I read the chronicles of Vilhjalmur Stefansson, hungrily, wishing I'd been there, glad sometimes that I wasn't. When Stefansson lived among the Eskimo of the Canadian Arctic in the winter of 1906–1907, snow was still the stuff of life. When time came to find shelter for the night, his Eskimo companions, Ovayuak and his wife, would watch their footsteps for the signs of a house. If their mukluks left no dent at all, then the snow was too hard; if they sank in so that the whole footprint showed, then it was too soft. If their prints were just barely visible, then the snow was right. The drift would be probed with a caribou antler; did the antler push in evenly or snag and rush through uneven layers? Only thick and uniform snow of the right wind-packed texture was good for snow houses.

The cut blocks needed to be handled with care or the edges would crumble, and the snow used for chinking between the blocks was soft, but by morning the millions of snow crystals had knitted, metamorphosed, bound; and ten men or a polar bear could stand on the domed roof and it would hold.

Often on their hunting trips along the coast the Eskimo would take along a carefully wrapped rectangle of freshwater ice. When they built their snow house they would place this pane in at breast height. Inside and under this window they would make a kitchen table of snow blocks on which they put a blubber lamp. Soon after the lamp was lit it would be warm enough inside the snow house for the men to go bare-chested, and the babies would be naked on their skin rugs. If the heat from cooking was too great the Eskimo woman would shield the pane of ice with a flap of sealskin. Later, when the family went to sleep under their layers of skins and over more layers of skins on their snow-block sleeping platform, the woman would put the lamp out. Rubbing her fingers, which were oily from pinching the moss wick, she could push the sealskin aside and see the moon. It was a dimpled watery slice of light like a moon reflected in a pool; but it was the moon, still.

Holes

I am going to all the ponds that I know of. I want to find a way into them, under them. I want to see what's there.

A freshwater biologist who was a teacher of mine once said: "There are a lot of things which go on under the lakes in wintertime which are amazing, and have never been documented or studied very well." It is a dark and a cold world and is difficult to get into, and so it has kept its secrets. "The waters are hid as with a stone," said God to Job, "and the face of the deep is frozen."

In January, all of the ponds and lakes here are plains of level snow-paved white, somehow artificial-looking, as if they were queer tennis courts or parking lots that had been plunked down in the middle of the woods. In order to find out anything there one has to find a way in; and in wondering how, I found myself haunted by an odd experience which changed my view of water for all time.

Even in summertime water is difficult to find on the hill

where I live, and eight years ago when I needed a new well a friend of mine promised to dig one for me; but he said that he didn't altogether trust himself about water. He said that he was pretty good but not very good — hardly the words to inspire confidence, but I didn't have the slightest idea what he was talking about — and he asked if I would mind if he brought a friend up to help.

The friend was a dowser. He came to the farm one morning in a new red pickup truck; he was tall, thirtyish, with pale blue eyes, and a handsome face marred with premature shirrings of worry-lines. He asked where I kept my apple trees. I took him out to the orchard on the brow of the hill, and he cut a forked twig from my old Duchess apple tree with his penknife and began to walk over the field with the twig held out in front of him like a steering wheel. He walked slowly, concentrating, as if he were driving a car, fast, over difficult ground. After twenty minutes he told me that the only spring on the place was at the base of a rock ledge below a big white pine, eight feet down and running southeast; it was a stream of water the size of his wrist, he said. He said that he couldn't guarantee it in a dry summer, but it was the best we had.

On the strength of the dowser's divination my friend dug a hole by the rock ledge at the base of the pine, and eight feet down and running southeast was a stream of water two inches wide. We stoned the spring in and ran a pipe to the house. Several years later, in a record-breaking drought, the spring ran dry for a week.

The dowser charged ten dollars for his services, and had made it clear that he expected to be paid only if things came out the way he had predicted that they would, so after the spring had been stoned in I went to pay him. When I handed him the money, he pocketed it slowly, and said that he didn't really like dowsing anymore. He said he'd sworn a dozen times never to do it again but that his friends talked him into it. He said that he didn't need a stick to find water anymore. Sometimes he would be driving along a road and he'd get a *jolt* when he drove over a spring or a strong vein of it, and that bothered him. All he had to do now was to drive up to a piece of land where they were looking for water and he'd know right away where it was. He only used the stick now for show because no one would believe him other-wise.

He told me that the whole center of the earth is filled with water, and that it wells up and circulates like blood through live tissue, feeding the whole land: soil, crops, trees, ponds. Where it arrives at the soil in a steady arterial flow it is a spring, and out from the spring veins of it run, weaker and less dependable for supply than the springs themselves.

Looking for open water in January, I found myself wishing that I had a dowser's gift. But I could do without — he was quiet about it, and quiet-spoken, but it was there — his terror.

Beyond the farm the road runs straight along the spine of the hill and then plunges, twisting down through the woods to Elligo pond. Elligo is a mile-long crease in the hills, part pond and part marsh. At its most pondlike it is more than a hundred feet deep, clear, clean, full of brown acid water. In winter no rain falls in and groundwater barely oozes, and unless there is a thaw Elligo gets very little water from the hills around itself, and the river that pours over its lip, spill-ing down the valley, dries to a trickle.

Once the ice forms, like a metal skin on the pond surface, it conducts heat fast out of the pond and into the chilling air. Once snow covers the ice, most of what little sunlight there is reflects back into space as though the snow were a mirror; and the pond underneath darkens as if a black tarpaulin had been laid down.

The pond is laid to rest, chilled, masked, shut.

But between two islands near the western shore of Elligo is a hole, a hole that comes and goes all winter, a live eye in the mask; an entrance to the dowser's jolting and compelling world. A warm pulse of spring water must rise there, having slipped over layers of impermeable rock, through a fissure in the shales, a hairline crack in the granite. There it rises, a column of warm spring water pushing its hands against the ice, melting it back. On shore, looking across at the hole, I see a circle of darkness; but what would it be like if one were down there in the lake? The hole would be an eye of light, the brightest thing anywhere, shot with gleams like an opal. What is attracted, pulled in to the light there like squid to fishermen's lamps? There is hardly a living thing in water, no matter how small, how apparently eyeless, that won't deploy itself toward or away from light.

We are at the mercy here of strange properties of water. Once chilled to 39°F, water is at its densest and heaviest, and it sinks to the pond bottoms. The surface continues to cool and stays where it is. And since it is colder, less dense, lighter, it chills toward ice; the least-dense water form of all. Here is the miracle; that water solid is lighter than water liquid and *floats* . . . think if it sank! We would inhabit a world of frozen-solid oceans and lakes whose surfaces might defrost a bit in summertime; swimming holes and fishponds would be floored in perpetual ice; world wind and weather patterns would shift, sea-change, be colder everywhere. To these quirks of a single molecule — its inflection point at 39°F, and the fact that ice is lighter than water — these quirks that exist because of the unique molecular geometry of this simple two-hydrogens-and-an-oxygen compound we owe our world as it is. Our winters as they are. Perhaps our existence.

Think of the juggling that goes on, the minute whirling machinery here. Chilled to the freezing point, the water molecules twist and lock into a solid grid. As they lock in, immense amounts of heat are released — 80 calories per gram, 144 BTU's per pound of water frozen solid. All this heat needs to be sucked away before freezing can happen. It takes days and nights of cold for the lakes to freeze, weeks of April heat and rain to plug those BTU's back in so that the ice can melt again.

Ice forms first as tiny disks called frazil ice. In rivers that are too turbulent for sheet ice to form, slushy masses of frazil disks collect and stick to rocks, wrenching them loose, carrying them off. Heaps of frazil ice collect in narrows and stick onto ice dams and bridges and under the plates of ice at the river edges. In quiet ponds and river backwaters the frazil disks float singly to the surface and sprout spicules, sharp freezing dendrites that mesh the surface into the first thin dark film of solid ice.

The surface waters of forty-eight percent of the northern hemisphere freeze every winter: nineteen million square miles of meshing dendrites.

The ice grows in layers: the black ice of freezing water, the white ice of frozen water-soaked snow. In the layers themselves are spangles of air bubbles; ice's strict lattice structure pushes its dissolved air out in packets, suspended spheres.

On a cold clear January evening there are noises, violent crackings as the surface ice cools and shrinks, breaking away from deeper warmer layers, leaving white blisters where it has broken, and making deep hollow booming sounds; the muffled explosions of cold.

When I left Elligo I went down to the spring pond over the flank of my neighbor's field. It is an old man-made pond with a derelict bathhouse sagging on one bank. The ground curves down toward it as if to spill one into space, the Green Mountains loom across the gulf of the valley — it is three townships broad, this scoop of valley — and the mountains and flanks of hills wear a dark stubble of leafless trees. Through these wooded slopes chins and juts of snowy ground show, the snow a fragile film over which I walk, leaving foot-dents in a wandering line; a chain of prints each with the fishlike reticulated shape of a showshoe.

My ducks used to winter on the spring pond, and that is how I guessed that there might be open water there. And there was: only half of the pond was frozen over and a stream

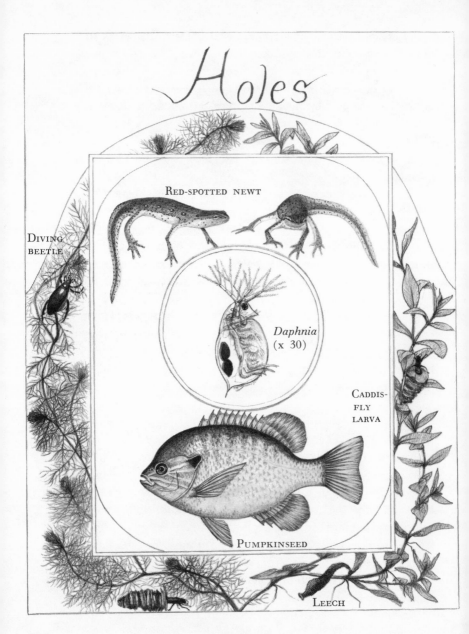

Holes

RED-SPOTTED NEWT

DIVING BEETLE

Daphnia (x 30)

CADDIS-FLY LARVA

PUMPKINSEED

LEECH

from some warm source spring ran in from the east, twinkling and muttering over its stones like a summer stream full of collected and reflected light. On either side of its inches-wide span were banks of snow, white pure, cold, diamond-bright. The stream was a crease in the snow mantle, full of greenery. Two kinds of leafy plants were massed in the running water and poked their branch tips just into the air. Farther downstream a patch of grass was growing in the streambed, green and lush, like a piece of spring lawn seen under glass. The pond itself was clear and had a soft brown mud on its bottom, and hundreds of caddis-fly larvae were crawling in the mud, leaving squiggly tracks. Their presence said that a good soup of micro-life simmered in that mud all winter long making food for them. The caddis-fly larvae are a kind of makeshift mollusk, pasting bits of their environment together into long cups which they tote around on their hind ends, and into which they can disappear at will, plugging the doors with their heads. They are choosy by nature. There are thousands of species of them worldwide, and each seems to like to make its cup out of different stuff. Some will use only sticks, others use grains of quartz sand, others use discarded snail shells, and these were using bits of plants — fragments of black half-rotted leaves and pieces of live green leaves which they had scissored out of the plants in the stream, using their jaws like shears. The harvested bits were stuck together with a waterproof mucus. The result was a lightweight pliable tweed, in emerald and black.

Standing up to my knees in snow, I watched the inch-long cases jerking about their business; it was like watching fish through the glass of an aquarium. Their world was six feet away, forty degrees Fahrenheit warmer than my world. Through the intercession of a warm clear spring things grew and were green there, things seethed and changed. Snow began to fall as I stood and watched, the tiny flakes disappeared soundlessly and without ripple or pause into another dimension.

How different was the winter world of these caddis-fly larvae from their summer world there? Not much, I thought, not much.

After leaving the spring pond, I walked up the quiet curve of snowy field and drove east over the ridges and the marsh-lands between. There are very few houses out that way, and my tire-tracks were the only tracks in the white road. Miles out, the road dipped and skirted a narrow little lake between the hills; Keeler pond. Close to shore and easily visible as a dark swatch in the wholly gray-white landscape — it was snowing still, tiny flakes slanting by as if the air itself were shivering — was another hole.

It had been a week of the coldest weather; it hadn't come more than a degree or two above zero F for five days and nights, but the yard-wide hole was open still, its one edge just covered with a fine film of new ice, stippled all over with extravagant flowers of hoar. The open hole steamed and the steam had congealed into this florid ice-lace; decorations. Within the hole itself was a mass of blackened vegetation, covered with flecks of coppery iron and sulfur sediments, which stirred up at my touch like snowflakes-under-glass. There was a faint smell of bad egg in the air, a whiff from some sulfurous agitation underneath, a reminder of eruption and quake here, and of our privileged place out on the cool, and nearly quiet, rind of the planet. Shoreward of the hole, clumps of coarse grasslike sedge burst through the ice and snow like sand-colored fountains, sprays of horny foliage. Beyond the hole was the long blank expanse of frozen pond, then fir trees and the white sky. Down there in the hole, through a film a scant molecule broad, spotted salamanders dangled like embryos in amnion. They seemed made up of the simplest materials — a darkish gel, a gilded eye-sparkle, kohl spots, mere wriggles and twists — more adjustments than motion. Their hole, their swatch, their microcosm offered them more warmth and light than anything anywhere could for miles. I fished one out and took her home in a jar.

Two days later I went to the Pond in the Woods, which had no holes of its own, so I had to go about making one. It had been two days since I had been to Keeler. It was 2°F at my house when I left, and out on the pond there was a wind, and a fine ice dust hissed over the surface and had packed into a tough, crackerlike crust. The snow on the pond had a riffled surface like beach sand; the image of sterility, pale and lifeless grit. The wind stirred the ice dust into my face and it hurt — burned more than hurt — so that my eyes watered and I turned my back into the wind and trotted, crunch crunch crunch, across the pond to the little bay where I wanted to make my hole.

At least once every winter I get colder than I like to be, and I knew right away that this would be it. My hair was coated with white rime from my breath and froze into a snaggle of wire, my cheeks and mouth stiffened. I pushed with mittened hands to get the hair out of my face and my hat slipped over my eyes. Under my collar there was a precious pocket of warmth, and as I fumbled with the Velcro catch of my hood my bare hand went numb instantly and turned a purple red. I couldn't make the catch catch and the wind blew my hood up and whirled the pocket of warmth away. I could feel my scalp tighten, my toes begin an ominous ache. I danced and danced as if the ice were hot. There is a place and time when hot and cold cease to have meaning and there is just hurt; this was close. Close.

I had an ice spud to make a hole with, a heavy metal pole with a chisel-like business end. I began tamping it in a circle and chipping the ice away, chunk chunk chunk. Pause. Chunk chunk chunk. I chopped away in my circle doing a kind of ceremonial dance, turning and turning on an ellipse of ice the size of a pail. Finally the spud hit pay dirt, ah, water, welling up yellow as urine with dissolved humic acids. The ice itself was a gray white, clean and layered like a cake. When the ice lump floated free, I shoved it back under the ice with the spud. It was too big and too heavy to haul out, but lovely; glossy and bubbled and faceted like a boulder of Steuben glass. Then I scooped the little shards of ice out of the sloshing hole. The water was dark, warm, 35°F according to my thermometer, and the open hole smoked faintly against the air.

I lowered my trusty net into the darkness. The net was a miracle of spur-of-the-moment engineering made of a broomstick, a coat hanger, wreath wire, and a pair of paraplegic panty hose, with one leg lopped at the knee and the other at the thigh and both knotted shut. The pond bottom was not far off; four feet or so, no more. I scooped down, feeling the soft sludgy bottom, the texture of another universe. There was a drag like strings breaking and then I brought in my haul, a netful of muck and brilliant green plants — leafy *Elodea*, *Myriophyllum* — and things squiggling, the tip of a worm, a beetle all glossy; quick quick dump them in the pail fill the pail with water! The cold is deadly, this was like hoisting them into outer space.

After I'd spudded away for twenty minutes my feet were warm and my hands were warm and I felt elated and packed with an effervescent energy: WHOOP! It was like working in the woods in winter: there one gets into a rhythm of working, ax and saw, chop, bend, rise, haul; the bad time is always stopping for lunch and then everything begins to go — nose, ears, fingers, toes, all chilled, rigid. It was time to leave the pond; the spud was frozen to the ice, the net crackly as a discarded snakeskin.

Running back into the wind, I was suddenly concerned about frostbite. After some desperate fiddling I closed my hood to a funnel, but first my cheeks disappeared and then my nose and I puffed and panted up the hill above the pond, aware that my feet were numbing to lumps. I had a surreal prize, though, sloshing in the pail, a netful of wonders brought up from a warm dark core which *goes*, somehow, under this desert surface. But they have their own lot of problems down there. Yes they do.

Most sunlight that comes to the pond in the winter bounces back, but some light — especially the shorter, bluer wavelengths — gets through. In the shallows the light is absorbed by the dark bottom muds and reradiated as heat; on a sunlit day the shallows are the warm places. And light can be — blue light is good for this — absorbed by plants and harnessed to the wheel of photosynthesis.

There is a simple experiment: one can take two bottles, one clear and one painted black, fill them with equal volumes of pond water and equal-sized sprigs of pond plant (*Elodea* is the classic one, an easy keeper, as happy in fishtanks or bottles as in ponds), and then lower the bottles by strings down to the pond bottom whence the *Elodea* came. Twenty-four hours later the bottles can be pulled up again by their strings and the contents tested for oxygen. Even after a cloudy January day the clear bottle holds more oxygen than the dark bottle, proof positive that *Elodea* was working with what light there was.

But — and it is a big but — after the experiment even the light bottle has less oxygen in it than it started with. In January, under the ice, even the live plants are using more than they can make, working at a deficit. In the red.

The ice has sealed the pond off from air like the lid on a jar. With no wind to stir them up sediments settle, and the microlife that feeds among the debris settles, too, so that pond life becomes concentrated at the bottom. As these live things breathe, the pond's dissolved oxygen is used from the pond-bottom up. Carbon dioxide builds up there, too, as the winter goes on, and through a chemical juggle it winds up as carbonic acid; and the pond water becomes more and more acid the longer the ice lid stays on. Ammonia also builds up, another waste product, excreted by nearly everything. At the same time the nitrates needed for plant growth run low as the bacteria that are responsible for cycling the ammonia back into usable nitrates quit their jobs for lack of oxygen. And salts accumulate; more life waste, more excretions.

In spite of acids, poisons, darkness, lack of air, the pailful of Pond-in-the-Woods-bottom was a seethe of life. There were two kinds of diving beetles, one long and oval, one round as a pearl. They whirled and bobbed like windup toys, perhaps convinced from the light and the sloshing-in of oxygen which I had provided them that spring was here. There were three kinds of pond plants, all very green, all capable — according to a consulted text — of photosynthesizing at ten percent of their summer rates in January, given light. There was a single *Tubifex* worm, a rosy-brown creature which has the nastiest lifestyle of anything I can think of. *Tubifex* worms live head-down in mud, eating mud, and breathing through their tails. *Tubifex* worms like to group up in colonies and lash their tails in unison to make a current of water flow over themselves, all the better to absorb what oxygen there is. When oxygen is lower they lash *faster* and still in synchrony, which means that they must be in communication somehow, the "lash-now" nerve pulses zipping through the mud between the worms. There was also a single tiny leech in the pail, an acrobatic mini-monster capable of any shape from a tendril to a sphere, and of shrinking/stretching from one shape to the other in a half second flat.

In dipping, peering, tweezing these creatures into separate glass dishes on my table, I couldn't help feeling that I was practicing up for something big. After all; when we do make contact with life forms from elsewhere in the galaxy the chances are that they are going to be at least as different from us as a *Tubifex* worm is; they may be *bright*, all right, but they may just have evolved in an environment as different from ours as a winter pond bottom. And we are going to have to make them welcome somehow, dignitaries smiling, flags waving, bands playing "Hail to the Chief." In respectfully tweezing the *Tubifex*, I am getting ready for Universal Diplomacy. Starting here.

With an eyedropper, a glass slide, and a microscope I took the exercise a step further, navigating the visible brink into a world of the nearly astronomically small. There were a lot of copepods in the pond water — round *Diaptomus* like spinning jewels, ruby, citron, sapphire, colored by the oil droplets which are their food store and which give them buoyancy. There were jar-shaped *Cyclops* with a kind of mustache of tentacles flowing from their round front ends, the females towing panniers of eggs. The pond copepods migrate up and down in the wintertime, coming to the pond surface at noon and retreating to the depths at night. In summertime when hungry fish are out and about in the day, the copepods will reverse their migrations, coming to the surface only at night to feed. It seems incredible that these creatures, as tiny as motes of glass, can change and shift; are drawn, repelled; have strategies.

I also found a few *Daphnia*, big plump-eyed water-fleas, with treelike tentacle arms flailing over their heads, doomed to a mad life of whisking their whole selves around in backward circles. With these surprising arms they drive a current of water through their translucent shells where algae and oxygen are filtered out, and in a kind of pack-saddle on the *Daphnia*'s back, eggs form.

Daphnia has a good wintering trick. It isn't just a wintering trick, it's a general hard-times trick. In the spring and summer when algae for food and oxygen for breath are plentiful, all the *Daphnia* in the pond are female, and they make eggs that hatch out into more females; but if there are changes — the hint of famine, the bite of low oxygen — *Daphnia* can make eggs that hatch out into males, and then the *Daphnia* mate, and eggs form from this mating that are different. They are hard and dark, encased in a tough sachel which outlives the parent and can drift and rest like a resistant seed. A *Daphnia* resting-egg can survive freezing, drying, can travel on the legs of migrating geese, can live through digestion by fish and animals, poisoning; time.

Some kinds of *Daphnia* go through the winter as adults, too, and they migrate like the copepods, in layers, schools, up and down with the faint rhythm of the winter light.

I spent hours behind the microscope — more translucent motes tumbled by, flailed, whirled. There was a chain of linked squares called *Tabularia*, each greenish square glistening with internal circuitry like silicone chips. There were lots of green new-moon curves of *Scenedesmus*, another alga. A paramecium spiraled by like a whirring grape; a rotifer bounced like a dancing jar; a translucent raspberry of a *Volvox* revolved lazily in some current of its own; there were humble immobile lozenges of bacteria.

All of these things survive various winter tortures by re-organizing their chemistries of breathing or feeding, by changing their behavior, or by forming resting-eggs or encasing themselves in hard, resistant cysts. Most of their arsenals of survival defend them less against the cold itself than against the effects of cold on the pond — the lack of light, food, oxygen; the buildup of acids, ammonia, salts. Most of their talents must have evolved well before the plants and animals themselves had anything to do with winter. They defend just as well against summer suffocation, stagnation, pollution, drying out — in the tropics just as well as here. Judging from an eyedropper or two full of their world, their winters are well prepared for.

What my net didn't scoop up was fish. I know that they are there because I have caught them in the summer, the little fish which go by many names — yellow sunfish, sun-bass, pumpkinseeds. They are nearly round, disklike, and glintingly colorful like small full moons. They like the quiet weedy bays. They come to the surface in summer mornings and bask in the sun, turning their flanks up and circling with their fins for balance. They can be caught on hooks baited with any small local talent; dragonfly nymphs, mayfly and midge larvae, worms, snails, water boatmen, larval salamanders. They nest and hide among the water plants — part of the community. When the pond cools and ices over, they pen up together over the deepest part of the pond or over the up-pulse of an incoming spring and go into a kind of semidormancy, just riffling their fins to stay put. Scuba divers who have gone under the pond ice in wintertime say that they can come up and touch the pumpkinseeds and swim among them, pushing them aside like leaves in a forest.

In some years when the ice goes off, the shoreline of the lake will be littered with dead pumpkinseeds, pale bellies up. The winter fish-kills seem to happen in those years when the pond freezes early, or when there has been a lot of snow in February and March, snow which lies deep and late, darkening the pond well into spring. Suffocation — lack of oxygen — is the greatest threat to wintering fish, and after the ice lid clamps down on their world, they are, oddly, at the mercy of sunshine more than ever. Until the ice goes off in April no oxygen can be absorbed from the air, and only if enough light gets through to the green pond plants can it be recycled, replaced, put back into circulation again. It depends on the pond, the winter; one year out of — how many? fifteen? thirty-five? six? — the sun doesn't get through in time.

I take the plunge; holes are everywhere, holes into and holes under, some deeper than others. Some lakes are so deep that water gets stuck in the bottoms of them and never moves at all. Fayetteville Green in New York's Finger Lakes is the textbook example of this; it looks normal on the surface of things, but the unmixing unmixable layer in its depths is a kind of chemical hell. It is so stagnant that there is no oxygen at all, a crystal calcite rain sifts down from the sunny upper layers, peculiar sulfur chemistries percolate, the water is thick with salty by-products of decay; and the salts make the stagnant layer so dense that it won't mix with the water above and has sunk forever like vinegar under oil. Plaques of purple sulfur bacteria — which can wrest energy from light and organic matter without benefit of oxygen — drift there in heavy layers. These holes are a kind of harking back to the time before air had oxygen in it, when earth had an atmosphere of methane and ammonia and carbon monoxide, and the earth surface was clawed by lethal ultraviolet radiation. The purple sulfurs were here, then, hunkering under a radiation shield of water.

In Antarctica there are ponds which are frozen solid down to bedrock, and which never have holes in them at all. Now when it is winter here and summer there, the day-long Antarctic sun is shining to those pond bottoms, and the stone and sediment are absorbing the light and warming up, defrosting the ice from the bottom. There is a layer of free water over the bedrock now and blue-green algae live there, under meters of perpetual ice, and they live there much as they did when they were the first and only plant anywhere on earth. They form humped mats, a felting of live soft darkness, spangled with bubbles of the oxygen that is their gift to us all.

Farther still, farther still, barely showing as a fleck of light through the long-lensed barrel of my old telescope is Titan, the largest of Saturn's many moons and the only one with an atmosphere. It is a yellowy ice moon marbled with darkish stains and riven by fractures in its ice crust, huge cracks made as the Mercury-sized moon heaves under the tides of its home planet. I wonder what the dowser would make of the tides of Saturn? According to the astronomers who have been deciphering the photographs and other data from the Voyager satellites, there may well be water under the ice. The darkish stains on Titan's surface are probably organic tars made in its methane-rich atmosphere — which is not so different from the atmosphere that Earth once had. Water, organic stuffs; the combination is tantalizing, too good to believe. Titan, it happens, might be a candidate for extraterrestrial life, perhaps the first such life that we will actually scoop up and carry home. Life will, if it's there, be ultra-wintry life, having lived always under miles of ice, perhaps wobbling and flailing its way toward the lights and gases of the latest in tidal ice cracks. The holes of Titan; perhaps the time for Universal Diplomacy isn't any further off than that.

Round and Round

I have a gray box on my shelf that is a kind of archive of enchantment, full of loose-leaf notes and articles and scientific papers, each of which explores or describes something about the survival of winter that has left me aghast. On the end of the box, written in black ink, is the title: Wonders.

This is a kind of leafing through, then, a rifling of a wizard's sanctum. The secrets in it are well concealed; the most secret worlds of all are those which are invisible, locked in the minutest expression of live form: in chemistry. Chemistry is the gyre of life; swirled globes of atoms snapped apart like Pop-it beads and snapping together, wringing their bound shapes endlessly. Most wintering technologies are an alchemy of sorts, a world accessible only by test tube, pipette, centrifuge, experiment, the careful compounding of elemental stuffs. If cold and the effects of cold are unfriendly to life, then living things must have defended themselves with carefully wrought incantations, and that things *live* is proof of the charms — look, we are hexed ourselves, and rolling!

So I see the world from one body and from one place. When I studied drawing in school, I liked the part about perspective; it was clear, mathematical, precise. You draw a horizon line at the level of your eyes and a "vanishing point" at the center of this line, and then you draw in a surround of lines converging on the vanishing point, the central infinity, like the rays of a star; and along these you can arrange the walls of a room, the legs of a chair, the plane of a table top. And they all come out looking just the way they do *look*. But if you suddenly lie on the floor, or walk a step forward or backward, or cross your eyes so that there are suddenly two separate points of infinity — one imposed on the other — then all of your carefully drawn lines are suddenly wrong; wherever you are, *what*ever you are, the world is a different place. How can I see winter from the perspective of a salamander? A fish? A butterfly egg?

I unbind, stretch, and shrink; to know their magics I have somehow to see the world from the perspective of these other live things. I have to flail, suck other air, swim.

The salamander that I took from the hole in Keeler pond has golden eyes, and she stares out at me from her glass dish eye to eye as all eyed things stare, but out from a world as distant and malleable as mine seems, suddenly, to be near and strict. Between seventy and eighty percent of my daily caloric intake goes just to heat me up, so that the intricate chemical stew I call myself can go on staring back at the salamander, writing notes in a notebook, humming along with the radio. The salamander, like most reptiles, amphibians, insects, crustaceans, and microorganisms, is free of the great gluttony of an internal furnace, and gram for gram she needs far less food in order to stay alive than any bird or mammal does; an economy model.

A chemical mixture poured or sprinkled or bubbled into a laboratory flask, a mix all set to undergo a chemical reaction (the bonding of chemical A with chemical B to make chemical C), is heir to the quaint phenomenon known as the Q_{10} response, which is roughly this: if you warm the mixture up by ten degrees centigrade (18°F), the reaction will usually progress between two and three times faster than it did before. All living things live by chemical reactions. Sugar $+$ oxygen $\rightarrow$ energy $+$ carbon dioxide (basic metabolism) is chief among them. If you put the salamander in a sealed laboratory flask and measured her oxygen uptake or carbon dioxide output while you warmed her up or cooled her down, you would probably find that the salamander has a nice predictable Q_{10} of about 2.76. I can't do this. No warm-blooded creature can. We run at full throttle all the time. If my body core cooled or heated more than a few degrees either way, I would lapse into deadly hypothermia or be cooked by fever. The salamander is a more flexible arrangement. But there are limits to the salamander experiment, too; if she gets too cold she lapses into chill coma, if she gets too warm she expires from overheating, but her range is tens of degrees broad. Too far either way, though, the salamander dies, and the chemical reaction no longer goes. But between these limits, for every 18°F the salamander cools down, she uses 2.76 times less oxygen and food than she did before.

But . . . if you keep the salamander at a new and different temperature for a few days, if you scoop her out of a cold pond and keep her in a warm room, the *whole system, all of your measurements, change.*

The salamander has been doing something in her new warmer place, tinkering away in there with her metabolic chemistries, twisting hormonal dials, adjusting the kinds and amounts of the enzymes that push her energies through. This is a kind of metabolic magic-show. Salamanders acclimate, adjust to new temperatures.

Her acclimation process isn't fast. It takes half a week for a salamander to adapt to a place which is colder or warmer, and microorganisms can adapt much more quickly. But given time, and pond water chills and warms gradually enough, she can function equally well at 36°F as she can at 77°F, just by tinkering with her internal chemistry. Along with her metabolic rate her lethal chill-coma and heat-death limits change, too. A salamander scooped out of a pond in January can survive at colder temperatures than one which has been scooped out of a pond in August, even if these two creatures happen to be the same salamander; with the golden eyes, and the elegant double line of black bordered spots on her back.

Things shift, make shift. Shifty-eyed means not to be trusted. Look around; the *Daphnia* in Elligo pond are red right now, and in the summertime they are not red. In the summer they are as clear as spangled bells, afloat and whirling-grazing on the algae, like cattle in a three-dimensional pasture of pond. When oxygen gets low in there, they make hemoglobin, a red pigment spoked around an iron atom like a molecular wheel; the finest carrier of oxygen from a source to a place where it is needed that life is capable of making. It is the same stuff that makes our blood red. In summer they don't need it, and don't make it for themselves. They can rely then on simple diffusion, on oxygen moving from water to *Daphnia* without any vehicle at all. They are a signal for us all: red *Daphnia* = low oxygen. Pink *Daphnia* = sort-of-low-oxygen. Clear *Daphnia* = plenty of oxygen around.

Breathing, breath, can be a movable feast even among mammals. Whales and porpoises have a "diving response," an alternative oxygen-using style they can switch into when they go down to airless depths for a long time. They can switch their fins and tails into an oxygenless mode, a kind of partial metabolism, which chops sugars into two bits of a mildly corrosive chemical called lactic acid. It is a move that liberates some energy (not much, though) and uses no oxygen whatsoever. They use their small store of this good gas fully to power their vital core; their gut and brain. If I run very hard so that I can't breathe hard or fast enough to keep up with my legs, my legs begin to ache as the lactic acid builds up in the muscle tissue — do the dolphin and the whale ache? Once I saw a pond turtle swimming around under the ice, prodding the bottom for edibles. She was breathing through her cloaca, her one anal opening, which pulsed like a lung, but she was living mostly off that same anoxic half-metabolism as a diving whale — does the turtle ache?

Even the frogs in the mud have to breathe. Why in mud? Perhaps because if they wintered in water too much would flow in across the simple slick barrier of their plastic-wrap–thin skins, and they would not be able to pee out enough of this excess water — frog kidneys, like all other frog organs, function sluggishly in cold — so that they would blow up and pop like watery balloons . . . awful. But mud has much the same salt content as a frog does, so water isn't so inspired to move there from mud to frog. Since their idea of breathing is a flexible arrangement anyway, their skin is as good as lungs, as tender, as permeable, mud is a fine sort of place for a frog to be.

Speaking of breath, of oxygen, I read last winter about a creature called an icefish, a horrific monster if there ever was one. They have made a weird hocus-pocus of their breathing arrangements, opposite completely to the clear/red flexibility of the *Daphnia*. Icefish are six-foot-long distant cousins of the pond pumpkinseed. They live in the fjord bottoms of Antarctica. They have huge heads equipped with crocodile-like toothy jaws, and narrow, scaleless bodies trailing behind like an afterthought. The water that they live in is always cold, varying a few degrees at most between winter and summer, but it is full of oxygen — and full of fish. The icefish eats other fish. He spends his time there lurking among the kelp beds waiting for likely prey, and except for the occasional snap-and-gulp he can stay nearly immobile. It is so cold where he lives that his energy needs, as long as he stays still, are minimal. His sluggish lifestyle and the perpetual chill of his ocean allow him to live in a state of total anemia. He has no red blood cells at all, the hemoglobin-containing red cells that fetch and carry ninety percent or more of any other animal's oxygen supply. His blood can contain, at maximum, no more oxygen than seawater. He is the color of ice, cleverly camouflaged by his own transparency; a live ghost.

Because of its saltiness, most seawater won't freeze until it is 28.6°F; well below the freezing point of freshwater, and well below the freezing point of *fish*. So the icefish, and the shorthorn sculpin of the Arctic, and other very northern or very southern fish, have a special problem of their own: how to live in a subfreezing ocean and not freeze solid themselves. The answer is that they can survive there by stoking their tissues with antifreeze; with special proteins and sugar-proteins that mechanically wrap the strict lattices of ice, so that it can't form in their flesh. In the autumn the sculpin begins to make up antifreeze long before the water gets very cold. This antifreeze-making seems to be mediated by hormones which are cued in by the shortening days that come before the ice cometh itself. By midwinter nearly sixty percent of a shorthorn sculpin's cell fluids consist of antifreeze protein. When there is no more risk of his freezing solid, the antifreeze disappears. This is a biochemical sorcery in which both the conjuring and that-which-is-conjured are invisible; but without all the genetic abracadabra, the wavings of the sunwand, the fish would simply — disappear.

Often when we are cutting and splitting firewood in February, we find insect larvae tunneled under bark or into the wood itself. There are larvae which make perfect polished holes through the wood of the beech trees, packing the space behind themselves with beechwood-colored droppings. From maple branches that have been dead a year or more the bark slips off like a sleeve, revealing rows of bark-beetle egg tunnels, each as descriptive as a Chinese pictograph; the bark beetles killed the branch. The oval galls of the goldenrod stems that still poke above the snow harbor minuscule bright orange grubs, brown pupae like grains of rye, and half-inch-long flies of a wonderful iridescent green with black antennae like the horns of an oryx; are these different stages of the same thing? Is one a parasite of the other, a sibling, a guest? Whichever it is, they all have the same problem there that a sculpin has — how to live in freezing places and not freeze themselves.

These insects make antifreezes, too. Once I picked up a brownish grub from a peel of maple bark, a larva as stiff and cold as a stick. It snapped easily between my fingers, and from its center oozed a syrupy stuff like the filling of an expensive candy. The grub was, had been, alive; its fluids concentrated to unfreezable syrup. In January, forest tent-caterpillar eggs clumped along tree limbs can survive internal temperatures of –40°F. What does winter look like to one of these?

The hunting work of chickadees lets me know that a single tree, a spreading system of trunk, bark, twigs, and buds, must be a planet-sized world for insects; a world inhabited by fungal forests, bark-ranges of mountains, materials for tunnel-making, a variety of juices and live food. And wood is good insulation against the pitches and yaws of weather; an averaging medium. A kind of arms race goes on here between the insects' cleverness in finding places to go quiet and dormant in, and the birds' ingenuities at hunting them down and eating a lot of them anyway.

The soil is a warmer, darker, rainforestlike world of deep and deeper layers; ninety-five percent of all insects spend at least some of their lifetimes in the soil. Though the monarch butterflies migrate from Canada to ancestral tree groves in the Mexican uplands, they have no monopoly on autumnal movement; even immobile eggs and pupae fall to the ground in October with the leaves that they are glued on or webbed into.

The water is filled with insects, too. The upper layers of the spring pond in January were thick with mosquito larvae, barely visible to the naked eye as tiny flexing hairs. Under the microscope they enlarged, clarified, bulgy and bristled and with enormous heads, like the worms that lie in wait at the bottom of a nightmare. Stonefly nymphs also lived there in the spring pond, clinging among the green plants like aquatic crickets. Winged adult stoneflies emerge from the water in midwinter looking like sluggish gray mosquitoes, and — according to my insect book — they mate then and lay their eggs back in the pond during the brief span of a thaw.

The world of spiders and of insects fascinates me but makes me uncomfortable. Insects are *everywhere*, and are so elegant, so coolly efficient. Many spiders eat their mates; the mantis eats hers as a part of the ceremony of sex, starting in casually with her lover's head; the young ant queen sips the juices of her own eggs. In peering at mosquito larvae under the dissecting scope, I am perhaps too aware that on a planet with lower gravity than ours the insect's external skeleton wouldn't weigh him down as it does here, and there would be no problem at all with a spiderlike or insectlike form growing large; even very large. In the denser, more buoyant "atmosphere" of the oceans, where the pull of gravity-on-skeleton isn't such an issue, there are giant spider crabs; not too distant relatives of spiders, which have a leg-tip-to-leg-tip reach of more than thirteen feet. How would Universal Diplomacy go with an intelligent extraterrestrial that had the appearance, not to mention the ethics, of a spider?

Cold-blooded creatures as a whole live in a place apart, in another energetic dimension, as if their world were subject to odd swellings and distortions; the perspective bolluxed in a biological funhouse mirror. The salamander stares me down, but what is she watching for? Is it fair to ask? Even time goes around differently where she is, there, in her glass dish. Since temperature is the greatest controlling force of the rate at which cold-blooded creatures *go*, when it is cold fewer things happen. Brains, muscles, hearts, lungs, eyes all work more slow . . . ly. On a summer afternoon a warm cricket will make more chirps-per-minute than a cooler cricket. Chirp frequency and cricket temperature can be correlated with mathematical precision; but according to the cricket himself, his chirping may always be going along at the same rate. In the world of cold-blooded things time and temperature are coupled, as if these creatures lived by a clock with a thermometer for a mainspring.

Winter, for an insect egg, can't be long at all; a passing dream, a single sleep.

The other day I held a deer mouse in my hand, the skin of her neck pinched between my thumb and index finger so that she couldn't bite me. I had trapped her in a box that was set on the ground and roofed so that snow couldn't get in, and that had a small metal trap set in it, baited with sunflower seeds and provided with a ball of cotton fluff. There was enough fluff so that whatever might get caught in the trap would have enough bedding to keep warm in while waiting for me to come along. From the trap the mouse was shaken out into a cloth bag, and then with much fiddling and prodding and shaking of the bag she was brought out, safely pinched, into the light of my kitchen.

The world of the deer mouse isn't so far from mine. Winter is as long to her as it is to me. She has had or will have a family to defend, and I can feel sympathy for the panicky waving of her feet, and the whiffling of her nose, which is her way of trying to make as much sense of me as I am of her. When I had admired her and written her vital statistics in my notebook, I let her loose back in the woods, and she climbed a fir tree like an acrobat swarming up a rope. With the large eyes of an animal that sees well in the darkness, she looks very much like the first mammal-like creatures who evolved in the time of the dinosaurs, and who were endowed, as the deer mouse is, with the great inhabiting miracle of warm-bloodedness. She keeps going, busy, warm. She has fur and fat to hold heat in, and — with plenty of dormant insect eggs and beech nuts to fuel it — a metabolic furnace that keeps her warm from the inside out.

All great ideas seem to be discovered again and again. What

is it the French say? *Plus ça change, plus c'est la même chose.*
Birds, for instance, which evolved from a different branch of
the reptile family than the mouse's ancestors did, also become
warm-blooded after a time; and the primitive pre-mammals
gave rise to marsupials, and true mammals, and here we are.
But it is still happening, the tool for the control of one's core
heat is being endlessly reinvented, rediscovered; life goes round
and round back to the same conclusions.

Several years ago an Atlantic leatherback turtle was caught
off Newfoundland, by mistake, in a fishing net, and while the
nine-hundred-pound turtle thrashed on the deck of the ship
someone had the idea that it would be interesting to take his
temperature. How this was accomplished history does not
relate. Perhaps with some instrument akin to the thermistor
probe that I used on the beaver lodge, and with the aid of
ropes and assistants with which to belay the turtle like a
Gulliver in Lilliput. The turtle had been netted in water that
was 45.5°F, and once the technical difficulties were overcome,
it was discovered that his internal core temperature was
77.9°F; 32.4 degrees warmer than the water he had been
swimming in. I wonder if the wielders of that thermistor probe
doubted their black box as I doubted mine. Turtles — mere
reptiles, after all — are not supposed to do *this*.

The leatherback has a thick, oily, fibrous layer of flesh
beneath his soft shell, which makes a fine layer of insulation;
like blubber, fur, or feathers. He is big and he swims fast, and
so he may heat himself up by simple effort — why not? We,
the established, have no monopoly on good ideas.

We have ideas, though. That seems to be what we are made
for. Recently people have been busy rediscovering what the
sun does. We talk and tinker; solar collectors proliferate on
roofs, there are pocket calculators and electric-fence-chargers
powered by solar arrays. So it suddenly occurs to us that the
springtails which leap and twist through the February snow
might be black for a reason, that frogs' eggs in spring pools

might be black for a reason. In the light of this new idea of ours we take a fresh look around. Other things have had this idea before. Solar technology is old, ancient; one dinosaur in particular is a case in point.

Stegosaurus, the "covered lizard," left a lot of signs of himself on three continents and over tens of millions of years. He was a humped, elephant-sized, plant-eating dinosaur with a long spiked war club of a tail, a walnut-sized brain, feet like umbrella stands, and a double row of huge, laterally flattened plates running down his back. So one asks: "What are those plates *for*?" For defense; ah, yes. But as for questioning what defensive purposes a long line from skull to tail of immense vertically oriented plates could have . . . wouldn't they be more useful for defensive purposes and be less likely to wedge in low branches and poke uncomfortably into sexual situations if they lay flat, like a shield, a turtlelike carapace? Of course they would. Why are they sticking up, then? Now some people have begun to think that a stegosaurus's plates were for the sun.

Covered with a dark layer of skin that was well supplied with blood vessels, the stegosaurus's plates would have made a handsome array of solar panels. Standing broadside to the sun on a cool morning or evening — all lizards stand broadside to the sun — the stegosaurus could have heated his huge bulk efficiently. Once warmed up to his happiest operating temperature, he could have shunted the major blood supply away from his solar array, conserving his heat in his own roundish massive self; for defense, yes. A warm stegosaur may well have been able to outrun, outeat, and outwit his chillier — and so more sluggish — enemies.

The magician's closet is large, full of still-invisible corners, vials of unidentified chemicals and fossil shelves; a universe of possibilities. Cold is unfriendly to life, but living things survive it, pop up, persist. They survive where they are. From where each live thing lives the world is a different place, skewed; even time and space have a new significance. What of us, then?

"To be in any form, what is that?" Walt Whitman asks. How many forms do we take on ourselves, here? First we are egg and sperm fused, a single round cell; hours later we are like a microscopic raspberry, a cluster revolving toward the uterus like a *Volvox* in pond water; later we develop an inside and an outside, a front end and a back end, we curve in on ourselves and a heartbeat flickers into steady pulse; we bud salamanderlike limbs with nubs for digits; we kick, grow hair. Ejected from the amniotic sea, we breathe air, then learn to warm ourselves against the chill of the cradle. Finally we suck a little sugar-water or milk, and take for ourselves.

I think we are more malleable than we know, more change-able than we feel, full of hidden talents. Several years after I had begun to live on the hill, a group of friends from the university gathered at my house one day, and we some-how got onto the subject of human body temperature. One friend told us about his bout with hypothermia, a near-fatal cooling of his body core that had happened when he had been caught raincoatless in a mountain storm on an autumn day. First there had been an uncontrollable shivering and then a weird lassitude, followed by a spiral into unconsciousness. Three companions had saved him by crawling naked with him into a heap of sleeping bags, an experience which he had been too groggy to enjoy but which had warmed him up, and warms him still, I think. Another friend told about her brother, who had experienced minor brain damage in an automobile acci-dent, and as a result of it had lost control of his body tem-perature for several days and had to be kept in an incubator like an infant. He had recovered completely. "You could never tell that anything had gone wrong," she said. But after the story we were all feeling our brows, smoothing our hair, feeling the egglike case in which our thermostat lives. I re-member telling about my own brief loss of temperature control after having given birth to my son, an hour of blizzardlike sheets which I still think of with amazement.

We are tropical mammals. Birds and animals who live in cold places can let their extremities stay cooler than their core in order to conserve heat; a cool ear loses less heat to a cold environment than a warm ear, and so reserves more net energy for the all-important gut and brain. Arctic animals are supposed to be better at this than tropical ones. We are tropical ones. It may be better to risk a finger than risk the self. We do this trick to some extent; we "take our temperatures" — meaning core temperatures — in armpit, gut, or mouth, because the rest of us is cooler than the center. How cool can our extremities go, anyway, without becoming painful?

We decided to test ourselves, and we put a potful of ice water in the middle of the table, and then one by one we put our hands into it until we couldn't stand it anymore, and then we took the temperature of our chilled hands — a game of how low can you go. Some went lower than others. A neighbor who had lived on the hill for ten years beat us all. He kept his hand in the ice water twice as long as the rest of us could and said that it wasn't painful at all, and when he took it out it was ten degrees colder than anyone else's hand had been. After working out-of-doors and living with cold winters awhile, had he managed to change? To sense cold differently? Were his hands adaptive, or damaged? We came to no conclusions, but we were surprised.

Some people had gone to the brink of the possible. Here is an image culled from my stove-side reading of old books: in the winter of 1908–1909 when E. H. Shackleton made his expedition toward the South Pole, he and his three companions took their temperatures every night. Deep into the march, when food was very low and their last pony had disappeared in a crevasse, when they were hauling their sledges by hand a dozen miles a day over the endless white plain of the polar cap, their temperatures sank to 94°F, and then finally disappeared down off the temperature gauge altogether. They suffered from fierce, constant hunger. "If one of us dropped a crumb, the others would point it out, and the owner would wet his finger in his mouth and pick up the morsel."

The navigation of polar cold is an exercise in the limits of the beast; we are tropical mammals. Or are we? All of us? The magician's closet gapes, things glint and beckon there; and somehow it is the magic of ourselves which amazes most.

For instance, this: the Yahgan Indians of Tierra del Fuego. When Darwin saw them from the decks of the *Beagle*, they wore very little clothing and lived most of their lives in the open weather. He describes nearly naked Yahgan women with babies in their arms, the falling snow melting where it touched their skins. The women would swim in the seawater in which lumps of ice were bobbing about, their toddlers hanging onto their necks and floating behind, their little faces drawn into grimaces of distaste. *Distaste!*

I stretch, suck other air, swim; and congeal into myself in my own house again, by my own fire. I slap my thighs, run my fingers through my hair in disbelief; the wind moans by the house wall and snow falls from the pines in clots. I have been mesmerized, summoned by a kind of witchery to feel that Arctic water and tree limbs and the crevices of bark can be as comfortable as this; but *here* I am.

BOBCAT

V ❧ *Honeymoon of the Owl*

*"I am no more busy than I am now," she said.
"People fancy that I am always making new
beasts out of old, but all I do is sit here and make
them make themselves." Then the lady smiled
down at Tom and said: "If you are to remember
the way to the place you seek then you must
look at the dog when I am not here to look at;
for it knows the way well enough, and will not
forget it. Another thing is that you must go back-
wards all the time. If you look behind you, and
particularly keep your eye on the dog, then you
will know what is coming next, as plainly as if
you saw it in a looking-glass."*

— CHARLES KINGSLEY,
The Water Babies

Branch Dance

Think of this: you live in a world whose economy slides and vaults from boom to bust every twelve months on the button. When it's bust the shelves are bare, the heat is off, it is very cold everywhere, the lights come on only a few hours a day, it is almost impossible to move around because the roads are clogged with three to five feet of heavy stuff: sand, say. When it's boom you are showered with glory, you can dance over every roll and swale, the world is lit, warm, there are edibles hanging on every twig. What are you going to do? How are you, for instance, going to go about raising a family? You have to settle down somewhere, seduce and be seduced, give the kids plenty to eat and a safe place to grow up in. Let's say you can get through all of this in six weeks to six months: you are going to have to choose your time and place very carefully. Very. If Darwin is right, and reproduction is the most important thing we ever do — biologically speaking — then these are the most important decisions that you will ever make.

Everything else here, with the exception of people, lives in this economy. We live with it, though; oh, most definitely with it! So. Midwinter is bust time. Like everything else, I am waiting.

Here the turning of the year is announced by owls. I need it announced. The furnace sucks in wood as fast as I can remember to put it in; my hands are full of splinters. I'm not sorry for myself; I'd rather be here and cold than down south and warm and not having mountains and needing to lock my doors every night . . . still. I'm really warm only when I'm in bed, and even then my one hand that's out in the open holding a book feels as cool and smooth and foreign — when I turn out the light and pull it in against my chest — as the white ceramic jug full of orange juice that sits in the fridge. This isn't my hand, no, this is a white ceramic hand. I need to know that things will change. The singing of the great horned owls in the swamp is my signal: I hang my hat on that peg as if I had already arrived at May.

I heard them begin their courtship one night at the end of January when I was on my way back from doing chores in the barn. It was dark and the hills were locked in black and silver frost; and then: "Hoo-hoo-HOO-hooo-hooo-hoo . . ." The owls' booming ventriloqual song filled the whole air. And again: 'Hooo-hoo-HOO-hooo . . . !" There were holes in the singing, pauses, oases filled with a vertiginous sky full of stars; and then another burst of "hooo!"s came — from where? It was as if mountain trolls were tooting granitic bassoons.

It went on all night. And later I went out in the snow by the apple trees in my boots and coat and nightgown, just to listen. The prickle of the hackle-rise on my neck was not just from the cold. I had felt that unconscious itch only once before, when the coyotes yammered from the swamp in October like a coven of idiot witches: *Coming to get me!* My black dog, Dunbar, was crouched between my feet, shivering.

Owls have always suffered from bad mythological press. That hackle-rise — that pressure between the shoulderblades

— must be universal, I think. Even Dunbar got the message; an audible something that bypassed all reason, went straight to the backbone, and spooked into the skull like a Halloween apparition. It is a direct message; it makes one imagine and believe the worst. The Sumerian goddess of the underworld was Lilith, an owl-demon complete with sycophant owls and ropes in each taloned hand: ropes with which she measured and judged the lives of men. The Chinese called owls "the bird which snatches away the soul." All across Europe and Asia owls were the spirits of witchcraft in particular and doom in general; the bird of passages; midwife and prophet of birth, deflowering, death, damnation. According to Pliny a fresh owl's heart placed on the breast of a sleeping woman made her tell all her secrets. (From what demonic pharmacopoeia did you get that one, Pliny?) Until less than a century ago it was a common thing in England to nail dead owls to barn doors and walls to keep storms away, as if the bird of destruction — skewered by nails — were a kind of vaccine against the live powers of chaos.

It was the most clear and quiet night of the winter. No muzzy glows of northern lights dulled the black of space and the stars shone steadily, unperturbed by the wobblings of atmosphere, which astronomers say is as distorting as water. The owls sang again. The dog shivered.

"It is only the owls dancing, Dunbar, hmmm? Only the owls." He stopped shaking and looked up, his eyes glittering in the starlight; my scalp-itch smoothed.

The owls were beginning something that would end in spring or even high summer; they trust their gonads in matters of song and dance, which is just as well. Like other birds they have a sexuality which is hinged to the year; which operates in the blind faith that the year is to be trusted. The owls were singing, dancing, mating out there.

In A. C. Bent's *Life Histories of North American Birds of*

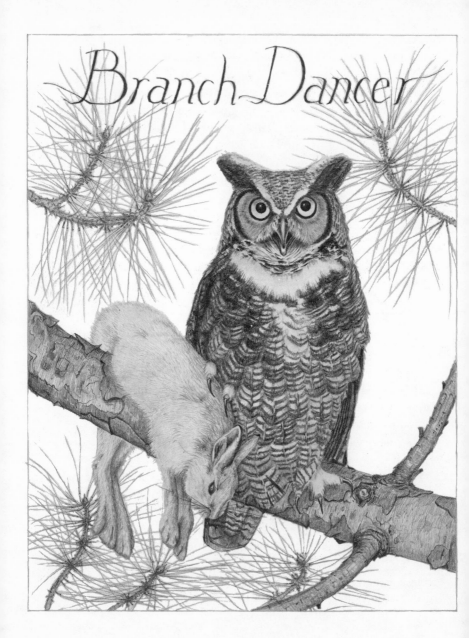

Prey there is a letter from one Floyd Bralliar describing the pair of great horneds that he saw, once, just before the singing began:

> So [the male owl] began bowing his head, ruffling his feathers, raising his wings in a curious manner. Aside from watching his antics, [the female owl] took no notice of his presence. Growing more earnest, he began hopping from branch to branch, continuing his maneuvers and snapping his bill fiercely as if to show that even tho he was not so large as she, what he lacked in size he made up in bravery.
>
> Finally, he attempted to approach and caress her but she ruffled her feathers and rebuked him sharply. He took flight, sailing up and down, around and around, evidently doing all the stunts of his race, now and again punctuating his efforts by snapping his bill. After a few moments he alighted again and began his bowing and dancing all over again.
>
> A rabbit came running down the bank and its white flag caught his eye. Rising in noiseless flight, he sailed downward without the flap of a wing, caught his prey from the ground, glided back into the tree, and presented his offering to his lady love. Apparently, she was convinced of his sincerity. Together they devoured the rabbit, and when he again began his love dance she joined in with as much enthusiasm as he.

The rabbit is important; more a proof than an offering. In order for them to settle down in one patch of woods for several months, and for one owl to be able to hunt for two, or three, or four owls all that time, there has to be plenty of game. The male owl has to be able to catch that game. If there isn't or he can't, the female won't play along. This is written into her genetic program, too; a fail-safe, a guarantee for the success of the venture.

There are years when the owls don't sing from the swamp in the winter. I know by the absence of the song that times are

Honeymoon of the Owl ⸱ 177

hard; and that they are not only hard for the owls who will do without their honeymoon this year, but for all the other animals they would have eaten, if they had been plentiful. So one learns something about the state of the woods, even from a winter silence.

What the singing says is this: by February the female owl will be brooding her eggs in the high spur of their chosen tree. Great horned owls have the reputation of being nest-filchers. They like to take over a nest once built by another owl or a red-tailed hawk or even a squirrel, and line the bowl of it with their brown breast-down. They want the nest as far away from people and as high in the air as possible.

The female will brood her eggs for a month of some of the deepest cold and worst weather that the year has to offer. Owl and nest will be covered with snow and sleet and ice; through all that time the male will hunt for them both. If there is prey enough, though, it is a good time to hunt. The woods floor is paper-pale against which the life that runs there shows clear. There are no crows or blackbirds to mob and bother the owls. There are no leaves to confuse the view. He catches anything small enough to carry off: chipmunks, mink, weasels, house cats, porcupines, shrews, grouse; the hares, in spite of their zigs and zags and stop-deads are caught and hauled off by the dozen. In February and March the male skunks will be out, dragging their bellies through the heavy snow of the earliest thaws and looking for female skunks; it is their time for mating. Against the snow their stripes stand out like beacons: easy game. I found a great horned owl's nest one March because it smelled like a dozen skunks; tatters of black and white fur littered the ground under the pine that the owls were nesting in, and the atmosphere stung the eyes as though someone had lobbed a tear-gas bomb.

When the fledglings hatch in March, they will be blind, naked, and helpless; they will stay in the nest for another seven weeks or so and won't fly for a month after that. Even after they can fly on their own, the young owls will follow their parents and beg from them, even into October. Hunting is a complex skill that owls have to learn from their own hard experience. I remember talking to a woman at Cape May who had raised a great horned fledgling herself. She said that he was lazy and clumsy, that he bumped into things, that he sat in the porch rafters and fiddled with his talons, clacked his beak, wouldn't attempt to hunt at all unless she half-starved him. She said that he started by hunting in daylight until he was hassled by the mobbings of little songbirds, by jays and blackbirds and swallows; and that he seemed so frightened and shocked by their rude behavior that he learned after a while to fly in the open only when they were asleep. He began to hunt the margins of the day: dusk, dawn. He would swoop and miss his prey, swoop again and miss again, click his beak like a frustrated child, swoop again and land on his breastbone or bash a wing-tip against a branch that he hadn't noticed; but he learned, stubbornly, resisting all the way.

Though February seems an odd time to lay eggs, and though the parent owls will have put in nearly four months of hard labor in getting their owlets to April, April will shower the young owls with easy food. Migrant birds will be coming back, many of them weakened enough by their long flights, disoriented enough by their stopovers in unknown woods, to fall easy prey even to something as awkward and ignorant as a young owl. Insects are beginning to emerge then, drowsy in the spring cool, and many a great horned has begun by honing his hunting skills on caterpillars.

The January booming of the owls in the swamp is a promise, then, a promise that there will be warblers in April hedgerows; that the trees which stand still and naked now will be fleshed with leaves and filled with insect hummings and the morning badinage of returned birds.

This is what it promises to me. Sex, birth, are chancy acts and are made — this is the nature of them — in faith. So I seem to have mythologized the owl myself; not as Chaucer's prophet of "wo and myschaunce," or as Athena's bird, ripe with her divine wisdom, ancestor of all of the Wise Owls in children's books; but as an omen of sexuality and rebirth. If the owls are singing, can Easter eggs then be far away?

Soon enough, on the second of February, comes Groundhog Day (or woodchuck day if you live north of the Mason-Dixon line); either way it is a formalized portent of spring which has a history older than Christianity. In Britain there is a badger who is supposed to come up from her burrow on the same day as our groundhog and for the same purpose, and in Germany it's a bear that emerges to predict the course of spring. The ancient Celts celebrated their spring on February first, and druidesses lit a votive flame that night to the goddess who would come forth next day to foretell the future. The groundhog, the badger, and the bear are her descendants. Old gods aren't often discarded: they simply change form.

But the real groundhog, hibernating under the lilac hedge, doesn't come out until March; and then he will come out for his own reasons — not to predict the future but to mate. To ensure that there will be a future. The fat that the groundhog put on last autumn will be nearly intact when he emerges. He won't have burned much of it at all in his months of hibernation; he has it to burn in this one month of the year when he can live with a mate (if he finds one, if she accepts his tail-wagging dance of intention) in her burrow. There will be no feed for either of them, then. They have to have their fat to live on. The male will be ousted from the female's burrow and the young will be born just when the grass begins to grow, so that the young groundhogs will have the whole summer to grow up in. This is the point of the exercise: that the young groundhogs will have the whole summer to grow up in. The autumn fattening, the winter hibernation, the spring mating-dances and chances, have all led up to that.

⚡   ⚡   ⚡

The earliest signs and portents of spring come in code, most of them unexpected, unlooked for. I was lost in the woods once in February up on the side of a mountain near my brother's farm, north of here; and I wasn't looking for anything then but a way out. I had never stuck to any trail and had misjudged the light as well; the light was going fast and the mountain seemed to shift around me though I had thought that I knew the way well enough. At last I came to a fall of icy rock down which I didn't dare to go, and from which I couldn't see the farm or any building. There in the new snow of that morning was a trail of footprints: the track of a bear.

I followed the bear. She had gone around the rockslide, she was going down, and she seemed to know her way. In one place she had torn apart a rotten log to get at ants and grubs inside. Shards of wood were scattered and the snow was roiled. Farther down she had clawed a fir, and tatters of bark hung where she had chewed at the thin flesh of the tree and licked the sap.

There was just enough light left to follow the wide, almost-human prints. I was running on my snowshoes, and I remember thinking that the wind was in back of me, that she would certainly smell me and get out of the way before I ran smack over her. But I remember remembering too that bears are unpredictable by nature, and that they are in a nasty testy humor when they are newly roused from their torpor, in February.

The woods leveled and changed. The bear's tracks stopped at a low twisted tree on which a few spheres hung dark against the sky — apples! An orchard! The bear had eaten some of these freeze-dried remnants of September's harvest and turned back toward the mountain, but I went on. Over the next rise a neighbor's house lay yellow-windowed in the night.

Half an hour later, nursing a cup of cocoa in a chair by the fire, I shivered to myself less because of the painful thawing of fingers and nose than at the thought of the cold and dark that I had been led out of. Snow hissed against the windowpanes in a rising wind. It seemed to be the heart of winter still, but if the bear had seen fit to stir from her den then so must spring be rousing, stirring; stirring the bear, stirring me.

One spring bear was enough. I can take it on faith now that bears are on the move on February afternoons, that the earth is on the move. As it moves there are plenty of signs to collect as evidence: the prick of a crocus tip after a thaw or a chipmunk spiraling up a dooryard tree. I seem to be led on every year out of the winter, and I like to know what it is that pulls the pussywillows from their protective buds, and what it is that launches geese.

What they come for is sex pure and simple. When the pussywillows in the jar on the table shove out and shed yellow dust, I throw them out on the brush heap; they are dumping polleny sperm by the hundreds of thousands.

The urge and the mechanics of sex are inborn, part of the circuitry of sexual beings. But most of the plants and animals here have a sexuality which unlike ours revolves around the winter, which takes the hard fact of winter into consideration first of all. Aside from all of that, the language of seduction — among birds and animals, anyway — seems familiar. In November I watched a ewe stare back around her flank at the ram, who was pushing her rear with his shoulder; it was a level expressionless stare, but a stare which was longer than a look. It's the way men and women meet each other's eyes sometimes across a room; the message is clear. Then she looks away. She looks back again. He is still looking.

For proof of good intentions and as a promise of care, a rabbit is as good as a diamond.

Face to Face

After the owls have stopped singing it is quiet again, but I feel the year's upward motion as though I had been pushed in a swing. If life is passed on here like links in a chain, the owl's song is the first audible clang of a link forged; others are harder to hear. The beavers in the swamp breed in January, the bobcats and coyotes, solitary hunters, are beginning their searches and dances of seduction now, too; the bears have given birth and are suckling their baby bears, which are no larger than puppies. I know about these things, but they are difficult to understand.

They are difficult to understand because textbooks make seduction and sex and birth among animals sound dry: mechanical processes done at the command of the genes. Yes, they may well be done at the command of the genes, very little that anything does isn't; but I am sure that they are not dry. Genes are clever devils. They not only dutifully go about deciding things like hair-color and shoulder-muscling, they dabble in emotions. Emotions are in the driver's seat whenever an animal is bound to another animal; whether through dependence, protectiveness, desire, or friendly partnership. Emotions are not dry. The only thing that is dry is the textbooks; that must be it. I chuckle when I read them; scientists are so coy about being the least bit anthropomorphic that they have succeeded in robbing beasts of both emotion and dignity, and themselves into the bargain. Come now, I want to ask, when have you ever felt sexually *driven* because you analyzed the situation and decided that yes, folks, this is it! Do you feel bound to your family because it's *logical!* Isn't it feeling that binds us up? Okay, conclusion: animals bind, therefore animals must also *feel.* I am not saying anything new. But suddenly the woods, quiet as they are, seem charged with life.

My son has no problem in seeing the world this way. His

world is dancing with fellows, nothing is immune. When he finds a stone that he likes, he washes it carefully and puts it on the sill where it can watch him eat his supper. When a red squirrel chitters in the pines, he leaps up and down at the window and "cheee! cheee!"'s back. When the neighbor's heifer comes up to him in the barn with her head lowered, he raises his fists and makes a razzberry, which the heifer understands far better than when I pat her on the head and say, "Nice cow!" She isn't a particularly nice cow. She keeps her distance from my son, though, because he's understood her; and thinks, very rightly, that I'm a fool.

When I read to my son in the evenings, his head lies round and heavy in the crook of my shoulder, and when I put him to bed — thumb, blanket, pillow, bear, quilt — and smooth his hair back across the curve of his forehead, I feel I am caressing and nesting this small skull as though it were a magic egg, a purring communicant, complete and intricate beyond belief; full of a folded force like the egg of a phoenix.

Later in the evening I read by the stove with my feet on the fender. I have a gray rocking chair that I sit in, low and old-fashioned, with curves that fit my back. The stove ticks with heat, the coals collapse with rustling noises as if the woodbox, like the human mind, held a bright and captive bird. The windows of the house are black and blank; part of the walls that seal us away from the outer world. I am encased in concentric layers here — house walls, beds and chairs, heavy clothing, flesh and bone — protected, firmly centered, and shut off. I know that there are moments when I am taken by surprise and off my guard even as a well-guarded adult, and the bird of the mind flies loose on its own business; and then I can and do connect with some live thing which is not, for once, only myself. Perhaps this happens because of the way that the mind is made.

In any case, it does not happen often.

✦ ✦ ✦

This winter I have been reading about the ways that the brain is built; the ways that it works. I have garnered this information now from two sources: that we are constructed in mental layers, spheres of influence, each one an evolutionary *oeuvre* and a capping embroiderment on the thematics of the last. Each one is a fresh exploration of the theme of *being here* like the separate but ascending movements of a symphony.

First there is a sober overture, the brainstem, the brain-machine which runs the body-machine. It keeps track of the basic rhythms — heartbeat, breath, blood chemistries in counterpoint. Then the brainstem is enfolded by the R-complex, a brooding scherzo in a minor key. The R-complex evolved in the skulls of reptiles hundreds of millions of years ago. It is in charge of the basic rites: possession of territory, aggression, ritual, sexual behavior, a competitive drive for higher social caste. The R-complex is in turn surmounted by the limbic system, a mammalian andante full of soft tones and rocketing dynamic notes. The limbic system manages emotion and feeling; sorrow, depression, ecstasy; it promotes respect-for-age and care-for-youth, and fierce identifyings-with and loyalties-for lovers, infants, family, and clan. Capping all of these things is the cerebral cortex, of which our species is so inordinately proud. Along with the dolphin, we have the largest cerebral cortexes on the planet. The cortex makes up two-thirds of our brain bulk, it is the mass storebank of memory, it manages logic, analysis, the intuitive muses. Other animals have cerebral cortexes, too, of course, but, with the exception of the dolphin's, theirs are neither so large nor so important for their survival as ours is.

What I like about this structure is that it shakes me up. It makes it difficult to be quite so separate from other live creatures, which is inconvenient. Now that I know that large and vital hunks of our mental structure are common ground, it becomes more difficult to be objective about other animals, who after all share much — most — of what is us. I have always had a horror of zoos, because the animals do not like to look me in the face. They have the purposely averted stare of revolutionaries who are without manifesto and stripped of their arms. It is almost worse when they do meet my eyes because then they have the look of almost suicidal indifference which human prisoners have, at once detached and despising; and in the case of monkeys and apes their natural sensuality seems to have become self-destructive and obscene. I cannot afford to think, anymore, that these observations are the result of an overworked imagination. If our brains are nearly the same, then our capacity for pain must be also. We are heir to the same ills: hooray.

Even a sketchy knowledge of these brain mechanics also makes it more difficult to think that it is right or good to be separate from parts of myself. The whole is always greater than the sum of its parts; let the whole work, then. Our layers are not separate, but they are often enough (almost always) in uneasy synchrony, the sections jarring, discordant; worse: in pitched battle one against the other. When I am overly analytical, objective, I wall myself off further. If the whole mind functions together, suddenly, drawn out in a flare, then I can be — for this flash of time — a communicant in truth. This is what I want. Sometimes, slumped in my gray rocking chair, I feel a pipping at the base of my skull just above my ear, and a rustling of something unhatched there, which, if it were let fly, would burst the seals of the self. If it would sprout, hatch, join the world. If there are seasons of the mind, then this would be spring!

In February I went out to spend the evening with friends in the next village. Late in the afternoon it began to snow, spatters of graupel, little separate flecks. At first the flakes melted and the branches of the trees glistened, and then slowly the snow began to collect; wet flakes settled on the tips and crooks of branches, clumping against the winter buds, and then thickening along branches and in the road. All evening when I looked beyond my friends' faces, over the tables with their candles, the lights of the streets and the houses beyond held dense veils of falling snow, like a shaking fabric. Cars traveled slowly behind halos of light as if they were swimming in a fluid, as if they were submarines navigating the seafloor among swarms of tiny shining fish. When we all got into my car again to go home, we entered a bright tunnel of flakes as though we were a star-ship navigating at time-warping speed among galaxies of stars.

"But they don't *touch* us, they don't *land!*" said one friend.

"They make me dizzy! Oh, I can't look at them. Don't look at them, Di, you're driving, you'll go off the *road*," said another friend. It was a strange world. I stared at the road as if the snow were going to bite me. The road. The road.

After I had let my friends off at their houses, I went the long way around the hill, up the valley carved by the Wild Branch river. The roads were thick with snow, and slippery. The hill that I usually take to get home was too steep to try; this one was more gentle. The Wild Branch lay in a gape of darkness beside the slowly climbing twisting road, an abyss bordered by guard rails. These guard rails, which were plastered with snow, marched confidently beside the curves. There were no other car tracks at all. The road was like the surface of a pile carpet, floored in thickening white. With just my low beams on, my vision narrowed and I could see only a few feet ahead. The sense of isolation grew; the sense of being in a submarine or spaceship, out of my element, surrounded with pressure or vacuum. Suddenly the guard rails tilted out, disappeared, then appeared, tilting, again; a toothy gap where some other car had swerved and gone off the road, perhaps months ago. I gripped the wheel, hard. Then there was another gap, full of crazily twisting cable. Then another.

I heard the pipping inside my head again, just over my ear. I began to remember things. Events that collected themselves, whooshed up, as it were, by the adrenaline which was making my cheeks throb, my hands as wet as if I had dipped them in soup. *We are granted these glimpses*, I thought, *when we lurch*

*off the path, crash the fence; when electricity flares and some
built charge empties in a crackle, a spark of touch!*

I remembered one early contact that was like this: one evening when I was driving home up the hills with a friend, in
one of the first light snowfalls of November, we saw a lynx
ahead of us in the road. She didn't move, and we slowed and
came very close to her so that we could see her extravagant
ruff, the dark tufts on her ears, the bobbed tail with its black
tip, the heavy gray-white mottled coat. She looked at us. She
looked at the car, blinked, and looked back at us, from one to
the other. It was difficult to breathe.

Finally she turned and began to trot away up the road, as
confident as a dog in her own yard. Her hind end was pale and
thickly furred, her feet very large and soft, and she trotted
ahead of us for a quarter of a mile, lazily, voluptuously. This
is south of the lynx's usual range; no one that I know remem-
bers having seen one here before, or has seen one since. What
remains from that glimpse we were granted is her utter confidence, her sense of repose, her aura of comfort; even of
sensuality.

Years later, in the summer, in the middle of the day, my
sister was driving up along this same road and a bear crossed
in front of her, so close that she had to stop the car to let him
pass. It was a big bear, and he had stopped and glanced up at
her "as if," she said, "I were a tree. Or no, as if I were a
stranger in a shopping mall and had bumped him with a
package. It was a *normal* look." My sister told us about it only
hours later, while we were drinking lemonade on the porch, as
if the event were of no consequence; after all, it hadn't seemed
of any consequence to the bear.

Once when my friend Dick was cutting firewood on his knoll
in the autumn, he looked up and saw a bobcat lying on a fallen
log not ten feet away. She was watching him as casually as if
she were a house cat resting on a wall. She stared at him, from
his own level, straight back. After a while the bobcat jumped
down from her log and trotted off. Ever since that moment the

log — and the part of the knoll where the log is — have always been haunted; full of a power that Dick himself can't explain. Except to say that he can never go there without *looking:* here I have seen and here I have been seen, face to face.

These are casual encounters. There was no sense of threat in any of them; sensuality, perhaps, grumpiness, curiosity; afterward there was a feeling of having been granted a gift. Not so much because one has observed but because one has been noticed, and noticed fully, and taken in as an animal, alive and whole; at that moment you can't analyze. You can't be logical. You communicate; *fly.*

There have been rumors here for years about lions, pumas. At hunting time every year one or two hunters come back saying that they have seen the tracks of one ("Pads as big as my hand, man, I swear!") or the puma itself, lying up on a rock, or walking on the other side of a river. Perhaps we need this contact so badly that we even make up beasts to take care of the deficit; this lion is a fairy tale, a fanciful wonder of a beast: but it may be a real lion, too. In the range map of the puma in the Peterson *Field Guide to Mammals*, up in the northeasternmost corner of Maine, there is a small black question mark. That question mark isn't really so far away from here. Pumas range over a hundred miles, and are hard to see at the best of times. They are solitary hunters like the lynx and the bobcat. How much *is* out there that we never see?

I hope that there are lions here. I want them to be here; the woods the richer for them. There are plenty of bobcats around, though. I have never seen a live one myself (except in a zoo; Lord preserve me) but I found the trail of one along the bottom of the pasture one March afternoon three years ago, surrounded by scatters of grouse tracks; I wished him good hunting.

My contact with bobcats has been more intimate. It happened a long time ago, but I can see by the notes and questions in my old notebook that I started wondering then about this difference between objective and subjective knowing; the difference between knowledge *per se*, and the contact, empathy, of being in eye-contact with something other, both the same and different. When we are face to face with an animal in her own home, present out of her own choosing, perhaps the feeling of *flight* comes because we are touching and using freely those older, deeper minds within ourselves which we keep so well hidden, and subject to the logical mind; their heads bowed and glances skewed like animals behind bars.

When I was first studying biology, the professor of my environmental studies class got three bobcat stomachs from a trapper. We wanted to know what the bobcat ate, where he fitted into the scheme of the winter woods. Opening the stomachs and examining the contents was a job that went to me, partly because — living on a farm as I did and having slaughtered my own animals — stomachs were nothing particularly new or nasty, or I pretended as much; and partly because no one else wanted to be reminded that the bobcats involved were dead.

Relying on information that I had read somewhere about Red Cross crews which had been involved in digging through the rubble of an Andean village two weeks after an earthquake had claimed the lives of half of the inhabitants, I ate half an onion and stuffed cotton up my nose before starting in on the stomachs. Then I made my way with sharp little scissors, tweezers, a spray-bottle of water, laying out my finds on a tray lined with paper toweling. In the first stomach there was deer hair; lots of deer hair, and fragments of large splintered bones, and a leg bone of a vole or a shrew, and the leaf of a blueberry bush. In the second stomach there was a cherry stone, several apple seeds, a shred of leathery material that looked as though it might have come from a rabbit's ear, the yellowed incisor of a squirrel, and squirrel fur, and rabbit hair, and a small twig, and a mass of fibrous barklike material, sand, a shred of rubbery hoof, and one tiny feather.

"All right in there?" The door of the lab opened and a fellow student looked in.

"Loog ad dis! I found a fedda, deer haih, ad . . . wad sob codden?"

"Oh, God, no *thanks* . . ." The door closed.

Another stomach: parts of a rodent skull, three long black hairs from a horse's tail, tiny tiny broken bones, more deer hair, three oats, half of a beetle carapace . . .

The door to the lab swung open and another fellow student poked her head around the door. "Want some help?" she said.

"Yes, sure! Loog ad dis, I foud a beedle ad seeds ad . . ."

"Ooooh . . ." The door slammed and there were noises from the lavatory down the hall. Then the door opened and she came in again, wads of cotton protruding from her nostrils.

"How cad you stad da smell!" she said. Her face was an odd color.

"Wad sob oniod?" I suggested.

"Oniod? Ooooh, no . . ." She disappeared at a run, there were more rummaging noises down the hall. No one came in again, but someone somewhere, obviously operating from the remotest possible control, turned the ventilation fan on high: it sounded as though a helicopter was coming in the window. I thought about those Red Cross crews. I thought about the bobcats.

I began to see a live cat out of the corner of my mind's eye, soft and mottled, indistinct as a shadow. He padded through the snow, wallowing, lifting his feet, leaping from a stone to a log to the snow-shadow of a fir, moving, then stopping and pricking his ears and turning his head like a radar antenna; sensing the woods, moving again. Slowly he quartered the slopes of ground between familiar trees. He sniffed around tree bases and stones, the dark hollows of a bent clump of brush, catching rich updrafts from the undersnow-world. He came up to an old deer kill, slowly, chasing off a flock of bluejays in a rush and watching them scatter off calling into the high branches with quick tilts and turnings of his head; an academic exercise, like a house cat watching birds at a feeder on the other side of a pane of glass. The deer kill was an old one, months old, familiar to the cat as a meal of last resort; a deer wounded by hunters in the autumn and then killed by dogs and gutted by coyotes. The cat lay on his belly and set to work on a haunch, on a rusty-looking knuckle, gnawing off tatters of skin. Enough. He went on to an opening in the woods that was full of blueberry bushes and chewed the twigs, his head bent sideways like a house cat chewing grass. He nosed under a log, pawed, licked up insects. He heard something and froze; then ran on again, and crouched in the snow, his eyes like lamps. He listened, smelled again, his neck stretched, nostrils wide; and homed in and then with a click like a snapping branch the trap bit. Later he was slapped by a bullet, rolled, and skinned; his belly fur immortalized as a jacket sleeve in a city shop. These are the rites of the living for the dead: these sprayings and tweezings, these layings-out.

After I had finished with the stomachs, our class weighed the traysful of fragments; we identified the hair and bones where we could, and we ended up with a nice analysis of what bobcats ate in January: so much of this, so much of that, this percentage of such and so. Vegetable matter, carrion, insects, small rodents, miscellaneous, etc. We were learning. How to reduce a bobcat to quantifiable bits.

I began to think that something was incomplete about that analysis, though I couldn't put my finger exactly on what it was. Someone could wade through a thousand bobcat stomachs and get a more complete picture, with conclusions drawn from a larger data base; but something would still, I thought, be missing. By analyzing, you keep your distance. The "analyzed" is still an object, to be known, managed, controlled. The beast is still in subjection; he is not alive, not *met*.

I thought about each of these things, separate events, hearsay and experience, as if I were turning the pages of some book and longing for the end; the snow was falling as thickly as ever, it hissed against the belly of the car. I turned up into the final hill, the snow swarming in against me like flies. And it came clear suddenly: *What we meet with is here, what needs meeting is here!* I thought, and I tapped myself on the forehead with one fist; the car swerved, tires spun in a muffling of snow; I swung the wheel, the car groaned and pulled straight again and went on; oh, for God's sake, Di, keep your eyes on the road. The road. In two miles I was home. The house and fences looked newly padded. It was very quiet. My son was already asleep and I took the baby-sitter home, and came back and lit the fire.

Fly, fly! I thought; this snow is like feathers from a burst pillow. I have had moments, I will have more; each one frees me further from the bondage of the self. Does a seed feel this? When, time ticked off and light measured and oxygen and water absorbed, each sense satisfied, *at last: nothing can contain me now!*

The Following of Light

There is one thing that you can always count on here, and that is day and night, light and darkness, alternating like the ticking of a clock. I don't know how to read time by sunlight; by *time* I don't mean the hour of the day; by time I mean the passage of the year. Almost everything else here knows how to do this, though, and I watch them. Showers of small signs spatter across my days and I try my best to collect them singly, as if they were thrown grains of rice, or coins. Meanwhile, the rising light is worth something in itself — the fundamental wind that blows into the energy economy here, the rush of particle-wave cash that showers down impartially, like a law. It will change the face of the world.

✦   ✦   ✦

My days begin with the squirrel; like a circus show starting with the single baggy-panted buffoon at center stage, setting the audience (me) at ease and setting the tone. Just below the pines where the maple woods begin, my path through the snow goes right over the roof of a flying squirrel's den. When I have gone just beyond, I turn and wait. On cue the squirrel pops from the snow and climbs a maple sapling paw over the paw and then stops, slung there, poised like an acrobat in his angle of branch and bole, his whiskers a-whiffle, and looks down at me from enormous black liquid eyes that sparkle like bobbles of ink. I laugh at him, also on cue; he is very funny. He looks shocked at my laugh, which must seem to him like a bellow of territorial rant; perhaps he is annoyed at my impertinence in tramping over his house, which, since it is a hollow log, must boom and resound with my daily snowshoe steps overhead. At one end of that log the maple sapling rises, silvery and sparsely branched, with a small hole-door at its base which must see all the squirrel's comings and goings to the outer world now; the tree is his path, his silvery upward wand.

Then up he goes again and outward, tentative, on a tiny branch, and teeters onto a twig, flails his tail for balance, launches — and blinks open like a parachute.

The underside of the squirrel-parachute is as pale as un-bleached cotton. Beyond this slowly floating square the flat brown tail lashes, holding him on course. He drifts down and sideways to an ash tree and at the last moment he lowers his tail-flaps and tilts up for the approach, landing gear out, and — disappears.

Illusion: a moment ago he was a pale lozenge against a pale winter sky and slowly descending; now he is a brown flying squirrel again, stopped on a brown tree: light to dark and dark to light — gone. His illusion done, he goes on, skipping and hoisting himself in ascending spirals up the ash; I see him again only by chance, ten feet up, another animal altogether. Unexpected. Even though I see this performance almost every day, I still lose the squirrel when he meets the tree, without fail.

Once he bashed into a branch in midflight and fell, with a sudden scrambled twist and somersault into the snow, like an animal shaken out of a box. He righted himself and hopped and ran and hopped, rooting for a soft drift or convenient hollow into which he could scuffle and be sucked out of sight; disappear. Disappear.

Now he finds himself another angle of branch to hang in and stares down, hoping I will go. Have I been fooled? The anxious bubble-eyed face watches me carefully. My daily show is over, and I walk on down the slope into the hemlocks: thank you! There is applause sounding somewhere, a faint mothlike batting under my breastbone. I lean back on my snowshoes and trot down the path into the maple trees.

Only the light is changing; not the scenery, or the cast. Now the light is strong enough so that I have to slit my eyes against it in late morning. The light reflected from the snow brings the canted slope and the leafless trees rising from it — like twigs stuck into cotton wool — up into a high simmer of brightness. Just for an hour or two at midday. No more than that.

At noon it is eight degrees above zero; I stop my ax-trimming of trees to find my pack, left hours ago in a beech stump, and rummage for my coffee thermos and a sandwich. While I'm leaning there having lunch, my hands and feet slowly chill and stiffen but I watch, with awe; a sift of snow on my dark blue wool pants shrivels into beads of moisture. The snow on the metal ax head, which is lying on the stump in the sun, coalesces into domed splashes of water that steam, gently. A liquid drop ignites and sparkles at the southern corner of the sugarhouse roof; an icicle begins to grow. Here and there on dark surfaces the light is being transmuted to enough heat — forty degrees above the temperature of the air — to melt snow. There the rigid crystals are collapsing. There it is a watershed day. In the shade the snow is still as soft underfoot as dust; in the light something else is beginning.

✦   ✦   ✦

Our planet is aspin on an elastic ellipse; we are set tilted and wobbling here like a top spun across a floor, doing obeisance to a star. Here at this place in our elliptical year we are gradually heeling over more and more toward this star from which, eight minutes ago, a nuclear burst scattered energy our way; here it comes; the light puffs, scatters, fills our sails; steady as she goes!

My ax is facedown in the snow, my arm slung around the hard-muscled trunk of a young maple; I begin to feel the whirl and I brace my feet against the surge as if I were riding the deck of a ship over storm swells; here we go boys, hup! This one'll poop her sure enough! The decks are awash with light, boys!

An odd thought. I hear the shudder and bang of stays — are they branches? I have had my sealegs for thirty years, but I still get these attacks of vertigo when I feel the vulnerable fragility of this ship, overfreighted as it seems to be with people and their blundering works, but heaving and spinning steadily enough. At night I can see this ocean in its true color: black. Absence. Strewn with an archipelago of other star-ships, all unthinkably far off. We have been sending messages out by radio for years now — soap operas and symphonies and Pepsi ads — and are all set to catch a reply. Out in the Arizona desert huge dishes of antenna-ears scan the galaxy for language; we have launched the Voyager spacecraft like messages in bottles: "We Are Here!"

Will we send one more, someday, a last bottle thrown from a tangled deck strewn with sail tatters and slick with congealing fluids: "Here We Are! Holed by our own hand and sinking fast!"

What would we expect then? Aren't we are already dreaming of lifeboats? Manned by beneficent gods, perhaps? Ha. Fat chance. All hands on deck; there are enough live things here to do God's work. A good Captain, a fine crew. There is no other land in sight. I retrieve my ax; the maple has steadied me. Thank you. More sub-breastbone applause for you, old salt. Little do you know.

One day in the first week of February the woods, suddenly, changed. It was a sunny day and the dark needles of the evergreens gathered the light, transmuting it to the longer wavelengths of heat; by one o'clock they had gathered enough to melt films of water under the snow that they held in their branches. The snow began to slide off, hissing and plopping, cratering the snow on the ground. It began in the high lit branches of the spruce and the hemlocks and gathered momentum until, at dusk, coming home up the hill, I saw that the pines around the house had shed their loads completely and were standing with their branches up.

Even things that were only just darker than the snow began to become solar transmuters and stores. Where the trail of a fox crossed a clearing, the grayish tracks became so widened and distorted by melt that they might have been the trail of a timber wolf. Tree trunks and stones warmed and melted the snow away from themselves; the snow was pressed back in gentle half-moon shapes. Every lit day quarried these hollows deeper. By the end of February they had become pots of air that surrounded and held whole trees, stones, even weed stems, fenceposts.

Near the end of February the gray birches opened their catkins and strewed their seeds. Minuscule brown airplane shapes of the protective scales and the tiny oval seeds surrounded by translucent curves of wing were everywhere in the snow. Blown by the wind, they gathered in hollows; my snowshoe path, squirrel tracks. They blew off across the fields in the fresh light falls of snow. A swarm of twig ends pokes from the white expanse of the old potato field; it is a field full of young birches, evidence of February strewings and blowings four years past. The new seeds eddied in behind them.

The rising expanding parabola of the sun is having its more subtle effects. One day just after the squirrel show I noticed a snow-speck only because it was moving. Legs spraddled, it walked over the snow with that single-minded intent that only insects have. I bent and let it climb onto a finger of my glove and there it moved steadfastly on its way so that I had to turn and twist my hand to keep it from going off the edge; it was a winter crane fly. I put my hand down and let it go. It was wingless, mosquitolike, and slow; it took up its journey again, in another direction.

It had all my attention. The purposes of its travels were not, I hope, as mysterious to it as they seemed to me. How could it survive and move there on the snow, cold-blooded as it was? What was it up to? Mating, perhaps. What pushed it out into a world still snowed in? Stupid questions — winter crane flies are made to be out on the snow; but it seemed a wonder of wonders. I hadn't seen any insects except houseflies for months. Either the expanding light or some sudden rise in temperature or humidity in the stuff of the woods where its chrysalis nested had joggled it loose: You! Time to move!

Every few weeks through the winter I went down to the lake near Dead Creek to watch the waterbirds wintering there. They were very shy, and wary of me; they had been shot at enough. The ice had walled them in to a few bays and corners of the lake, and in one place in particular I had found a way to sneak up on them, belly-crawling through a ravine full of raspberry canes and then hunkering behind a big cottonwood by the shore.

There were hundreds — sometimes thousands — of birds gathered there. I watched the mergansers diving for perch, always attended by scavenging gulls who would try to snatch the perch away once it was caught, chasing the duck through its scandalized quacking flock; the merganser's only hope was to gulp his fish on the run. Canada geese tip-tilted along the shore, and preened on shelves of ice, and slept there with their heads curled back. Mallards and black ducks gleaned the cornfields over the rise and flew in and out in small subtly quacking gangs to rest on the slopes above the water. By noon even in early February the snow between the stubbles and the sheet of ice on the open lake put out a white resounding glare, against which the dark shapes of open water and leafless trees quivered and were indistinct like mirage shapes in a desert.

Then one early afternoon — it was February the second; I have it written down — there was a song: "Leee deee . . ." A pure two-tone song. Again: "Leee deee . . ." I stood up carelessly, my spotting scope and tripod fell over, the mergansers turned in unison and paddled away like a brigade on the march, mallards rose in a quacking swarm and tilted up along the fields; where . . . ? Again: "Leee deee . . . there! One chickadee high in an elm, head thrown back. Singing his private claimant's song. Only February. And already.

It was the first sign that the migration-reverse had begun. Not because the chickadee had migrated anywhere; he had wintered here, but the mechanics of the movement are the same. The growth of light had sent its messages to his pituitary gland, the pituitary had shunted its own brand of hormonal messages directing his testes to swell and produce; the testes in turn made the hormones that sent him to claim the elm as a boundary post of the place where he could mate, brood, feed a crop of young chickadees: did he know that? Maybe. Probably not. He was just — *singing*.

A broad-winged hawk soaring over the Florida keys has his inner chemistries changed, too, by the growing light. Light penetrates the thin skulls of hummingbirds wintering in Mexico, sparrows in southern New England, and blackbirds in the deep South. The messengers of the blood pulse on their business, testes and ovaries swell; and with them swells a divine discontent. Each bird will come home in its own time and by its own path.

Soon enough the waterbirds on the lake will be catching the drift of all this. There will be more quonking and quacking and gatherings and nervous short flights along the lake; then the mergansers will make their way from marsh to lake to marsh to Nova Scotia, the Canadas will be off to Newfoundland, the

Honeymoon of the Owl ⟵ *199*

three snow geese — which lost their way to Delaware and wintered here with the Canadas — will launch themselves, too, on their private trajectory to the north shores of Hudson's Bay, perhaps even as far as Ellesmere Island. The little tip-up-tailed ruddy ducks, bobbing between the geese like rusty bathtub toys, will go west to the Rockies and the northern plains. Most of the mallards and blacks will go north, too, into the marshes and backwaters of Canada. They will go home soon, toting a good layer of fat under their wings; fat gleaned from Champlain Valley perch and waste corn and tons of roots of waterweeds and crayfish and waterbugs; it will carry them into the expanding continent of the spring.

Watch by Night

Lambing time begins at the end of February, and as it closes in I catch the drift of other birthings on their way, out there. There are thousands of blackfly eggs clustered in the streambed of the Tamarack, the great horned owl embryos are turning yolk and white and filtered air into themselves, bobcats are scenting each other out, grinning and hissing, waving a claw-full paw — the ancestral movements of our smile and handshake. According to astronomers, stars give birth to stars among coalescing clouds of celestial trash, and even the universe was born once from a pinpoint of compressed energy smaller than the dot on this *i*. Under the snow the winged maple seeds are hankering for water and light. The first spring that I lambed the big flock in this barn I was pregnant myself, all the side-buttons of my overalls undone.

It is February. It is cold. But the air seems charged with bursting and immanence; that one animal gives birth to another is a grand magic. It is plainly magic; I have seen the birth of more than a thousand lambs now but familiarity hasn't bred contempt here, if anything it has only heightened the sense that dozens of linked and intricate biological sleights of hand steer the work through. I recognize some of them, now. (Ah, another coin palmed! I saw that, I watched!) Once the lamb stands and suckles on its own, its ewe-mother sniffing at the base of its tail, the harvest is in: a bright scarf whisked from an empty bowl.

I was expecting more than 300 lambs, and they would need more watching than I could give them myself, because it was still very cold. So two friends of mine, Betsy Gillette and Marca McClenon, had agreed to apprentice themselves to the lambing trade for the spring, and after they arrived at the farm we began our work by hauling cartons of paraphernalia into the "warm room," an insulated and heatable corner of the barn which would be our headquarters for the next month. As we tramped down the road to the barn in the snow, Betsy and Marca sang a song that they had heard on the radio and laughed. We kicked out our booted feet like a chorus line. What was so funny? We were overalled and scarved and mittened against the wind, which flung the snow across the meadow in a stinging fog. We plugged in the heater in the warm room and arranged our gear in the cabinets: gallons of alcohol and iodine, bins of boiled syringes and needles, bottles of serums and anti-serums, antibiotics and oil and soap, loops of coated electrical wire, disinfectants, salves, splints, adhesive tape, a walkie-talkie, sheaves of record sheets on a clipboard, a single electric burner, a cooking pot, cups, jars of instant coffee, tea, cocoa, honey. We swept up a year's worth of dead flies and dusted the easy chair and folded a clean blanket over one arm; I have never yet managed to sleep there. No one has. The blanket is a formality.

I thought about the does in the ravine, swelling toward May and June. I thought about the insect eggs measuring quanta of light and warmth inside the oval wombs of goldenrod galls, the clusters of spawn ripening in every female frog's ovaries like winter fruit, the Nashville warblers in Guatemala feeling the good urge to come back and raise another brood among the little trees in the sheep pasture; none of them have midwives. But 12,000 years ago — a mere eyeblink ago — neither did sheep.

The lambs began by coming slowly, two or three ewes birthing a day, and then the rhythm picked up and suddenly there were lambs in the kitchen, in the shed, newborns were walled in with their mothers behind hay bales because we had run out of little pens to keep them in. There was a premature lamb that needed feeding by tube every two hours; an automatic feeding-bottle that needed constant cleaning and filling with fresh milk to feed the orphan lambs; in the mornings we made the rounds of the newborns, tagging their ears, weighing them, giving them their vaccinations, catching up on the records. When there was a difficult birth, I made Betsy or Marca go in and correct it while I leaned against the wall, handing them loops of coated wire or disinfectant and talking them through:

"I can't tell if this is a tail or an ear!"
"What is it attached to?"
"Oh."

"There's just a bunch of hooves, nothing else."
"Push it all back in and start over."
"There are . . . wait . . . five hooves, that's all I can find."
"*Five* . . ."
"I found a tail!"
"You don't want a tail. Find a head."
"No head."
"The head may be curved back around like this. All you'll feel is the curve of the neck. Keep going till you find an ear or something."
"Oh, God!"
"Don't worry, there's plenty of room."

"I found it! God, it's way back there! How . . . oh, no . . . can I have a wire?"

"Is it coming around?"

"Yup. There's still five hooves, though."

"I can't feel anything. Just a lot of moosh."

"It's a lamb's back then, probably."

"This one's a *monster*, must be a yard long!"

"Find the head?"

"Yup. But there's only one front leg."

"It's hiding the other one under its tummy, maybe. See if you can fish it out."

"What would you be doing if you weren't here?"

"I have no idea. It's Saturday night . . . the Greenwich Village jazz clubs open in an hour. If we drove all night we'd get there in time for a set before closing."

"This is more fun, dammit. I got that leg, now what?"

One can't help noticing that some special things happen once the live lamb is on the ground. Our job at lambing time has always been to ensure that they happen the right way. Two years ago I read an article about problems with premature human infants; it seems that many babies that are born weeks or months early end up with a worse record of child abuse throughout their youth than infants that are born at full term. The abuse record doesn't seem to correlate with anything else except the prematurity. A team of researchers tackled the problem. They did a lot of their experimenting with sheep. It turned out that at a certain timed interval before a mammal gives birth a special set of hormones open an emotional window in the mother, through which the infant is meant to enter. In sheep this window creaks open a day or so before the birth, in people it opens a month or more before term. If this window isn't open, then the bonding between mother and infant can't take place. After a while, the window closes. If the child is locked out, its life will be hard. This emotional window can also be forced open ahead of schedule to let a premie into the sanctum, but only through plenty of intimate sensual contact: plenty of smelling, tasting, touching, feeling. Many premature infants used to be kept away from their parents for days or weeks, and were cared for by nurses. The upshot of this research effort was that all of that has changed. The sensual acts of bonding have become hospital policy.

If you take a lamb away from its mother-ewe at birth, just for an hour, and then give it back to her, she will bang it against the wall with her head. Any shepherd could tell you that.

Finally in the third week of lambing it was my turn for a week of night watch, which I have always liked best because there are no interruptions and it allows me to be awake for dawn; the clean, holy hour. After dinner I went out in my freshly washed and dried overalls with one pocket full of boiled lamb nipples and the other pocket with a little box of raisins in it to keep me going in the wee hours. I was not expecting the sky: a brilliant strew of stars which seemed, in the still and cold, to have taken their places, not on any steadfast bowl or dome like a planetarium ceiling, but near and far, each hung with vast distances between, so that it was this distance more than anything else that I saw when I looked up. There was a watery whirring glow in the north sky, a lace curtain of aurora borealis stirring faintly in the solar wind.

I didn't look up much. The night was big. Fingering my box of raisins, I kept my eyes on the road and walked carefully in the trampled ruts; I was reduced to an iota, a speck, an awed collection of atoms moving down the slope and hoping against hope that I wouldn't be sucked off.

The barn kept me busy and it was hours before I went outside again, clutching a mug of honeyed tea, to sit on the hay cart under the sky. The aurora had gone wild against the stars. It was pulsing in white gouts here and then there; long jabs of light were hurtling to the zenith and fading and glowing like fire and hurtling again; my instinct was to duck and take cover, but I crossed my legs up on the cart and sipped my tea. *Hold on to yourself*, I thought. *Hold on.*

The Eskimo and the Tlingit peoples thought that this flow of light was the reflection from the dance fire of the ghosts. Pagan Germans thought that it was the reflected glory of the warrior women's armor — the glow of the shields of the Valkyrie. True to the spirit of the times, most scientists now believe that it is a gigantic TV show of the moods of the sun. As the sun flares it sends a gust, a storm in the constant solar wind of subatomic particles that stream off into space. This solar storm then activates the earth's magnetic field, which performs like an immense cathode-ray tube. Somehow this stirred magnetic field generates electron beams that project an image on the screen of the upper polar atmosphere; a gyrating oval of light. The greater the storm, the wider the image. A huge solar convulsion will send the show as far as Mexico.

I drank my tea and ate my raisins and watched. The tea and raisins were comforting, they held me down, they gave me a gift of gravity.

Back in the barn everything was calm. More than a hundred contented lambs were asleep in heaps under the central light. I had an idea for a moment that at last the armchair and blanket might get some well-deserved use, but one ewe stood by the west wall, her head down below her shoulders as if she were listening intently. She shifted on her hind feet. I made another mug of tea. There were hollows in front of her hipbones and her belly looked pear-shaped, dropped, from the rear, not held high and round as it had been. She shifted, shifted, then turned and lay down, and lifted her lip in discomfort.

Her legs pushed at the straw. Then she lay quietly awhile, still looking as though she were listening hard. She chewed a cud and stood up. I walked in the alleyway and drank my tea.

The ewe turned and pawed at the straw, and sniffed at the

spot where her behind had been, then turned and turned and finally lay, slowly, down, and pushed and strained again.

A pale balloon of fluids emerged and burst, loosing a flood of clear, jellyish stuff. The ewe rose and sniffed and licked at the fluids in the straw, and whickered (*where . . . ?*) and lay down, pushing, puffing, straining, her neck stretched back, her spine bent. She paused and looked back toward her rump (*where . . . ?*) and looked, ears cupped, toward the black barn cat (*is it . . . ?*); the cat stalked across the barn and climbed a post with a rattle of claws (*no . . .*) and the ewe stood, and turned, and lay down again, and strained; her whole body taut and heaving, her nose to the sky, hind legs rigid against the ground. She got up again slowly, with difficulty.

I could see two cloven hooves now when she pushed, covered with a shining welter of mucus, each hoof clothed in the white birth-slipper of cartilage that protects the ewe from the sharp horn cups. As she lay down and pushed again, I could see a black nose tucked flat between the front knuckles of those feet, and the ewe strained, heaved. She answered another lamb's bleat, the high baby-cry of hungry-for-milk-in-the-night (*is it? No, not mine, where . . . ?*).

She pushed again and the head and shoulders of her lamb eased out at last, steaming in the cold, and glistening in membranous packages; the lamb's head thrashed, thrashed, beat against the straw wham wham . . . wham wham . . . It sneezed, shook its head, its ears flapped loose and it sucked air. The ewe, her head aimed back under her belly, sucked air. The lamb lifted its nose and the ewe rose and turned and whickered and the lamb came all the way out finally with a wet slap, and the ewe rumbled, and licked and licked and the lamb, and rumbled (*here! and here!*) and the lamb cried, a wobbly "Aaaaaa . . ." and turned toward the lapping tongue.

I could see another reddish fluid-filled sac emerging from the ewe's behind, and in it the pale cloven hooves of her second lamb. The first one thrashed in the straw, trying to get to its feet.

I went in then, to do my bit. As always when things have gone the way they should, I was generally ignored. I picked the lamb up and carried it slowly into one of the maternity pens, which had been limed and floored with fresh hay. The pens are bonding insurance; they allow the window to close around the occupants; and nothing else. Without a well-bonded mother, a lamb dies. The ewe followed at my heel, rumbling, like a trained dog. Once in and with the gate closed, lamb and ewe took up again where they'd left off, nosing and whickering and "aaaa . . ."ing. I sat the lamb on my knees, cut the cord close, and doused it with iodine from a jar. I reached under the ewe for her teats, each as big as my thumb and taut, and pressed a long squirt of milk out of each one; the ewe licked the lamb and hunkered, giving me more room (*oh, yes, that . . . is . . .*) and I splayed one hand under the lamb's wet breast-bone, and aimed him in under her flank, feeling — under the slippery textured wet of its hide — the bird-fragile cage of bones with a quick inhabiting flicker. The lamb's mouth pursed, searched, its head bumped the udder, the lamb slipped from my hand and thrashed in the hay. I tried again. I poked a teat into his overeager mouth. There was a sudden thrumming in the lamb, then suddenly (*oh, yes, there now . . . !*) a whuck . . . whuck . . . whuck of the milk galloping into the lamb, and the lamb sagged, relaxed . . . whuckety whuck whuck . . . I could feel his belly swelling. The ewe turned to smell and lick under its frantically wriggling tail (*yes, this is mine, yes*).

It was a perfect circle; ewe nose to lamb tail, lamb nose to ewe teat. The second lamb eased into the hay and I put it out in front of the ewe; and it all began again, all over again.

It was almost morning. Through the open door to the pens I could see the faint line of woodlot trees like an illustration done in washes of ink. A window high up under the barn peak showed a lozenge of graying sky where there had been only dark. We were a lighted ship afloat and going; afloat in a circle, a charmed circle.

COYOTE

VI Pond in the Woods

Who can say of a particular sea that it is old?
Distilled by the sun, kneaded by the moon, it is
renewed in a year, in a day, or in an hour. The
sea changed, the fields changed, the rivers, the
villages, and the people changed, yet Egdon
remained.

— THOMAS HARDY,
The Return of the Native

The Lab with a View

I go and sit on Steve and Jan's porch by the Pond in the Woods when I've been too busy and I need to breathe, and let myself be. No one comes to the camp in early March, and the wide porch offers a snow-free place to sit and look out on the iced and snowed expanse of pond and the curved bounding hills penciled in with grays.

The feeling there of Absolute-No-Event is a key to winter anyway: but now it has less the feel of absence than of prescient hush. Months and months ago the forest orchestra finished its autumnal grand finale, and now the solar conductor stands strong again with his arms and baton raised: some other music is on its way and no matter that the hush will last weeks — the bows are on the fiddles, mouths are pursed on the mouthpieces of tubas and piccolos, drumsticks are raised for the opening boomp.

The weeks that will pass from now until the beginning of April when the ice goes, and then the four or more weeks that will go by until the leaves come out on the trees — these will be a time of greater change in and by this pond than anywhere else I know of. This time of thaw and refreeze and thaw again will mean that the whole bulk of winter snow and ice will be flung from solid and nearly impervious crystal, to free solvent liquid, and then back, and forth, and back again. Whole hills full of thaw water will come in through the clearinghouse of the pond and then down through the tipped rushing of the pond brook and out through the valley river. Water is the way that nutrients move here, through a tree, or a deer, or through a landscape.

These things would happen soon enough; but I went there in March first of all to contemplate the No-Change, the flat white expanse of pond that hadn't budged for months. It is a peaceful place to be, though sometimes it's too peaceful, like a television screen which has been turned off: gray, depthless, emptied long ago of all of its dancing lights. And I went to the pond, too, because I wanted to know what it is that all these new things which are on their way will begin from. This, then!

I walked to the camp in the afternoon and sat for two hours until dusk, working my way through a chocolate bar and watching and waiting for whatever chose to be revealed on the snow-gray screen of the pond. I began by showing myself an old mind's-eye home movie of a strange story that Steve told me years ago. Steve used to have a big blue-eyed male huskie who loved to chase cows and sheep, and so the pond in winter was one of the few places he could be let just to run free; a kind of rural Central Park with nobody's tempting heifers in sight. One afternoon when the dog was running there with Steve close behind him, a stag came out of the woods and the dog saw the stag and froze, for one second, two seconds; and then burst, *shot* after the stag like a gray rolling ball, and the deer saw the dog and began to run, zigging and zagging, and the dog bunched and ran harder, cutting his quarry's evading curves like a pirate ship gaining leeway on a treasure-toting galleon. In minutes the dog had the stag by the throat and dog and deer fell together kicking, on the ice. It was a perfect docu-drama of a kill; a kill done by wolves hunting deer or elk or caribou; by weasels hunting meadow voles, by lynx hunting hare, foxes hunting grouse; a chase, and a hit; and a final silence, after which nothing was the same. Steve had watched it all, and I watched the mind's-eye film run through and finish, with a flip flip flip at the end of the reel.

After that I thought for a while of what was going on under the ice, in that rich wintering world I dragged up a bucket of months ago on that cold — too cold — day. And I realized with a sense of shock that there was something vital that I had missed. Not that it was visible. Or that it ever has been visible. Only that it is central; the wellspring, font, source of the flow; of the live flow here. Not the water flow now. After all, water is only a blind and dumb chemical that freezes, melts, and vaporizes according to set laws of temperature and pressure, and rolls downhill by the easiest route; hauled and engaged by the force of gravity. Forces and laws are what water obeys and it obeys them simply enough. If you had, say, two thousand years, and a computer hooked to enough memory chips to fill a room, you could write a formula and draw an intricately shaded map of exactly what will happen to these hills full of snow in the next eight weeks. But you could never, ever, devise a formula for what is going to happen to the life in the pond. Or for what is happening there, now. Not so much the ongoing business of its life but the larger work of transformation, for which the pond life is hooked up to the universe by sprays of raging energy. Every second, in through the ice-snow water shield of the pond, these sprays pour.

Even now when we take it for granted, the idea of Darwinian evolution has the power to shake the soul. I wouldn't dare to say that these subatomic "sprays" are responsible for the actual creation of anything; but they are responsible for the amendments to almost everything. By amendments I mean a lot. It is as if all that had been created were a single organism, simple as the one word *yes* — and then through constant trial and error, through the adding of single letters, a phrase or two, here a line, there another line transposed, all of them chance happenings and chaotic inspirations and all of them subject to the hard editings of survival — one had finished up with the

Encyclopaedia Britannica. No — a million encyclopedias! All of them subject to countless mutation-revisions and selective-reamendments. All of them! But underneath the almost infinite variety of the complex live beings that are the result of all this, one can still touch that original assumption: the *yes*.

All the rest is frill.

These sprays — which are cosmic rays and their almost equally powerful daughter rays — are very small and very fast. They slice in through the atmosphere in chance bursts. They do their work with as much grace as a soft-nosed bullet. They can be heard as clickings from the gut of Geiger counters and seen as brief trails of light in cloud chambers. They work just like the ionizing radiation that results from a thermonuclear blast, and they are wanton, destructive, and everywhere. Like the dog after the deer they do their work with a zing, a hit, and a following silence; after which something somewhere is not the same. All of what I know about ionizing radiation — cosmic or domestic in origin — I have learned by reading the writings of scientists who have worked long and hard at their business. So I take it on faith then that this goes on. But I did learn something from my own experience around the fringes of this subject, and that experience has a good deal to do with why I am not a scientist myself.

In my early days at college, when I was looking for something to achieve in the way of real scientific work, I spent several months of afternoons peering through the eyepiece of a Nikon microscope at specially stained ultra-thin sections of sunflower roots, in search of root cells showing signs of damage. The damages had been inflicted by me in carefully measured doses.

These damages were the interesting part. What there were of them had been done by ionizing radiation — gamma rays, in this case. To get enough of them I went to the hospital where a doctor who was in charge of radiation therapy for cancer patients agreed to treat my seeds after hours. They needed hours. Seeds are difficult to damage.

It was late at night when my turn came and the doctor and I stood out in the hall sipping coffee while the gamma-ray machine hummed on the other side of the door. There was a thick oval of glass in the door, through which we could peer in, like the window of a deep-sea submersible. The seeds sat in glass dishes on a padded table made for prone cancer patients. Nothing seemed to be happening to them there. I took it on faith that something was. At the beginning of the session a slug of radioactive cobalt, barely larger than a piece of chalk, had been wheeled from its locked repository down the hall and inserted in place in its machine. At timed intervals we would turn the machine's eye off and then go in and remove one dish of seeds and then leave with them and turn the machine's eye on again. The seeds that stayed in there the longest absorbed hundreds of times the full body dose of ionizing radiation that would have been sufficient to kill a man.

Gamma radiation is subatomic particles crazed with energy. They zip through space until they meet another solid bit of matter — some particular small molecule quietly going about its business — and they cut it apart; they slice it into two frantic charged pieces each of which whirls in its own right and attacks the nearest molecule and rips it apart, and so on. The damage spreads like a stain.

Take a cocktail party, for instance, at which there are twenty happily married couples, and give three of them instant, irreconcilable divorces, and see what happens. The party is a party no longer. This was what was happening inside those sunflower seeds.

Afterward I took my seeds home, each in labeled vials according to how much radiation they had absorbed, and planted them. When they grew — which most of them did, with varying degrees of speed and garblings of leaves — I extracted a root or two from each one and looked carefully at the visible damage. The invisible damage was long over by that time. What does the community look like six months after that cocktail party? Something like that.

The lab that I was working in had a floor-to-ceiling window at one end which looked out over the valley and into the hills beyond, a nice architectural detail which made life in the lab more humane. One afternoon in late March when I was working alone there, I made the mistake of looking up. Whole careers are blasted to smithereens by mistakes like that. The sky outside was gray and full of rain so that the tree branches were wet, and red, and whole ranks of hill upon hill were furred with this wet red forest, which had patches of evergreens nested in it like dense hair. There were plumes of mist rising out of the old snowbanks, and scudding tags of vapor trailed among the hills like the veils of dancing girls. I looked up from my microscope and saw those drenched hills (and just how many roots are out there sucking in juice?) and something in me leaped and expanded so that the sensible casing which I held around myself cracked and fell to the floor. I felt naked as a jaybird. I looked at the Nikon microscope and it made as much sense to me as it would to a jaybird; I packed up my slides and went home.

I never looked at the slides again. I gave an inconclusive paper to my science seminar, complete with requisite audiovisual materials, and when it came time to offer up my concluding statement I wished that I had had a special little device concealed behind the slide viewer. A device which I could just shove down with one insouciant toe. And when I pressed — carefully planted charges would explode, there would be a loud crack and a thundering noise, and one wall of the auditorium would collapse outward in a puff of splinters and cement dust, leaving a snaggle of electrical wires through which one could see those hills. Then with my arms waving I would shout, "Get out! Get out! Out! Out!" and herd my terrified fellow students and our professors through the ragged gap. "Let's get out and stay there! And if we live out there enough we can come back tangle-bearded and humble and courageous and full of the love of God and fish a microscope from the rubble and embark!"

This seemed like the only sensible conclusion to draw from the material at hand.

All of which goes to show that a lab with a view can be a dangerous thing. To do good science you aren't supposed to see the forest. You aren't even encouraged to see the trees. To get anything done you have to zoom in on one microscopic or submicroscopic — biochemical — bit of blended homogenized abstract Tree and stay there. If you want to see the forest? Then maybe the lab is as good a place to start as any, but sooner or later I think you have to leave.

Look at it this way: forests don't hold with conclusions. There are, for instance, more than five hundred pines around my house. They were planted in the same spring and were bought from the same nursery and were very likely bred from the same parent stock. They are a lot more uniform than any natural forest could ever claim to be. Each one of them has several million needles. There are certain things that you can say about those needles; almost all of them come in bunches of two, are half-moon-shaped in cross-section, turn brown and drop off after their second summer, are as long as a ten-year-old's hand, and come to a pale yellow point at the tip. But every needle is different from every other needle. No two of them are exactly alike.

This in itself is a conclusion, but it does leave room for things. Like the Hand of God; which is as good a name as anything else for the whimsical and creative forces that never allow nature to repeat itself. It moveth in mysterious ways.

According to present theories of evolution, this variability exists because of the constant amending of genetic software — inherent biological programming — by ionizing radiation, stress, chemical damage, or mere mistake. This program is then "used" (or misused) by whatever environment the organism happens to find itself in. A life *form* can't be separated from its environment any more than it can from its heritage; each pine needle — each form — is molded from within and from without.

There are certain things that one can say about ponds: they have water in them, a water "budget" (inflow and outflow) and an energy budget, and an array of live creatures which range in function and in size all the way from single-celled algae to large and highly visible animals, such as migrant geese and resident snapping turtles; but there is something else about ponds which is as certain as these other things. I have seen a friend of mine, a brilliant doctor of freshwater biology, stand wide-eyed and immobilized in front of her blackboard, chalk clutched in her hand, intricate graphs and formulae forgotten, because she has said, ". . . but every pond is different from every other pond!" and has just heard herself, with a kind of panic, admit that she knows nothing — nothing beyond the most bland generalities — about a subject on which she has spent half of her life.

I think I recognize that panic. The realization that one can't know about very much at all, that in trying to *know* one is always chasing the ephemeral, the rainbow-end; that yes, one can come up with theories which test out under most conditions and formulae which work a lot of the time; but that in understanding the limitations of knowledge one has somehow made the first step in a greater game.

What one can gain from this panic is an addiction to miracle. Unlike some other addictive habits, this one is cheap and easy enough to maintain. In watching this immobile pond from my seat on the camp porch — a bowl of dark water seething with interwebbed live things, held out to the sprays of cosmic radiation, flung through a cycle of seasons which seem, on the surface of things, all but impossible to live through, so different are their demands — I found myself shivering, my heartbeat doubled, my head nodding over the scraps of crumpled Hershey-bar wrapper in my lap: well, well.

The sun sets more to the west now, to my right behind the hill of hardwood, instead of over the spruce trees across the ice where it set in January. A million mouths are pursed on the mouthpieces of tubas and piccolos, a trillion microscopic drumsticks are raised for the opening boomp; I expect the music, the rhythm will be familiar, the variations (most of them) will be interesting enough. Spring is on the way. But perhaps, after the opening of the thaw, the curtain of ice will rise to reveal something absolutely *new*. Maybe one *Tubifex* or alga will have been damaged over the winter by the radiation rain, damaged in a way that has amended its genetic program for the better. The chances are admittedly small, and the likelihood of any person finding out about it even if it has happened is almost nil. But it is enough that, according to the evolutionary record, these things are going on here all the time.

Crows and Satellites

There is a superstition here that the crows come back to the hills two weeks before the maple sap begins to run; two weeks, that is, before the first serious thaw.

On March first, which was Town Meeting day, I saw two crows crossing the high ridge of the hill below the Martins' house. The next day Russell Martin boiled in five gallons of fancy syrup, the first hill syrup of the year. His sugar woods always starts a crop before anyone else's here does. His whole family was there to gather the pails — three sons, two brothers, grandchildren — and the women made doughnuts and hot maple biscuits in the house and sent egg-salad sandwiches down to the men in the woods. Russell's woods at sugartime are his assurance that there is hope in the world and green grass around the corner, there on the other side of sugartime, waiting for him in the wings as it always has.

The next day it was cold again and a wind sent fine snow across the fields in a low skin-singeing fog; it slid like smoke across the icy ground and the ruts in the road and the dull drifts. The pines held a filtrate of flakes, a white underlining in their branches. The sky was gray, low, full of soaking light, full of a brightness that melted through the cloud and hurt the eyes. From the east soft pulses of light came flowing over my shoulders like a breath: the change was on its way.

In the second week of March and in the midst of a snow squall, with the hills and the near trees fading in and out of flurries and waves of white, the crows came back again. A whole clan of them came scouting the woods margins, calling out to one another with the hoarse sounds of cornfields, death; a derisive daring-you-all cawing as if they were coming up to hawk some seamy wares, or as if they knew the soft underbelly of the world better than anyone; perhaps they do.

With the arrival of the crows we began to get our woods ready for maple-syrup–making. We stopped cutting timber and firewood and made repairs to the sap-collecting pipelines and we washed the tanks and the evaporator and swept the sugarhouse, and ousted the porcupine from his winter quarters in the woodshed; we watched the weather. But March weather, like crows, is not to be trusted.

There are bitter and reluctant springs here when the time comes for thaw and there is no thaw, nor any sign of one. Even the crows' maple-sap prophecy can go wrong; through they, at any rate, don't seem to care.

Three years ago we had one of those grudging Marches, and one day I was down in the sugar woods, inspecting — it seemed for the hundredth time — the empty sap lines that led forlornly from every tree. I was not expecting anything, least of all the faint moaned cry that came from the thicker woods as if an animal lay hurt there. A moment afterward a skein of twelve Canada geese came flying low over the trees, still bugling mournfully like a flock of ghosts. They circled twice and went off finally toward the southwest. There was no open water anywhere then except on the river rapids; the corn stubbles were buried, the marshes still encased in ice.

Although geese kept coming all through March and into

April — the laggards a kind of insurance against the reluctant springs — there are autumns when the southering flocks of geese seem scant. One can look at the rigors of the spring before and guess at a reason. Migrations are not without their missteps and horrors, even timed as they are on the sun, which is as infallible a timepiece as anything could be. The geese have been launched, but have no way of knowing what it is they have been launched toward. There are sleeting rains, winds which blow into the North too strongly and too soon. Each April and May the cadence of the morning hedgerow bird-chorus shifts; we are low on wood thrushes, or overwhelmed with bobolinks. In some years one can walk for miles through the woods without hearing a single white-throated sparrow's song, the grave gentle melody that only the year before seemed to emanate from every other clump of brush.

Waiting for thaw, we watch the weather in earnest; every evening on television I see the atmospheric goings-on from a satellite's point of view. I see a curve of grayish sphere with lighter markings; our slice of this planet against the black of space. Sometimes I catch a glimpse of the curled boot-shape of Cape Cod. "There's Cape Cod!" I say, overjoyed at a landmark found. I watch the clouds shift jerkily across the face of North America like smoke blown in a wind; but even the perspective of satellites, correlated by computers, transmitted through atmospheres, bounced across continents, and announced to all and sundry at six P.M. by a woman standing in front of a weather map with a pointer in her hand — can be wrong.

A warming trend is announced and reroutes southward in the night, leaving us with snow. A polar high comes and sits on us for eight days, eight days of gnawing cold and frozen maples and emptying woodsheds, and the woman points with aplomb to ninety-five degrees in Miami, a deluge in California. What we want here is a nice, fat, southern front to come drifting up for a few days; something to muffle the Arctic winds that barrel down on us around the lows; oh, bring

Pond in the Woods ⸱ *221*

us an easterly on padded paws, a balmy something from the Southwest! I watch the weather map like some people watch football: "Come on, Low! Go, High, go! GO!"

I often wonder if the miles of electronic circuitry, the mass of silicone chips, the hours spent by intelligent people in head-phones, all add up in some way to an ancient, well-buried neural center in a crow's flat skull. In March I watch both kinds of augury with equal faith.

Discoveries

Some of the changes in the woods are small, but their small-ness is deceptive. Put it this way; they can lead to the dis-covery of bigger things.

One day in early February the snow under the spruces and firs in the swamp looked as if it had been strewn with fine dark speckles. I was skiing and the sun was shining. The dark bits were sprinkled more thickly here and there, as if someone had come along in a serendipitous mood with a pepper grinder; nothing, I thought, that trees could make would be that regular or that small.

There were a lot more of these sprinkles around the dark melt-hole at the top of the beaver lodge in Carow Brook, the little tributary of the Tamarack. This time my skis were shed and I was face to face with the dark bits so that I noticed that the bits were moving. Each one was crawling through the interstices of the snow like a kid on a jungle gym. Once in a while a speck which I had my eye on would disappear, and I realized, with a sense of shock, that they were leaping.

They were springtails; the ones that are commonly known as snow fleas. They were slightly fuzzy and quite black, which meant that they were absorbing what sunlight there was and converting it to heat with fair efficiency. Their leaps were enormous in proportion to their minuscule size, and I wondered if the jabs of energy that they were releasing with each leap were warming them further. Leaps and blackness together were adapting them to life in the snow; these and other things, such as (according to one text) a unique oxygen metabolism that allows them to keep up their cold-blooded state in hot-blooded style. They were evidently feeding on something in the thin films of thawed water between snow crystals — what else would they be doing there with such acrobatic verve? — which meant that there was a lot of edible something in the snow which was subvisible to me, but of great interest to them.

It happened that these snow fleas were one of those easy-to-miss little silks in the raveling of the natural world. When one tugs on it, traces it along, keeping an eye out for the creatures themselves, and browsing through the library stacks with a mind open to interesting trivia, one can end up by winding off a whole wad of wonderful stuff.

Consider this: the earliest fossil insect that anyone has yet discovered is an odd-looking creature called *Rhyniella praecursor*. She was a few millimeters long and had stubby segmented legs and sucking mouthparts, and she lived some 370 million years ago in a forest that was two feet high. That was the height of the tallest land plants which grew anywhere in those days. The plants in that forest were leafless and skimpily branched and had creeping stems; they were not much more than seaweeds with just enough vascular starch in them to struggle up two feet closer to the sun.

Collecting a realistic picture of a past landscape and past events from the evidence of fossils is a process very much like the puzzle-piecing which an archaeologist does when he wants to discover the shape of some whole jar from a few random shards. (Is this fragment a handle? Or a festoon? Is it a pitcher's lip, a bit off a pedestal, a decorative animal's ear? What did it hold, this jar?) Even after the form has been determined from the fragments there is always some doubt as to what it signifies. Was this jar (creature, plant stem) the product of a common artisan, one of many from the evolutionary main-stream? Or was it a dead-end experiment, a mutant, misfired goods; the make of an eccentric, a genius, or a child? Most of the time it's hard to tell. But in the case of *Rhyniella prae-cursor*, we know.

Rhyniella p. is an easily recognizable springtail. If someone found her alive in the woods today (any woods, anywhere), they wouldn't think her unusual at all, and would simply mark her down as a newly discovered species; one among many. There are more than 3500 known species of springtail around nowadays each of which inhabits its own particular niche; all of them are variations on *Rhyniella*'s theme. Some springtails specialize in caves, some live in flowerpots, others skitter on the surfaces of puddles or saltwater tidepools or water droplets; one rotund sort lives only on lakes that are infested with duck-weed, another kind inhabits the permanent ice fields of glaciers where all it finds to eat is windblown pine-pollen. Some people believe that there are more springtails alive on this planet right now than all other animals put together; other people think that this dubious honor belongs to the copepods. At any rate the springtails, from high Arctic to hot tropics, are successful here, now.

What else is evolution but the piecing together of form from scattered, found fragments? A mutation is nothing but a change in some genetic bit, and the struggle to survive in myriad chancy environments selects those individuals, those finished forms, which are the best suited for the time and place. Some designs — only the most simple, adaptive, and elegant — with-stand the constant pressure to change without changing. These designs are, they must be, as near to perfection as nature will allow anything to come.

Springtails seem to possess such a design. They are all less than a centimeter in length, and they look like tiny segmented jars with the narrow end going along in front. They have six stumpy legs and anywhere from zero to eight simple eyes, no wings, and a spring. The spring is held against their bellies with a clasp and when the clasp is released the spring jumps out like one of those flick-knives which street gangs use, and then the springtail disappears. She hasn't disappeared at all but the leap is so immense in relation to the leaper that it looks as though she has. It is a useful illusion. Springtails also have retractable tubes called collophores on their abdomens, which can be used like an elephant's trunk to suck up water or to dab the springtail clean. Some species also secrete an adhesive stuff with their collophores in order to stick themselves to an interesting surface. Some have mouths made for chewing and others have mouths made for sucking, depending on what their business is. Their businesses vary.

After the first long thaws I went back to the Pond in the Woods. The whole forest there seemed suddenly sentient; there was a high creaking and rustling among the branches, and whole trees were waving back and forth as if they meant to pull up their roots and be off. I heard the "conkereeee!" of a redwing staking a claim along the pond shore. Other birds were back; I counted sixteen flickers foraging on the open ground, and a junco slipped between the branches of a fir, in the surreptitious way of migrants; it was as if he were a counterspy in dark sneak-thief clothing, moving quickly from cover to cover, all his movements expressing hurry and hunger. On the slope of hardwoods above the pond the snow had already melted away, leaving matted dark leaves with sticks poking up, and the whole ground had a wet crushed look as if it had been underwater, pressed down by snow-weight into a single sodden leaf-and-twig fabric. Only the week before, the snow had been pristine and omniscient, but now what was left of it lay in sullen gray heaps in the hollows and in the shadowed places under the firs.

I saw from a distance the flat white of the pond, still iced in. When I came close to it I heard a wonderful sound, a soft, wettish rustling, as if millions of tiny bubbles were rushing to the surface. The ice had melted out an inch or two from the shore, and its greenish bulk was carved back in curves and rounds like the interior of a Swiss cheese. The shoreline mud had been warming in the strong sun, and had melted the ice over itself. The sweet birch and the other brush by the shore had sleeves of clear water around their light-absorbing stems. Every spruce needle and twig and birch seed that had fallen or been blown onto the ice had warmed enough in the last three full days of sun to melt themselves down so that the whole surface of the ice was pitted with tiny twists and oblongs, and the edge of the ice and the inch-wide moat of melted water and the whole shore itself were alive.

There were millions and millions of springtails there, like a vast strewing of live poppyseeds seething over the water and earth and ice. This narrow shoreline was the warmest and wettest place anywhere around and was full of flotsam; the springtails were like chomping snippets of charcoal-gray felt or velvet; they crawled, leaped, crawled again. Farther on I found more of these mass invasions clustering around rivulets, floating in swarms over melt-puddles. Their coming out in such abandon let me know that their home in the soil was suddenly changed, and that the melting-freezing world was ripe for snowfleas and they would wait no longer to be Out! And I know now that they were the sign of other less visible blooms, less obvious jubilations, beneath the glistening mat of last year's leaves.

I have to struggle with dizziness to enter that world. Behind the lens of my microscope, I can shrink suddenly into it like an Alice who has obediently swallowed her potion. But entering the soil isn't just a struggle against the barriers of size; it is more like Alice's journey through the looking-glass into an opposite world where large becomes small, old is made into new, and where familiar things become, through a teeming of life, no things at all. The work of soil is decay. Progress is made there only by going backward.

The old fallen leaves are the interface of this other dimension as though they were the rough, glistening surface of a sea.

Soil is layered like the sea is, with heights and depths. Burrowing groundhogs sound down to hardpan like whales, and shrews and moles tunnel through like porpoises; billions of springtails whisk by like schools of herring. Shifting currents of tree feeder-roots interweave in the softening leaves of the year-before-last, and vortexes of taproots dive to bedrock. There are water animals there, scaled down to live in the microponds that lie between the raised veins of leaf fragments, and to swim in the streams which run between veins of quartz; minute shrimplike crustaceans, miniature, rotifers spinning away like jeweled food processors turned inside out; and nematodes curling like pale whips. Tinier still, the paddling protozoans and colorless single-celled algae, cousins of green pond scums and giant sea kelps, but algae that need no chlorophyll to make a living in their lightless world. Almost all of these soil creatures breathe oxygen in and carbon dioxide out just as we do, and through simple osmosis, the drift of gases in and out, the whole bulk of air in the porous, lunglike, top six inches of soil is renewed every hour like a breath.

Every organic crumb and fleck of mineral in the soil is an absorptive cell, an island in the soil-sea, well forested with fungal nets and with colonies of living things. A single ounce of soil may have a collective surface area of as much as six *acres*, and every square millimeter of this is crowded with some life form or other, busy multiplying, growing, dying, eating or being eaten. A teaspoonful of soil may hold 200,000 algae and fungi, five billion bacteria, and a million zipping protozoans that graze on them. There may be more than a hundred thousand springtails alone in a single cubic yard of woodland soil. If one digs down through that soil, the springtail species one can find there become smaller, shorter-legged, each with smaller collophores and shorter springs until, sometimes, six feet down, one can find only a tiny, white, blind springtail with no spring at all; a creature only just barely higher on the evolutionary ladder, and little different in function, than the Worm from which all insects ascended a long time ago.

According to one trustworthy source, all the trillions of soil-dwellers which inhabit each single acre of ground expend the amount of energy every year that would be roughly equal to the energy spent by hundreds of human beings. The soil-dwellers do their work in a city of immense age and complexity, and near-total darkness. The soil deprocesses all that falls to it: feathers and leaves, whole trees and deer, the sulfates and nitrates in the rain; boiling it all at last into a chemical broth which the trees can bring into their roots, and which can be translated into swarms of insects, and the creation of new leaves, grass, wood.

The soil is at its most active in the warmth and wet of early spring, and the ripe smell that the forest gives off after a rain then is the smell of earth-alchemy performed. The snow fleas are the soil's earliest spring ambassadors to the upper world, and I sometimes wonder what they make of the light and space here when they come up to discover it.

Hidden Waters

One morning at the end of the third week in March it began to rain, and when it did the maple sap began to run in our woods. As I drove along the hill road to home, there was a mist rising everywhere as if the ground were the bowl of a volcano; serrated ranks of spruce and fir rose through the streaming vapor like jagged teeth, rooted in ridges that curved like the jawbones of gigantic animals. I felt suddenly as if I would, any minute, be swallowed up by this thawing landscape, gulped in with no more eulogy than a steamy burp issuing between two ranks of champing spruce. Everything in and under the snow was suddenly awash, and as suddenly exposed to the sharp frosts that were still coming: what were the seeds, roots, meadow voles, doing now?

It rained for most of the afternoon and the mountains were sealed away behind a curtain that was the color of wet plastic. In the woods the sap tanks were filling steadily; next morning we would boil in our first syrup of the season. During the middle of the afternoon I put on my yellow coveralls and armed myself with shears and a pole-saw and went out to prune my apple trees, my rite of March; clipping dead twigs, disentangling conflicting limbs, and lopping skyward tendencies. I am a small woman and I can't pick apples too high in the air.

All afternoon I was aware of what was going on down in the sugar woods, and even involved as I was with decisions among the apple twigs, I kept my eye on the two small maples behind the house. They didn't seem to be doing anything at all; a hoax. If I were a maple in the spring rain, I would be swollen with juice, red in the face, my heartbeat tripled; I would be howling and dancing, threshing my arms against the sky! But trees are introverts. Everything that goes on there goes on *inside* until they are ready for their final statement of faith, for which we have to wait another month or two. Then they will let loose their flowers, a mist of sexually loaded parachutes dangling from little silks; and finally their leaves. Trees are like anything else — if one doesn't need to know anything about their insides, one can go on thinking that they don't have any. Ignorance can be bliss.

The Indians of the eastern woods were the first people to make maple sugar. It isn't difficult to see how they got the idea; in the first thaws every broken maple twig end and every porcupine-chewed patch of bark bleeds sap. Some of this sap dribbles down the trunk of the tree and is distilled by the sun into golden sugar drops; in March and April I have harvested these candies myself, picking them from the bark with heavy competition from a pair of overcharged, newly wakened chipmunks. The Indians — Pennacooks, Laurentians, Mahicans, Malecites — had their spring groves all over the Northeast and into Canada: they slashed the tree bark with tomahawks and boiled their sugar by dropping hot stones into birchbark troughs and hollowed tree trunks full of sap. It was a laborious way to boil anything, but the only way to boil in flammable pots. Then as now it took about thirty-two gallons of sap to make eight pounds of sugar. With the river ice going and the snow melting fast the men were off fishing, after fat hare, the first geese; and sugaring was women's work. It is still a common thing here for women to do the boiling, to keep all the float-valves set just so on the big steel evaporating rigs, and to keep the filters rinsed, and the hot syrup graded and canned.

I don't make my syrup alone. I've gone into partnership now with a friend. He cuts the wood and keeps the fire going and I help with the boiling where I can, and I make myself useful by climbing up on the woodpile and throwing down wood. In the evening I like to go out and sit on the stump of a beech tree that I cut many winters ago, to watch the towering geyser of sparks which explodes from the top of the smokestack when he shakes the fire. Sometimes I make fresh doughnuts to dip in hot cups of syrup, and I make coffee from boiling sap so that the brew has the gritty taste of the woods still in it.

I am always awed and stirred by these trees, perhaps because they seem so unmoved even in the midst of their most violent season. We don't collect our sap in pails; we collect it the modern way by more or less letting it collect itself. The sap flows downhill from the tapholes through a plumbing system made of plastic tubing. The tubes are hitched together with clamps and widgets like a giant set of Tinkertoys. The tubes run into small black pipes and the small pipes run into bigger pipes. A final two-inch pipe lets the whole thirty acres' worth of maples run into the holding tanks, from which the evaporator draws its slow supply. In the days when we hung pails in the woods a good run was signaled by the muffled plinks of dripping sap, which was a gentle enough sound, though the trees could still fill their attendant pails twice in one day if they felt like it. The pipeline system is more brutal. I have seen our two-inch pipe gushing sap as though it were a fire-hose. I have watched the holding tanks filling up at a brisk 300 gallons an hour. And all the while the trees stand; the trees stand on their slope, mute and unbudged. What — I have wondered this more than once in March and April, when my life is run according to the maples' fickle moods — what is *going on?*

In my last year at college I took an elective course at the Proctor Maple Research Lab. The work done there with maple trees is a kind of grassroots project, sponsored by the university and staffed by inspired people who do their science with their boots on. One year there they cut an entire maple, which weighed several tons, and hoisted the top part over the stump and monitored both the branch and root systems for months, only to discover that, no, the sap does not come up from the roots in the spring. Old Wives' Tale No. 1 debunked: what then? They discovered that some trees have sweeter sap than others by a factor of many hundred percent. They stuck hypodermics into baby maples and discovered that sweet trees are sweet from birth; that productivity varies in maples as it does in cows, in direct proportion to the quality of their parentage and the quality of their feed — a maple's feed being plentiful sunlight and dry sloped ground. They put sap-drip measurers and pressure cuffs and thermometers in and on their trees, and had a roomful of dials and recording needles to monitor the condition of their patients. They made detailed charts. They made maple syrup. They boiled syrup with oil, gas, and woodchips. They boiled syrup in experimental evaporators which looked like the rear ends of moonrockets. After a few years some patterns began to emerge from all of this, a body of knowledge which like all such bodies raised more questions than it answered.

For sap to run at all there has to be a thaw, with no wind to chill the twigs. For the sap to run well it has to have been below freezing for at least forty-eight hours before the thaw began. The sap run is a live process; if the thin films and spokes of living tissue in the tree are killed, no sap runs at all.

The fact that such a tiny rise in temperature can bring about such a huge response means that there must be some live "trigger" involved anyhow; an enzyme that kicks suddenly into play, completes its work, retires. What enzyme? What work? No one is sure.

The sap runs from the tapholes because the tree pushes it out; this is the unexpected thing. During a thaw the whole tree expands under the pressure of its sap. The tree in winter is a closed hydraulic system and during a sap run it can build internal pressures of up to twenty-four pounds per square inch. After a while — even if it stays warm, or instantly if the temperature should drop below freezing again — the pressures reverse and become negative. Given the chance then, the trees might reabsorb all of the sap that they pushed out hours before.

If the weather is right the sap will run from the trees any time for six weeks or so after the leaves have fallen — sometime in November — until the new leaves arrive. During winter warm spells the tree are grudging with their sap as if they were half asleep. After mid-March here the trees are at their touchiest and most responsive; if the weather cooperates then the trees *push*. What we wait for is classic sugaring weather — a span of icy nights and soft, clear, windless days. But weather can surprise everyone. It is as though the winter, being as strong as it is, omniscient, the ruler here, has entered a pitched battle with the forces that would have it go, go; and the trees and ourselves are caught in the crossfire.

In the first spring that I sugared here we had a monster run; there was a sleeting blizzard which lasted for three days, it was 33°F, and the trees were plastered with slush as though they were wearing bulky gray socks. The sap gushed, steadily, all that time. We boiled around the clock for three days and the sap tanks overflowed just the same. Two friends and I took turns firing, boiling, and dozing off. When we fed the fire we had to wear an extra pair of wool pants to protect our thighs from the heat, and asbestos gloves layered with silver duct-tape, and we had a seven-foot-long section of aluminum pipe to shake the fire down. Even protected as we were, we had scorch marks along our arms where our shirt cuffs had fallen open, and around our wrists where the gloves had slipped. By the third day we all felt as though we were locked in a losing war with the fires of the underworld. We took turns walking the three-quarters of a mile up to the barn to feed the sheep. I remember going down into the woods again through the timeless dusk of that blizzard, coming back to the sugarhouse, which was rumbling and steaming, its smokestack shooting columns of sparks that flew up like stars, and thinking that this was a forge built for dwarves. We looked like dwarves; swarthy and thick. What were the dwarves doing? Refining gold . . . ? Of course. Yes.

A run like that happens only two or three times in the career of any one sugarmaker, which is just as well. No one can predict it, though; so lay in a spare store of firewood, buy extra syrup drums; no one knows how the trees work. But we do know that after every run the bark of the trees has gained in water content and the wood has lost, and the frost resistance that was built up so carefully in the fall has been gently eroded; all the water columns in the sapwood have to be set in place again, ready for the leaves.

Toward the end of April the sap runs get scanty again as though the maples were moving on to other things. The syrup that we make then is dark and more and more heavily flavored, and finally it begins to smell and taste bad. The chemistry of the tree has suddenly changed; from one hour to the next we smell the change. The last rank syrup is shipped away for curing tobacco, and we pull our taps and wash the tubing and the tanks and the evaporator, and call it a year. There are spring beauties blooming then on the high ground under the trees, but the trees don't look any different than they did before. Except that if one looks closely at their buds one can see pale curves where the bud-scales once overlapped, and have, just, pulled apart.

Thaw Water

The water let loose by the thaws is a power in itself; five to six months of rainfall lies captive in the snow. Though the first warm spells release some surface trickles, the snowpack and the soil beneath it simply soak up most of this. We have to wait until April for the real thing; the stretch of warm weather that will take away the snow.

The thaw water moves things around; mineral grits, soluble chemicals, countless small lives, taking them from hills to lakes, and floodplains, deltas, oceans. It has, in the past here, when it was the melt of glaciers which were a mile or more thick and thousands of miles in length and breadth, transformed the landscape beyond recognition. This is what goes on here still, in April, though on a modest scale. The movement is here. This is what I want to watch.

Meanwhile, the thawing snow wrecks my fences, maims the young apple trees, gullies the woods road, and turns the soil of the fields into a quivering jelly. They call thaw time "mud season" here. In the days when everyone traveled by horse and cart or sleigh, mud season was the only time except for mid-blizzard when no one could go anywhere. Even now when the town trucks are good about hauling gravel to fill in washouts and collapsed culverts, one is likely to come around a corner on any hill road and sink without warning into a truck-swallowing morass.

Last year someone with a good nose for black comedy put up a sign on the brow of the hill: "SiMULATed MOON SURFACe NeXT 2 MiLeS," is said. After a week the sign disappeared; the hard-working drivers of the town trucks took umbrage, no doubt, and tore the thing down. Another sign promptly appeared in its place: "NO FISHiNG iN POT-HOLeS," it said. It's April. Winter's last laugh. Haul on your boots; the world is new.

There were a few days of hard frost at the very beginning of the month and then it began to thaw and rain, hard. Masses of tea-colored water roared down the ditches, which were still full of snow, and joined the swelling of the valley river. On the second day of rain I went and stood on a railroad bridge over the river and watched. The ice cracked under me with a noise like gunfire and broken floes shifted nervously in the current. Jagged cakes of ice battered and twisted against one another and piled up, grinding, like animals in rut, and slipped loose and tilted off downriver to wedge against banks, rocks, in narrows. The floodwater spread out and claimed the rich bottomland where Benny's cows graze in July, and gulped a few thousand tons of cornfield soil, and rolled grumbling boulders downstream a bit; but did not, as far as anyone knows, damage its own trout.

When I went out to walk my fences in the rain a week later, I thought about those trout. I like fishing in that river. I like letting the line move out and I like to watch the fly settle just so in a riffle and drift down over a rise. I don't fish very well. But when I manage to make one single cast the way I want to, it has all the emotional punch of having made someone cry; of having gotten through; of being a dancer poised on one toe, the rest of one's body flung up and out, the balance momentary only, impossible to maintain, the fall just caught by a leap; the moment when the audience says, "Ahhhh . . . !" Sometimes the trout leaps, says his last "Ahhhh . . . !" and swallows the fly. My hands are full of shudders. The line slices the water like a knife; I have gotten through.

Trout season opens on the second Saturday in April. The date is engraved on my year, replete with the glows and hopes of an Opening Night.

It was the fifth of April when I went out in the rain to look over my fences. The world was awash; there had been no sun for two weeks. Twenty feet from the door there was a

Pond in the Woods ⸱ 235

woodcock, a plump long-beaked little silhouette, like a fat man hurrying with a stick. There were other signs, too, of gentle things; the narcissus were poking up from the corn-snow and pine needles, still yellow at their tips; and the pines were full of robins who clucked and tchicked like small nervous hens. They flew from one hedgerow to another in fusillades of rust and dark gray.

The snow was nearly gone and the grass hadn't begun to grow yet at all, so that the turf was an indeterminate color like a soggy abused carpet, and thick with accumulated junk: blobs of sheep dung, thistle clumps like bristly starfish, sticks, a wad of wool. I kept my head down against the rain and began my fence walk past the barn and down the pasture road. The fences looked shoved and wobbled everywhere as if a flood had been through. In the lower pasture the welded wire was accordioned down on itself, and no strength that I could muster could budge the crushed folds upward again more than an inch or two. Branches an inch and a half thick had been torn off of the bottoms of the firs, when the snow that had packed in around them in midwinter had heavied and sunk with the thaw.

Squelching through the mud and water of the pasture road, looking sideways at the fence, I was busy calculating numbers of reels of new wire, pounds of fence staples, quarts of paint for the gates; and then, looking down, I noticed the water at my feet, running, making noise, full of glimpses of reflected twigs and sky. Today, in the rain, I heard blackbirds singing in the village. Hup, whoa! Think of this: things are on the move.

This was collected water going out of old snow, and rainy sky, and sodden ground. Through one route or another it was on its way down the woods to the ravine and the Tamarack, and down to the Wild Branch; and then thundering, white, roiling with accumulated purpose, with a watery mob psychology, with a higher cause than one could ever deduce from the gentle tricklings — on up to Lake Champlain and out finally to the sea.

Starting here. But as I thought of that flow I felt at the same time a reverse flow, a surge, coming back.

Two weeks before I had been down at the lake for another bout of playing at Peeping Tom with the winter wildfowl, and I had noticed the redwinged blackbirds most of all. They were hard to miss. There were tens of thousands of them in the corn stubbles mixed in with the ducks and crows. They didn't act like any birds that I had ever seen before. Near the cornfields were roads, their edges heaped with fine gravels from winter sanding. These road edges were solidly black with scurrying redwings, all running and pecking shoulder to shoulder, busily packing in grit to grind the stubble trash in their crops. They moved fast, rising and falling like swarms of flies. They went up in a rattling crowd every time a car passed and then settled again in a black glitter over the stubble or the grit. Everywhere through the valley they were moving in flocks that billowed and changed shape like fantastic Chinese kites: *hurrying.* A week ago there were a few of them, a dozen perhaps, perched like fat dark leaves in the big elm across from Benny's farm. Today I heard one singing in the village. Soon one will trickle up here to buzz and trill in the elm by my pond. Another will settle in the maple at the end of the north hedgerow. The birds are coming back — a melt-river in reverse.

Caught in conflicting flows, out on the tipmost tentacles of both, I looked at the rivulets at my feet again and then squatted down and watched. Something familar there had caught my eye. A trickle wound itself across the humped gravel of the road, branched, diverged, joined again, spread out again toward the bordering ditch. In each winding trickle bits of stuff moved. Fine pale silts, flecks of sparkling mica, tiny puffs of dark organic matter. Where the trickle was strongest a pebble rolled, stopped, rolled again. It was a doll's-house melt-river. Thaw water in miniature. The tiniest fragments raced along in the flow but where the current curved, flowing more slowly on its outmost flank, the silts settled in a pale band like the curve of a new moon. There it was again, and there. And there. Pickup, flow, deposition. I remembered then where I'd seen all that before.

I saw that in Svalbard, when I was standing on a glacier there and looking down.

I went to Svalbard with my husband, whose family came from Norway, so that he grew up with these mysterious northern islands looking over his shoulder. He had promised himself as a child that he would get there when he had the chance. So one midsummer when we had the chance, we went. Spitzbergen is the largest island in the archipelago of Svalbard, and Svalbard is almost as far north of Norway's North Cape as the North Cape is from Denmark. In summertime the northernmost sweep of the Gulf Stream pushes the polar pack ice away from the west coast of these islands until, if wind and current are with you, you can go within ten degrees of the North Pole by boat: nearly ten degrees farther north than Point Barrow, Alaska. Most of Svalbard is under a permanent ice cap. Little glaciers sit in their cirques in the mountains, and in the valleys there are big serious ones fed by the central ice, all busily calving icebergs into the water. In the fjords there were icebergs the color of blue sea-glass, and brash ice that rattled against the hull of our boat. The boat that we were traveling on was combination ferry and freighter, and in one place where it stopped to unload cargo for a Norwegian mining town there was a glacier snout clearly visible up the valley. I went up there, having always wondered what a glacier was really like.

The ice snout, hundreds of feet high, was fronted by a silty stony moraine which was like a mud-pie slapped together by the Frost Giants at the dawn of the world. Slick curves of melting ice shed wads of chewed and predigested landscape,

SEQUOIA

Svalbard: then

Metasequoia

GINKGO

MAPLE

MAGNOLIA

SVALBARD POPPY

and now

BIRCH

and among the debris were bits of fossil-bearing rock. Once I had discovered this I clambered through the glutinous mountain bent on treasures. It reminded me more than anything else of picking through the bellies of those bobcats; looking for legible signs in a sticky chaos.

The only plant that grew in the moraine was a tiny white poppy with fuzzy leaves. According to my wildflower book this poppy grows only in Svalbard, and seems to have made a specialty of moraines. I found it growing there among the fossils; perhaps making its new life from their flaking carbon, like a fresh tiny light.

As for the fossils themselves: I found lumps of pale rock which were imprinted with the overlapping patterns of broad leaves, like the pattern on a forest floor at home in October, after the leaf fall and a softening rain. Other flakes held long wide forms like the leaves of giant grass. Some were the stems (my graduate course in paleobotany was coming back to me) of giant horsetails, and the straplike leaves of primitive conifers. Many rocks held what looked like the impressions of fir twigs complete with needles; twigs of *Metasequoia*, the dawn redwood. The dawn redwood is a huge beauty of a tree that was thought to be extinct until a handful of them was found holed up in a few acres of mountain forest on mainland China; their last hideout from the ice ages, the worst winters of them all.

I had no idea whether I was looking at the records of one woods or millennia's worth of woods; these fossils were clippings and shards of a huge, rich, partly deciduous dawn redwood forest that once grew in unbroken cover over Arctic Europe, Siberia, Alaska, Arctic Canada, and Greenland, in a long beatific warm spell before the beginning of this present ice age. The ice age still holds Svalbard, and firmly, and this particular glacier was busy enough scrunching the ordered rock; a gargantuan bulldozer amok in the old forests' fossil library. The trees themselves have moved on. No plant taller than a cotton-grass grows anywhere on Svalbard now; there is only tundra there, and even that is scanty. The old forest has moved away. Maples, lindens, redwoods, magnolias.

Winter has its own convoluted history. With my pockets full of the evidence — no, the *facts* — of the immensity of time, the durability of life, the fragility of species, it was only I that was reduced to a shard.

I found all that I could carry. I sat on a boulder then and looked down. The moraine was full of clunks and rumbles as the streams of meltwater tore it away; below me a river stretched down the three miles of valley to the fjord where the boat sat like an abandoned toy. It was a "braided river," a half-dozen streams converging and separating again, and it made a noise like the rumble of a loom. The water was milky with silts. Where a stream curved and its water slowed there were pale curves of gravel bars; all the silts and sands were being swept out to the fjord, where they were piling up, summer after brief summer. The moraine was being sorted, laid down in layers by faster and slower meltwater, year after year; the fjord was filling its belly with silt and sand layers; a valley was being woven. A flat-bottomed valley with gently mounded walls. This, I thought to myself, is Benny's corn-field ten thousand years ago. The Connecticut valley. Almost any river valley in northern Europe or in the northern two-thirds of North America that you could care to mention. The valleys of half of the northern hemisphere. Some of the other half are still full of ice.

In April, in the pasture road, the work of meltwater weaving went on, in minuscule, under my feet.

By the time I had walked all the fences it was cold again, and after dark it began to snow. In the evening I sat by the fire winding a new spool of monofilament line onto my spinning reel and browsing through fishing catalogues; my downfall, my April indulgence.

When I had dogeared the catalogues I turned on the outside lights and turned off the inside ones so that I could enjoy the snow. The maples by the house were freshly furred with it, and millions of tiny flakes billowed against the windows, now swirling up, now pressed down as if under a weight, each one a separate point of light or a streak like a falling star so that it was more motion than form that was lit up. It was like being in the belly of a wave, below waterline in a surf traced by points of foam. Perhaps a trout sees a rapids like this, points of dancing foam, while he holds in an eddy, waiting.

By next morning the fields were padded with six inches of new snow but the wet spots were open; patterns of dark ground in which the crowd of robins was eking a living. They hopped in these smatters of open earth, heads up, attentive, then they would suddenly hop twice, bend and poke and drag a worm from the blackish grass. On my way to town to buy fencewire and a fishing license I saw two robins dead in the road, smudged packets of russet and black; this is cruel weather. Cruel.

On the way home I drove out and stopped at the bottom of one of Benny's fields where the river bends under a huge willow. The river was running around the corner there like a black muscle. The current barely rucked over the gravel bar where I have waded in the late spring and summer when the water is low, casting to both sides. Once in May when I was fishing there something happened which was very strange. There was a rain of black ants, winged ants. They fell in pairs, locked in sexual curls, their wings like slivers of silver. Knots of these hopelessly coupled insects were floating along by the dozen. The water boiled with rising fish. Nothing I could offer them worked. I panicked and cast wildly everywhere and as a result I lost my favorite handmade mosquito, fatally hooked among the willow twigs. I tried casting fake black ants; I was outclassed and outnumbered.

Trout belong to meltwater; they belong there, and nowhere else, unless you count fish farms. You can tell fish-farm trout because their fins are worn to nubbins and rags; trout aren't made for that life. They are quick, voracious, and wild, and they like water that dances downstream.

My father, who gave me the love of all things fishing, had a great respect for the unknowableness of trout. Salmon are the grand cousin of trout; their unknowableness raised to the highest possible power. Casting a fly-line on a river for either one of them is a tender and violent art, not to be confused too much with a science. You can get caught up in the technology of the thing, like anything else; the lures, leaders, reels and so on; or you can know the river, and learn to judge water as you would music; but a great deal is always left up to the will of the fish, who is as fickle as the water he lives in. A friend of my father's once caught a record salmon on the totally wrong kind of fly, which he had knotted to the end of a line in the wrong way and had dropped in the most un-salmonish part of the river to give his line weight while he rolled new backing onto his reel. When he had nearly reeled the line in, the salmon took it all out again and fought him hard for more than an hour, over half a mile of river. My father's friend didn't have his waders on and had left his net in his boat. He landed the fish alone by battling it into a shallow gravely pool and hauling it onto land, one hand meshed deep in the salmon's gills.

The lifestyles of these fish are as changeable as rivers. Salmon trapped by geological accident can live and breed landlocked for hundreds or even thousands of years. Some rainbow trout go to sea, salmonlike, to feed and grow; and come back to their native rivers to spawn, at which point they are called steelheads. The rivers they come home to may have rainbows in them which never move more than 300 yards from the gravel beds they were spawned in. Evidence of genetic, heritable differences between the seagoing steelhead and the provincial rainbow are very small, if they exist at all. The size that trout and salmon grow to seems to be limited only by the amount of available food in their river, or ocean, or lake. When enough time has elapsed, they become sexually mature, no matter what size they are. In the Tamarack a six-inch brookie is a big fish, certainly a grandfather, black as your hat and as feisty on the end of a line as only a born native of a mountain stream could be. I have a gray gnat on a hook the size of an eyelash for fishing the Tamarack.

Trout are aggresive, they hold territories, and eat anything they can find: caddis larvae, stonefly larvae, adults of both, nematodes, gnats, floating anything, goodies flushed down the tributaries in a thaw or a flood. Fed well, they grow fast. There is a classic study of trout "production" in the Horokiwi stream in New Zealand which came to the conclusion that more than 500 pounds of trout grew there per acre of water per year. But hear this, ye doubters of fishermen's wisdom: in order to grow like that the trout had to be eating more than seventeen times the tonnage of insects and other invertebrates that the river produced. Seventeen times. In other words, no one knows exactly what they *were* eating. This same discrepancy between trout growth and apparent trout food supply has been found in other places, too. It is a phenomenon known as Allen's Paradox. It is unsolved, as yet. Which goes to show that the unknowableness of trout in particular and fast-running rivers in general is more than just a fishermen's mystique.

No one is sure, either, how salmon and steelheads navigate. Do they use the stars, the arc of the sun, fields of gravity, a nose capable of the finest chemical analyses? Steelheads have traced their way back to their spawning rivers even when they have been blinded and have no sense of smell at all. Some things about these fish are certain, though: they are thaw-water fish, breeding in the highest rockiest streams full of clear water and tumbled-in oxygen; over millennia they have followed the glacier melt deep into the centers of once-glaciated continents, claiming the new rivers of the hemisphere. To breed they must have gravel beds, gravel that has been conveniently ground up for them in the craw of glacial ice.

When a river gets too muddy-bottomed or slow-moving, bass are there. At the ends of old rivers, among marsh grasses and warm rich water, there are pike. When a river gets too civilized — warmed too much because of cut forest cover, its gravels silted over by runoff from plowed ground, its chemistry overenriched by sewage — it is the trout which are flushed away.

Trout are a sign of raw original health in a river, like canaries singing in a mineshaft.

Requiem

On the twenty-fifth of April, when I came up out of the woods at ten in the evening, I could hear the news. We had been boiling dark syrup all day — the last boil of the year — and as I walked up under the solitary maple on the brow of the hill there was a trembling in the air, a nasal rattling; the ice was gone. The farm pond was open, and its opening was audible; not as the river was, which had boomed and thundered its release, but in the rough chorus of woodfrogs.

I am fond of frogs. They are easily caught and easily kept; easily caught in old pickle jars and easily kept in old pickle jars. I have watched frog spawn hatching in jars on the kitchen counter, a schoolroom windowsill, my own desk. Frogs are the golden geese of basic biology; every schoolchild and every hopeful pre-med student takes at least one of them apart, bit by slim pickled bit, learning the names of each carefully tweezed-up piece as if a frog were the map of a country no one would ever visit, a country fallen like the language of Latin into a deserved disuse. I find that this attitude smacks of egocentric complacency. Of disrespect for frogs, mostly.

There isn't a better signal of winter's end than the woodfrog's song. You can hear it rattling away from drainage

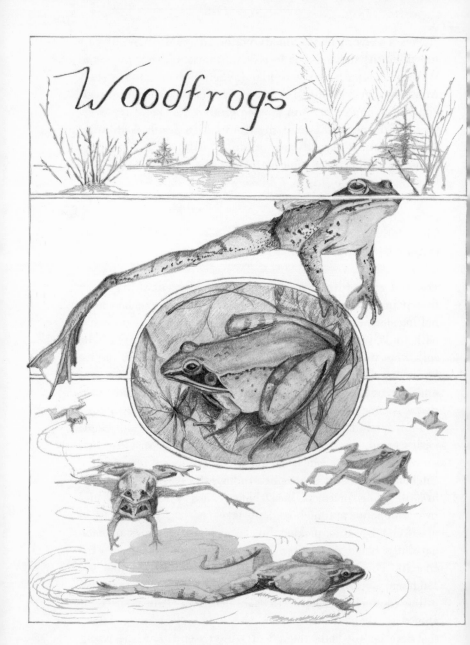

Woodfrogs

ditches and farm ponds and any leafy depression filled with snowmelt through most of Alaska, and Canada, and down into Wyoming, Kansas, New England, and the hills of Georgia. Another frog species, which is nearly identical in appearance and habits, ranges through most of the north temperate territory of Europe. While most frogs are content to be easygoing equatorial folk, woodfrogs practice a kind of evolutionary brinkmanship up into the edge of the high Arctic. Part of the way they manage this is to make an early start on the year.

They come in an array of colors; some are rosy red, or russet, there are local varieties of browns, olives, and grays. They have an opaline iridescence to their skin and raised ridges like piping down their backs. There is a sharp brown robber's mask stretching from their eardrums through their eyes and ending in narrow straps over each nostril. All woodfrog hind legs are long; our local frogs have legs two and a half times the length of their bodies. Woodfrogs are slim, alert, built for speed — except for the females, who are filled with eggs when they emerge in the spring, like rosy balloons.

The woodfrogs have a few days of wild debauch — explosive breeding, the textbooks call it, as if it were something dangerous — just as the ice melts off their spawning ponds. Otherwise they live in the woods, and winter there, under logs, stumps, stones. In the last big thaw the woodfrogs back up out of the leaf mold, blinking the old snow out of their golden eyes, having solved the problem of greatest importance to amphibians in cold climates everywhere with greater success than any amphibian anywhere; which is — finding a place to hibernate in that isn't going to freeze. Some hibernacula probably do freeze. Some woodfrogs don't make it. Not enough to make a big difference, though.

Their breeding is explosive because it happens all at once.

The night after they began singing it rained, and I went out with a slicker and flashlight to watch the frogs move. Across the slope of the field there were hundreds of them hopping and stopping like earth-clods tossed up. They know their way.

There has been a lot of research done to try to discover the mechanics of the frog homing instinct. Some of the experiments involved frogs wearing leaden hats; apparently frogs navigate by the stars, using a kind of third eye in the top of their skull. I could see no stars at all, but the frogs looked as though they knew where they were off to. They have their own home territories in the woods, and they go to the same ponds to breed every year. Moved far from their homes, most frogs will still hop off on the correct pondward compass course — most of the time. The system is imperfect, though. Under the most rigorous of test conditions and even without the disorienting leaden hats, frog experiments agree that there are always a few frogs who head off dead wrong. These are planned goof-ups, no doubt; how else would new puddles be pioneered except by goof-ups? Even Christopher Columbus had something other than North America in mind when he left Spain and sailed west in 1492. It seems to be in the scheme of things, here under the yaw of the stars, that something has to be left to chance.

The singing of woodfrogs isn't fancy. From across the field the collective chorus sounded like pebbles clattering in a pail, or a lot of duck quacks tuned low; not melodious. It doesn't travel well like the high sleighbelling of the peepers, the twang-plunking of green frogs, or the commanding, solitary summer call of a toad.

The next morning I lay on my belly in the grass above the pond and watched. The grunting-rattling was in full roar, but it was a difficult thing to catch a frog in the act, throat-sac inflated: "Quank!" Hundreds of male frogs were floating there, hind legs splayed, just their gold eyes and nostrils poked above the water, forelegs hanging.

Female frogs are attracted only by the songs of their own kind of males. Singing *en masse* gives the calling a choral authority, and attracts more females to the pond in question. But even within one species the songs vary a lot from place to place. There are local dialects; the northern dryness, the western slang, that old southern cornpone, even among frogs. A female cricket frog from New Jersey isn't interested in the song of a male cricket frog from South Dakota. Not my type, she thinks. A furriner, not one of the folks. The regional tuning has to be there in the ear of the listener as well as the throat of the singer, since many of the females in question can't have heard the singing before. It is a question of gentle genetic drift here — colors, songs — countless variations on a woodfrog theme.

Whatever the forces are for local change, frogs are cut from a pattern that is geologically ancient. Even the frog way of breathing, by using the wide floor of their mouths in much the same way that we use our diaphragms — to pump air in and out of our lungs — is a kind of quick-fix method left over from the lungfish. Through their shortish lives frogs make use of more ways of breathing than almost anything else does. In the spawn clumps the eggs exchange oxygen and wastes with the pond water through simple diffusion just as the tiniest and simplest of life forms do. Newborn tads have feathery gills, but they also absorb oxygen directly through the wide flange of their tails. Eventually frog lungs develop and tad gills are reabsorbed, and the tad-frog rests with growing legs and shrinking tail, half out of water, gulping air; at this tender half-made stage a frog can drown. He needs a beachhead to crawl half out of water on; it is his moment of truth, of betweenness, before he hops off. Even a grown-up frog can breathe directly through his thin blood-rich skin, and does just that all winter, buried in the soil like a root. He can even absorb oxygen directly through the membranes of his excessive mouth, panting, in July, in the leaf shadows, waiting for bugs.

In the pond in April the male frog's program is simple: clasp anything of appropriate girth (wide) and texture (soft) and hang in there. Male woodfrogs have even been found clasping lumps of mud and dead toads. On the second morning after the singing began, a few females had arrived and there were fights. There was a ball of wrestling frogs near the shore, each frog clasping various portions of each other's anatomy, and growling, and gaping; at the center there was one female, as fat and placid as a stuffed toy. I couldn't understand how she could manage to get a breath of air in the midst of her churning ball of suitors. Within an hour some of the outermost frogs, who were hugging each other's heads and legs, their hanging-on a kind of a gallant gesture, let themselves float away. Finally there was one victor riding his lady-love off to the depths. The female looked as if she were carrying a pack-saddle. She was in control then, and sooner or later, along with almost all the other paired frogs, she would head on over to the willow clump.

The willow clump is the favored communal frog-nursery in my pond. It is in a corner off by itself and is next to a drain-pipe, which brings a trickle of water out of the field and makes a nice music. The grassy bank is just above it and I watched the goings-on in the willow clump from there.

On the third morning after the singing had begun it was already crowded: I counted eight single males and three clasped pairs there, all in a space the size of a pail. They bobbed. They blinked. Waited. I waited. One has to move at frog-speed in this business; the sun shone, the ripples were like moons of bluish light, and the frogs looked freshly enameled. The drainpipe made its trickly music. The willow twigs stuck up from the water, as bright as if they had been newly varnished, their single lapping bud-scales were just pushed aside by small domes of starting leaves. One female frog positioned herself and her partner (he had nothing to do with positioning, his was not to reason why, his was but to hang on) until one brown twig was between her wide knees. She bobbed, blinked. Then the eggs began to run out of her like a dark tapioca pudding. As they rippled out the male hunched, shut his eyes, and ejaculated, his thighs quivering. He pushed slowly with his feet, packing the egg mass against the stem; she pulled from the other side of the stem with her feet, rounding and packing. It was all done in a little more than a minute. By the next day the gels around the dark eggs had absorbed water and expanded until the egg mass was three times the size it had been.

Two days later there was a deep frost and there was a filigree of ice around the willow stems in the morning. But a frog egg happens to be, by design, perhaps, one of the most efficient of passive solar collectors and stores: the core is black, the gels are ninety-nine percent water, and they store heat very nicely. On that cold morning the egg masses were still a measurable degree warmer than the surrounding water.

A week after the first sound of woodfrog rattling there were only a few hopeful males still waiting in the spawn clumps. Three days later they were gone, too, and among the willow twigs a few dark spheres of frog eggs were beginning to change. A frog egg like any other frog thing moves only at the speed which temperature allows. On my desk-top the distance from new egg to born tad was covered in less than four days, but in the pond where the water was only ten degrees or so above freezing the journey took two weeks. But by the time the parent frogs had disappeared a few dark rounds had gone oval; a very few were long enough to begin curving around on themselves, bending against the innermost gel walls. They had wide fetal bullet-heads with delicate heartbeats pulsing behind them, tiny wedges of tails, and they were as black as coal in the womb of the pond: the singers for next April and for Aprils to come.

Prelude

Late in April after the ice had gone I went back to Steve and Jan's camp porch. The dark clouds building over the mountains to the west were announcement enough, and the pond is a fine place to watch a storm.

There are several big spruces there between the cabin and the water, but for some mysterious reason, in the height of their strength, they all seem to be dying. Trees are heir to their own vascular ills; there are fungi which suddenly blossom and clog the tree's waterways with cottony filaments, there are softening ailments of the roots — more fungi at work down there. Some of the big trees are invaded by carpenter ants who hollow out airy castles at the base of their trunks. Whatever it is that is getting to them at least one falls down every year, and they have always missed the cabin though the outhouse has been flattened twice. Steve and Jan's canoe spent many years chained up to one of these trees and was mortally holed last summer, not by running aground on a rock or hidden snag but because a wind-toppled spruce hurtled down onto it from above. So every year the view from the porch clears.

With the ice gone I could see the wooden jetty running out into the water, wrenched free from its pilings by the ice and awash in the flop of little waves. In the summertime it is always a challenge to dash down its canted and unsteady length and hurl oneself off the end in a racing dive . . . all of those good times seemed nearly believable, even huddled as I was on the porch, in two sweaters, with an April storm rising in the west.

The first summer that I knew the pond I used to come there to fish for perch and pumpkinseeds once in a while. Most of the shoreline was unfruitful and I was always itching to get out into deeper water. I spent some time looking longingly at Steve's canoe but even then the key to its fetters was lost and best forgotten, and though I did mention hacksaws and cold chisels to my friends they were not enthusiastic and the canoe stayed imprisoned. So, on shore, did I, until one afternoon when I was scouting the pond edges I found an old chunk of a camp jetty that had been torn free by ice and had blown up into the brush by the shore. (There are two other cabins on the pond; both have been jetty-less for years.)

Hoping for the best, I tied my rod and my can of night-crawlers to a protruding nail, hung my tacklebag around my neck, and shoved off. When I reached the middle of the pond, I climbed aboard and started fishing. My raft was more waterlogged than I had thought and with me on top it sank eighteen inches below the surface, so that I was casting knee-deep in pond water. I stayed out there for more than an hour and caught a lot of little fish, feeling more and more like a seedy version of Botticelli's Venus with pumpkinseeds on my gill-line instead of dolphins.

The pond hasn't changed in the nearly ten years that have passed since that summer. All three of its cabins are if anything more deserted than ever. A seventy-acre pond is too small to support a motorboat. There are no firewood-ice-cream-showers-and-beer places anywhere nearby. No beach.

Only clean dark water. Only a horizon of forest and hills. In the summertime you can stand naked in the middle there for hours and play at being a minor god, if you like.

The wind rose, clattering the branches and bringing thunder. A sudden burst bent the trees as if a hand had been pressed over their tops. The clouds above the thinning spruces were purple dark and filled with a jittering light. There was closer thunder, a flash of freezing blue, and then the rain came pelting down like stones. The roar from the tin roof was deafening, like children banging on a can.

The pond roughened and whitened with waves. I couldn't see it happening, but I knew that it was happening out there: the turnover. All winter the coldest part of the pond has been the frozen surface and the warmest part has been the depths; but the surface has been warming up now for weeks. The dark pond sediments have absorbed April sun, the surface water has thawed, and now the whole business is at a uniform temperature — or close enough — so that for once it is all the same density, too. There is no barrier anymore to the whole pond's *mixing*. And now there was wind; waves, oozings and tricklings of fresh rainwater, wind wind wind — and the surface water, filled with wind-whipped oxygen, was folding into the depths, and the sour airless water down there, stuffed with a winter's worth of ammonia and carbon dioxide, was churning up. It brought sediments with it, fertile mucks, the bodies of diatoms, fragments of fish and leaves, winter spores of algae, and crustaceans' eggs and dormant protozoans, and in the oxygen-rich and nutrient-rich water they were hatching. Supplied with oxygen at last, the nitrite bacteria were beginning to multiply madly and chew into the ammonia, making the water more habitable and releasing tons of plant food. The microscopic multitudes were wriggling free, kicking, unfolding, spinning and swimming and tossing, feeding growing multiplying, eating one another up. For the next few weeks the pond would hold an invisible bloom of growth, and would be more (a biologist's word) "productive" than at any other time of year. It would, in other words, catch and capture more *light*.

Soon enough a new layering of the pond is going to begin. In a quiet day of sun the surface will warm up, and once it is warmer than 4°C it will float over the denser, cooler water underneath. The warm layer will stay there on the surface and never mix with the depths. The deepest part of the pond may stay close to 4° all summer long. I remember diving from my wretched raft and swimming down, as deep as I could go, that summer ten years ago, and I came down quickly into a world as chill and sour as any midwinter pond bottom. It was dark and cold there and I turned and shot back to the surface, to the summer and the light, as fast as I could.

As fast as I could.

Dance of Giants

After two nights without a freeze the maple seeds began to sprout on the slope by the Pond in the Woods. I only noticed them because there were sudden white squiggles among the dark leaves on the ground; newborn roots feeling the way out of their winged seeds like sensitive fingers. Some curved over sticks, other luckier ones had already penetrated the wet leaf-covered soil. Most of the embryonic leaves were still furled in the seed, but some of them were edged partly out, swollen and turning green, like insects in splitting husks struggling to be free.

A week later I found a cache of maple seeds farther up the slope. They had been packed away carefully last autumn in a six-inch-wide hollow and were laid round and round in a neat pattern, and even then at the end of April they were frozen, succulent, and crisp, laced with ice crystals. Red squirrel? Chipmunk? Something had rifled the hoard and the leaves were stirred up and seed fragments were scattered, but almost anything could have stumbled on them as I did, grateful for the discovery.

The sun was warm on the slope and the spring beauties had opened their pink stars overnight. Red and green dappled trout-lily leaves slanted up, and here and there a flower stem emerged among them coiled like a snake, ready to strike the eye with its yellow tongues.

Lying in the dry leaves, which rustled like paper, I had the old urge to stay put; if I stayed just there for another month I could see the trees dance. Passing through as I do, I can only trace the passage of that dance and can only imagine the flow, the reeling and bowing.

In these maples and birch and beech the branches reach out year after year, running skyward like the fingers of rivulets when water is poured on dry ground. Water is at the heart of

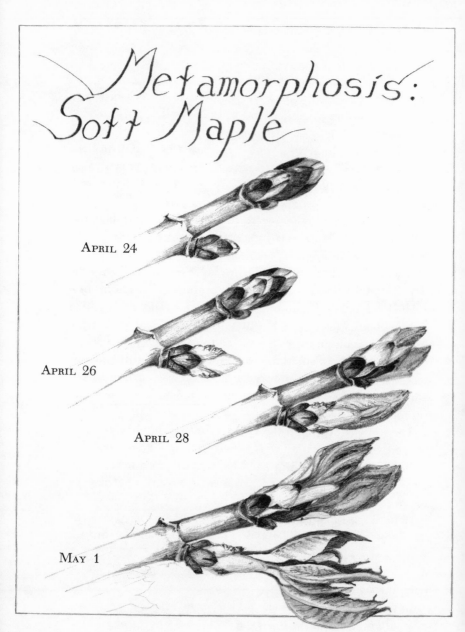

Metamorphosis:
Soft Maple

April 24

April 26

April 28

May 1

their form; they have the shape of river systems seen from space, or veins of blood, or nerves. Standing there, buds swollen, with a wash of deep red over them, they seem as lambent and as alive and as ready as anything on earth could be.

The annual running-out of the branch ends begins in May and will continue in slowing pace even into August, but the birth of the leaves themselves takes little more than a week, and in good weather even less time than that, so that in the movements of the tree dance this emergence of leaves would be seen as a flash, a flick, like the sudden unclenching of fisted hands.

Plants' movements are unmuddied by temporizing thought but are complex enough for all of that. In spite of years of biochemical research no one has managed to explain how they do most of their moving without the medium of nerve and muscle. Most of the time we zip around here too fast to notice that they are moving at all.

Movement is relative: a hummingbird goes by us in a blur; heart pulsing at more than 75 beats per second, metabolic core heat set at 105° F, flying along at fifty miles per hour . . . even the fastest human runner moves, from a hummingbird's perspective, as ponderously as a tortoise.

Plants choreograph their clenches and reaches in response to a great many things, but only while their tissues are still soft and young. Past midsummer the twigs and leaves stiffen and their position lignifies and becomes a permanent statement, like a photograph. Most plants move because of differences in growth rate between one bit of tissue and another, or because of shifts in water pressure within each fluid cell. Movement in plants is either an expression of growth itself, or an exercise in hydraulics, or a combination of both.

The newborn maple root is already intelligent about gravity, light, and water. It corkscrews, seeking an opening in which to poke down. Even in pitch-darkness a seedling orients itself by gravity, the shoot going up toward light, and the root twisting down to spread its absorbent network, hairy as a beard, between the crumbs of the soil. Once there it senses the presence of water and grows faster on its drier side, so that it curves and curves again to penetrate the wettest earth.

There is an odd little plant called dodder, and in the summertime the wildflowers that I pick are often twined with it. It is very pretty, leafless, tangled but graceful, like a snarl of fishing line drawn by a poet. It is a parasite. Its fine curling stems are pinkish and its flowers are a foam of white, but I can never quite escape from the knowledge, having read it once somewhere, that it can smell. It can smell a desirable host from inches away and will swing toward this good smell until it reaches its goal. The way it bends toward is the same way that any plant bends toward what it wants the most; by growing fastest on the side of itself that is farthest away from what it wants. So it curves. Its shape is the trace, the wake, of its motion.

In June the tendrils of my pea vines will hook the chicken wire I have put there for them, and, responding to the touch of this wire, they will spiral in a matter of hours and then stiffen. In October I will have to pluck these stiff coils off, themselves as hard as brittle wire, though the plants they held up to the sun are long dead and rotted away. The bog on the west hill has sundews that slam shut on ants and tiny flies in less than a half second. Maples with a patch of their bark gnawed away by a wintering porcupine hurry to send pale caramel-colored bulges of new flesh over the wound. Trees grown in the open are thicker of trunk because the wind has blown them, and they choose to thicken in the parts of themselves most stressed by their own bending. Trees in a dense woods where the wind can't push them are as thin as wands.

Look: I am watching this now as if I were putting together the countless still pictures I have accumulated, the befores and the afters and the durings, into one quick dance so that I can watch it happen, for once! I am tired of going into the woods in May and June and seeing leaves in mid-uncurl, ferns with a fist ready to punch air, twigs pointed like gleaming arrows. They look as though they had stopped their fling because I had stumbled on their private dance and was tactless enough to want to watch.

I have noticed that the bottom twigs of maples grow only an inch or two a year and that the top twigs may grow a foot or more in the same season, so that if one could see this month of their growth as a single convulsion it would be like the upward leap of a flame, as if someone had turned up the wick on an oil lamp. As they leap up the twigs wriggle. They make a hormone in their growing tips that flows back to where the cells are expanding, and it accumulates to the shadiest side of the twig and stimulates the expansion there, so that each twig bends independently toward the light. They turn in to each other and away, and in again until they have trembled to a stop in the spot most lit. Each single leaf does this same light-seeking dither, too, so that they seem to lurch and adjust like hands hefting a ball. The air around me suddenly fills with green commotion; the pond is lost from view, the air clogged with flutter, the path home closed with writhing leaves and with saplings and brush shuddering upward from their roots like sunbursts. Now the ferns careen from the ground, rolling upward and letting fly leaflets like the many limbs of Vishnu, until at last their tips flick over, wavelike, and a new green surf inhabits the shading ground. If you look up at the end of May here, the leaves are an almost perfect mosaic, there are few swatches left of the sky; they have become a web for the capture of the sun.

This seethe if actually seen in full boil could well terrify me beyond recall; except that I know that it isn't me they are after. I am as benign and unwanted as a rock.

I come back to the papery leaves, the spring beauties, the sun which reaches me here, now, unfiltered. The twigs, leaves, flowers, and ferns that are on their way are already formed, were made last summer and packed away in scales and sheaths; all they have to do is to expand like balloons, and then their branch tips will begin their hurry to make more.

As I went down the slope again, I reached into my pocket for some of the maple seeds that I had taken from the frozen hollow, and opened several and ate them; they were crisp and green and bitter. I know what you could become, I thought. I have seen you three centuries hence, massive as a god, pushing your ferment of leaves until you shade a quarter of an acre. I thought about the tribal warriors who ate the hearts of their enemies so that they would absorb the strength and intelligence of the adversary; you are hardly my enemy, O trees, but I want your grace.

The Watershed

When I go out for a walk I almost always seem to go to water. Gatherings of water, like mountaintops, make obvious destinations; a place you can go and say you've been to and returned from, having peered there into current or depths or over rolls of hills. Either way you have looked into something other than the bounded usual world of solid earth, straight horizon.

When I went out to walk the Tamarack one morning at the very end of April, I realized that this was the end of the journey that I had started months ago, centuries ago, it seemed, by going off to explore the muddy whorls of Dead Creek. I was drawn down there by the autumn wash of birds that follows the rivers and mountains south every July, August, September, October. That was the beginning; now all the birds are washing back. Everything is washing back. There is assorted flotsam on the wide beach of the year, and everything is ahead, inland, and green.

Besides, it is almost the first of May; and I have, arbitrarily, perhaps, chosen the first of May as the end of winter and as the end of this book. I set it up that way from the beginning and will have to stick to my guns, otherwise I might find myself whooshing on into June where I don't belong.

May first is arbitrary because who can say when winter is finished? Is it the first morning that the Nashville warbler chants his chant in the pasture, or the first evening that the woodthrush sings his song that is so joyful and sad at once that it swells my throat as if I were going to cry; or the day that I notice the sudden silence of the jays who are being secretive about their new home-place among the birches? Is it the first noon that I can go out barefoot and not scurry in in two minutes because my toes are cold? Is it the yellow crocuses suddenly wide open among the stones by the door, or the spinach seedlings up and green like long-winged insects, so that my mouth is watering for salads? These are arrivals, successful arrivals, announced with flourishes. Their journeys are finished. The making of food and the raising of families is summer work.

I went down to the bridge and walked up the Tamarack, drawn upstream. This was a watching and collecting trip, perhaps the last one of the winter. The sun was warm and a pleasure to be out in, and so strong that I had to squint my eyes against the light. The two-inch snowfall of the night before was moist like a fresh cookie, but full of sparkles, and by ten o'clock it was collapsing from the tree branches in little clinks and crunches and water dripped from the firs as if it were raining. The brook made a loud rushing under the bridge and avenues of clear water had opened in the Carow beavers' pond. Short chewed sticks — the beavers' winter trash — floated in small rafts against the alder clumps. There was a tiny centered ripple where an insect thrashed in the water. I saw each of these things, all new in the year, as signs; a language of separate glyphs that might run together into a statement if I read them far enough; follow the brook, I thought, higher than you've been.

As I went upriver I heard the thud thud thud thud thud thudthudthud of a grouse drumming, beating his wings against the air, claiming home space and strutting with his tail cocked and black ruff erect; it sounded as though someone were starting an engine in the woods, it was oddly ventriloqual, hard to locate. As I went on through the hare's spruce thicket, the thudding began again and filled the air around me so that I knew that I was closing in, and I walked carefully, moss clump to moss clump. The next time that the grouse drummed his thuds seemed to fill the space between my ears; actual shockwaves which made me dizzy. I fell clumsily against a tree, and from twenty feet away the cock flew up with a hammering of wings; and then the hen flew up.

Out in the open ground of the beaver meadow heavy clumps of reeds and grasses poked up from the new snow like a field of upturned broken baskets. I heard a woodpecker knocking, one crow cawed, a single gray-winged insect landed on my sweater. As I walked through the clumps hundreds of these clumsy flimsy insects flew up, like backward echoes of last night's snow. A deer had walked beside the river that morning, just as I was walking.

Running quietly through the open meadow, the Tamarack was free of ice, the water smooth, strong, quiet, dimpled at its surface with little rising whorls like a dissected muscle. Specks of silt and blackened vegetation were carried along and here and there they tumbled to the surface, glinting in the sun. Over the pale bottom sand some interior watery turbulence made traveling bubbles of darkness, rimmed with a golden light.

In one place there was a shallows glittering with mica bits; swimming over it was a school of tiny fish, no more than an inch long, wriggling like bits of mobilized mica themselves and darting among the drowned broken reeds.

A patch of moving gray along the edge of the forest caught' my eye: it flowed, stopped still, flowed on again. It was a coyote hunting the fringe of trees and nosing among the basketlike clumps. With their snow cover gone the voles and shrews that had been so common in the swamp in midwinter must have still been there somewhere, and easier game. I stopped still like a tree, half-hidden behind a clump of alders. The coyote was upwind and I watched him for ten minutes, fifteen. My side began to ache, something throbbed at the base of my skull. I forced myself to breathe, relax; my breath came and went in shudders. The coyote came closer. He looked like a small huskie or German shepherd but obviously belonged only to himself and the swamp; no domestic creature could move with such concentration or skill. He sniffed from one clump and tree base to the next, pawing where the smells required. Often he stopped and widened his ears, lifted his nose into the air, and then went back to his work. Finally he either smelled or saw me and I knew that he had, but he waited, stopped still and staring, nostrils pulsing; he was close enough, less than a hundred yards off, so that I could see his thick fur moving in the wind like long summer grass. Then he was off upriver and into the woods like a puff of smoke, gone.

While I had been looking at the coyote, my mind had split in a now familiar way; I could feel the rumble of dual machinery: one half was busy taking notes. Look how he quarters the woods, this is familiar territory to him. Look how he pauses at that tree and takes a long deep sniff, points his ears; he knows something is there. Look how he uses his whole body as a tool, all senses and muscle at once, in the kind of purity of concentration one sees in a master blacksmith when he has the iron in his forge, and snatches it at the correct moment and taps and pounds it and turns it on the anvil; or in a senior businessman at his conference table who is aware of everyone, who is assessing the speaker's goals and character, market strategy, world politics, quarterly profits, and his own power all at once; or in a cook who has long ago forgotten all exact recipes but who whisks, pinches, pours, adjusts heat and tilts her pan in just this way — with her head tipped downward and her eyes forward in just this same way — centered in her craft. Look; this coyote is paler than others I have seen, they do vary, they look different from one another just as other animals. I wish I could sketch this quickly, the way he holds his tail, his ears, the way he lifts his paw over a clump.

Why couldn't I sketch it then? Because of the other half of myself, the other and deeper whir. When I saw the coyote, I froze. I didn't think "freeze!" I *did* freeze, just as one snatches one's hand from a hot stove long before one has felt pain or told oneself, "Snatch away your hand, the stove is hot, you will burn it!" My pencil was in my hand, so was my notebook, I had been writing down notes about the little fishes — but I could no more unfreeze to draw than I could have put my hand back on a hot stove having once snatched it off. What was I waiting for? I was waiting for the coyote to pass out of sight without seeing me or to see me and freeze. His reaction to me was identical to my reaction to him. It was! So. Once mutually frozen we had several choices of action, which had to be mutually decided upon: sex, a friendly pat-wag-and-sniff, fight, flight, or utter indifference. The first two were out, since we were not of the same species nor of the same family. The last is an expression of defeat; the only resort of caged animals or emotions. Fight then? We had no quarrel, we weren't competing for anything, we didn't need to eat each other. Flight is what we were left with. The only real question was — which of us first? He had more to lose and so he ran. But there was a fraction of a moment when neither of us was sure. All of these decisions took a half-second.

What was I left with? No sketch, though my hand gripped my pencil as though I had been drawing for hours; but the euphoria of knowing that I was an animal, here, whole, and very much alive.

✓ ✓ ✓

I went upriver again with longer strides. Upstream the Tamarack lost itself in a thicket of alders, but I followed it in. While I was climbing over an old tumulus, the decades-old ruins of a beaver dam, I was struck full in the face by a gout of floury dust. A gold powder sprinkled my cheeks, sifted into the stuff of my sweater, speckled my boot tops. Brushing my face with my hand, I looked up; a cluster of alder catkins dangled there in front of my forehead, long and red and gold, loosing their pollen; the first flowers of the spring.

The little fishes, the drumming grouse, the so quickly melting snow, the open brook, the sunshine warm on my head, now these flowers; I would be tempted by all of these things to worship the sun again myself as the chief deity — except that I know that it is only one smallish star among trillions — because everything else here does. By worship, I mean obey. What do I obey, then, with such whole and abiding homage?

Something, I am sure of it. Something as pervasive and as powerful and as reliable as light. I shook my head hard then, like a dog assaulted by flies, both to shake off the tickly pollen and to rid myself of this pestering question. I went farther into the alders, as if by doing so I could either find an answer or, better yet, forget that I had asked.

Alders aren't easy to walk through. They come up from their root in a clump and send their branches sideways. Many of these branches are as large as my arm and angle off at the levels of knees and chest and interweave, so that going through them I also had to interweave, duck and step, slogging through wet ground and running water and trying (not always succeeding) to go around the deeper streams and watery holes which overflowed my boot tops.

I followed the main stream back as well as I could, but it wandered into the alders and I lost it there; it was frayed out and disorganized into a thousand rivulets and pools and finally un-rivered beyond recall. The watershed — what I could see of it through the leafless branches — was large and complex, a dozen slopes converging, each pricked with springs. I stopped, confused, at the edge of one pool deeper than the others, which held as much water in one place as I thought that I could find. It was as far as I was going.

I assessed, took stock. Winter was finished, there were signs everywhere. The snow was still sprinkled but mute and small, like a vagrant species of white fallen leaf. The lower limbs of the alders held ropes of matted leaves and reeds, evidence of the height and current of the thaw. The coyote's hunting had let me know that there had been, here, enough to feed him and that there was enough to feed him still; he was the visible tip of a live iceberg, all that supported him invisible to me, but implicit, obvious, part of what he was. The two beaver lodges held live beavers; that fact announced by the raw color of their winter twig-trash, which floated in the nearly melted ponds. And I was there, too, wasn't I?

Still there, straddling an alder branch. It is impossible to be in alders without either straddling or being straddled or both at once. My feet were cold, my socks sodden, my sweater held crisps of dead leaves, one forearm was scratched. There were trickling swallowing noises of water moving, and dark and light reflected up from water, and alder pollen as gold as a daisy-heart filling the air in various dilutions. These were the live things, the Created, there: the alders, myself, the muck soil of the swamp which gave us both unsteady footing. All the forces of physics were there — the gravity which would have all malleable things become as round as soap bubbles, the tidal pull of the moon; and all the traveling energies traveled there — heat, light, noise, cosmic and domestic ionizing radiations, the low pinging of radio waves, magnetic forces, even the background thermal radiation, which, at $2.7°K$, and coming from every direction at once, still announces the birth of the universe.

Astronomers and physicists have picked at the wound skein of being and found particles, waves, forces which give them motion. But is that all there is? I would like to believe that these are the clay, but to give any clay form there needs to be a potter. A potter who is never finished with pinching and glazing — a perfectionist, revisionist, endless fiddler. I submit to this: I am pinched, glazed, used. I am perhaps most pinched and hardest used by the wintering of my body and heart. I have (how many times? How many times will I?) spun a resilient chrysalis, concentrated my juices, dissolved form, survived, waited — and obeying again some program I can't know, emerged. Winter, work, relative solitude, that is all I have just lived through after all, but I feel a forming hand challenging my shoulders, my arms. It is spring, after the fashion of springs here, which are neither bountiful nor quick. Why does even the thought of emergence so terrify? Why does living hurt? Even beauty, knowledge, beauty most of all: I ask.

The alders nod in the wind, loosing another million gold sperm downstream; the alders are pinched, glazed, used. But do they ask?

I heard chickadees coming closer through the web of branches, chipping, chickadee-ing; idle perky chatter. I smiled to myself, shaken by the current of my thoughts, and brought to earth again by these old friends. They collected around me and went on toward the swamp fringe and the trees, and left me straddling and straddled beside my pool like a tattered Narcissus, only I couldn't see my own face reflected at all, only a dimpled swatch of air.

Do you remember the parable of the blind men who went out to discover the elephant? One of them felt the elephant's leg and so thought that elephants were rugged and cylindrical like a tree; another touched its tail and concluded that an elephant was a species of rope; the one who happened on the trunk decided that an elephant was a large snake. A wonderful story, very silly. I thought then — and still think — that I am like a pool in the heart of the swamp; that's as far as I'd got. It was almost literally all that I could see.

The pool reflected, darkly, just where it was, a patch of spiky reed, branches, cloud, dulled light. It reflected its place, but the water went on bringing and taking; the water that makes and is the pool was moving. The broken light of the riffles below and above gave the game away; the pool was an apparent stop but no stop at all. Even in midwinter when it was sealed with a cap of frost, there had been water trickling through, light, heat, fragments of supernovae entering and leaving.

Look at it this way: it seems to be impossible to be any one thing from one moment to the next. The breakfast that I had eaten three hours before — boiled egg, coffee, raisin bread — was being torn into chemical snippets small enough to pass in through the fingerlike frills of my small intestine and enter my bloodstream. There they went: feel the pulse at your wrist? There they go — your egg and bread, granola and juice — they pass into eyelid muscles so that you can blink the required number of blinks per minute, into brain circuits to process sense, store memory, drive emotion; at that moment some of my breakfast-bits were being shunted into the fabric of the knee that I had skinned the week before when I had slipped on a rock while crossing the Wild Branch river, and some of those bits were busy knitting themselves into fresh skin full of requisite hair follicles, freckles, and sweat glands; so when did the egg and toast stop being egg and toast and start being me?

Look at it the other way, the downstream current: I stomp through the swamp and the swamp is changed, the morning hunt of the coyote is changed. I have planted apple trees, and the number of species of insect that suck their blossom nectar in May would fill a catalogue of fine point larger than this page. I have given birth to a child who is busy changing his world in a way peculiar only to himself. Where then do I leave off being?

So I can explore my own watershed some and my own downstream flow some, feeling around the elephant of a life which seems, the more I explore it, not to be mine at all.

Whether of the year or of the spirit, winter is a kind of requisite battle; anyway, it is a hard journey in which old energies have to be put to new use, and it pushes to the limit whatever inventive and seminal resources life has. What survives has changed. Whatever it is that hurls planets and instills faith is at the helm: and the goal seems to be nothing less than transformation.

I am able to know a bit about a few currents and obstacles of the flow in which I am a pool, clearinghouse, and apparent entity. Like everything else I am too busy taking and giving in my watery net to absorb too much; but I know now that I am capable of damage, delight, change: always change. So is a tree, a fish, a star.